FOUR
FRENCH
SYMBOLIST
POETS

FOUR FRENCH SYMBOLIST POETS:

BAUDELAIRE
RIMBAUD
VERLAINE
MALLARMÉ

TRANSLATION AND INTRODUCTION
by

ENID RHODES PESCHEL

Preface by GERMAINE BRÉE

 OHIO UNIVERSITY PRESS • ATHENS

Library of Congress Cataloging in Publication Data
Main entry under title:

Four French Symbolist Poets.

The poems are in French and English.
1. French poetry—19th century. 2. French poetry—
19th century—Translations into English. 3. English
poetry—Translations from French. 4. Symbolism (Liter-
ary movement)—France. I. Peschel, Enid Rhodes.
PQ1170.E6F6   841'.8'08   80-29625
ISBN 0-8214-0557-8

Several of Ms. Peschel's translations of these poems were first published in somewhat different
form in the following places: Baudelaire, "La Chevelure," "La Musique," "Rêve parisien,"
"L'Albatros"; Rimbaud, "Tête de faune," "Le Bateau ivre," "Mémoire"; Verlaine, "Le
Faune," "Un grand sommeil noir . . . ," "La lune blanche . . . "; Mallarmé, "Brise ma-
rine," "Sainte," "Le vierge, le vivace et le bel aujourd'hui . . . ," "A la nue accablante
tu . . . " in *French Symbolist Poetry: Sou'wester* (Southern Illinois University), ed. Enid
Rhodes Peschel, Special Issue, Vol. 6, No. 1 (Winter 1978); Baudelaire, "Correspondances,"
"Spleen" ("Je suis comme le roi . . . ") in *Sou'wester*, Vol. 2, No. 2 (Winter 1974); Baude-
laire, "Femmes damnées" in *Sou'wester*, Vol. 3, No. 1 (Fall 1974); Baudelaire, "Un Fantôme
II: Le Parfum," "Un Fantôme IV: Le Portrait" in *Sou'wester*, Vol. 3, Nos. 2 and 3 (Spring
1975); Baudelaire, "Les Bijoux" in *Sou'wester, Vol. 4, No. 1 (Winter 1976); Baudelaire, "La
Vie antérieure" in *The Colorado Quarterly*, Vol. XXII, No. 1 (Summer 1973); Baudelaire, "Un
Fantôme I: Les Ténèbres" in *The Colorado Quarterly*, Vol. XXII, No. 4 (Spring 1974); Rim-
baud, "Le Dormeur du val" in *The Colorado Quarterly*, Vol. XXIV, No. 4 (Spring 1976);
Baudelaire, "L'Héautontimorouménos," "Un Fantôme III: Le Cadre" in *The South Carolina
Review*, Vol. 7, No. 2 (April 1975); Baudelaire, "Parfum exotique" in *Counter/Measures*, No.
3 (1974); Verlaine, "Crimen amoris"; Mallarmé, "L'Après-midi d'un faune" in *The South
Dakota Review*, Vol. 17, No. 1 (Spring 1979); Verlaine, "Streets:I," "L'espoir luit comme un
brin de paille . . . "; Rimbaud, "Vénus anadyomène" in *The Green River Review*, Vol. X,
No. 1 (1979); Baudelaire, "Le Vin des amants," "La Chevelure," "Harmonie du soir" in my
essay "Love, the Intoxicating Mirage: Baudelaire's Quest for Communion in 'Le Vin des
amants,' 'La Chevelure,' and 'Harmonie du soir' " in *Pre-Text/Text/Context: Essays on
Nineteenth-Century French Literature*, ed. Robert L. Mitchell (Columbus: Ohio State Uni-
versity Press, 1980), all rights reserved; and Rimbaud, "Honte" in Arthur Rimbaud, *A Season
in Hell. The Illuminations*, trans. Enid Rhodes Peschel (New York, London, Oxford: Oxford
University Press, 1973), p. 13.

ACKNOWLEDGMENTS

The French texts are from the following editions:

Baudelaire, *Oeuvres complètes*, eds. Y.-G. Le Dantec and Claude Pichois (Paris: Gallimard, Bibliothèque de la Pléiade, 1961).

Rimbaud, *Oeuvres complètes*, ed. Antoine Adam (Paris: Gallimard, Bibliothèque de la Pléiade, 1972). For "Tête de faune," "Le Coeur volé," "L'étoile a pleuré rose . . . ," "Comédie de la soif," "Honte" and "O saisons, ô châteaux . . . ," I used Rimbaud, *Oeuvres*, ed. Suzanne Bernard (Paris: Garnier Frères, 1960).

Verlaine, *Oeuvres poétiques complètes*, eds. Y.-G. Le Dantec and Jacques Borel (Paris: Gallimard, Bibliothèque de la Pléiade, 1962). For *"Nevermore"* and "Dans l'interminable / Ennui . . . ," I used Verlaine, *Oeuvres poétiques*, ed. Jacques Robichez (Paris: Garnier Frères, 1969).

Mallarmé, *Oeuvres complètes*, eds. Henri Mondor and G. Jean-Aubry (Paris: Gallimard, Bibliothèque de la Pléiade, 1945).

I am grateful to the French Cultural Services, New York, for permission to reprint the following pictures:

Baudelaire, photograph by Carjat
Rimbaud, by Coussins
Verlaine, photograph
Mallarmé, photograph by Félix Nadar

For their generous critical advice, as well as for their enthusiasm, understanding and help, it is a pleasure to express my gratitude to Germaine Brée, Robert Greer Cohn, Richard Ellmann, R. Étiemble,

Diana Festa-McCormick, Lloyd Kropp, Virginia La Charité, James Lawler, Robert Mitchell, Bill Morse, Henri Peyre, Richard Selzer, Stanley Weintraub, and Virginia Wilkinson.

PREFACE

One only really reads the poets one translates, remarks Professor Etiemble, himself a translator, in a preface to Enid Rhodes Peschel's subtle and balanced book on Rimbaud.[1] And, he adds, those only that one has translated well. The translations collected here show how skillful a reader Peschel has been of poets as complex and different, as great too, as Baudelaire, Mallarmé, Rimbaud and Verlaine.

The "extraordinary prestige"[2] these poets have enjoyed far beyond the precincts of France, they owe in some measure to the quality of the translations they have inspired. Poems are mobile structures, more particularly perhaps those of the brilliant constellation of poets grouped under the deceptive label of Symbolism. As the years go by and interpretations multiply, new translations must inevitably appear, for who would be entirely satisfied to sit down and accept another's reading situated in the past?

A poet herself, a scrupulous scholar too, Enid Peschel is highly sensitive to what I shall call, for want of a better word, the feel of the two languages with which she works. She knows what can and cannot be done as the poem takes on its new linguistic form, and the fine choices that have to be made so as not to impair, in the passage, its distinctive mood and texture. The undertaking is difficult. For these poets, while still working quite often from traditional forms, were seeking, and finding, each in his own way, new, elusive and deeply personal modes of expression. The range is vast, from the fluidity of

[1] Enid Rhodes Peschel, *Flux and Reflux: Ambivalence in the Poems of Arthur Rimbaud* (Geneva: Droz, 1977).
[2] Henri Peyre, "Verlaine: Symbolism and Popular Poetry" in *French Symbolist Poetry: Sou'-wester* (Southern Illinois University), Special Issue, Vol. 6, No. 1 (Winter 1978), p. 13.

Verlaine to the severity of design of Mallarmé, the shifting tensions and brilliance of Rimbaud, the variety of mood and complexity of Baudelaire.

Reading each poem for itself, but with the larger patterns of the poet's writing and sensibility, Enid Peschel has made certain exacting demands on herself. She has wherever possible kept the rhyme patterns, redistributing the syntactic elements without dislocating the articulation of the phrase and the rhythmic flow. There are instances, however, when a strict adherence to a rhyme pattern might tend to distort a mood or atmosphere or, combined with too sustained a rhythmic measure, recall, however faintly, the parodic monotony of English doggerel. In those cases Peschel has preferred to draw on the resources of internal sound patterns that echo the free-flowing yet carefully controlled musical texture that is the hallmark of these poems. Excellent examples are such varied poems as "Lethe," "Faun's Head" and "Evening Prayer," among others.

The reader senses the integrity of the translator-craftsman who has considered, beyond the linear structure of the poems, the balance of tension and shifting image, the recurrent allusion, cadence or design. But the translator does not sacrifice the original statement for poetic effect. This respect for both reader and poet may at times detract from the multiple echoes the original poem awakens in the language, the vistas that open out from it in multiple directions, but it does preserve as accurately as possible the matrix that is the poem.

These translations are no journeyman's job. They call upon more than technical craftsmanship, which Enid Peschel certainly possesses in abundance. Each one draws upon the full range of the translator's intimate knowledge of poetry, her imagination and sensibility.

For those who wish to elucidate further the nature of the prestige these poets enjoy; to locate their role in the development of our contemporary awareness; or merely to test their own readings of these poems, there could hardly be a better incentive than this volume. It will prove invaluable to students and lovers of poetry everywhere.

Germaine Brée,
Kenan Professor of the Humanities,
Wake Forest University

Past President,
The M.L.A.

For Dick and for Colette,
with love

CONTENTS

Selections from the "Pièces Condamnées" ("Condemned Pieces")

Selection from the Third Edition of *The Flowers of Evil*

RIMBAUD
Selections from "Poésies" ("Poems")

Selections from the "Derniers Vers" ("Last Poems Written in Verse")

VERLAINE
Selections from *Poèmes saturniens* (*Saturnine Poems*)

Selections from *Fêtes galantes* (*Gallant Festivals*)

FOUR
FRENCH
SYMBOLIST
POETS

INTRODUCTION

Symbolism, or the Veil of Words

> *Were I called on to define, very briefly, the term "Art," I should call it "the reproduction of what the Senses perceive in Nature through the veil of the soul."*
>
> POE, *"The Veil of the Soul"*

In its strictest historical sense, symbolism describes the French and Belgian writers of the late nineteenth century who, rejecting realism, tried to suggest ideas, emotions and attitudes by using symbolic words, figures and objects. Around 1885 to 1895, they produced manifestoes, sponsored literary reviews, met in various literary groups and discussed points of artistic doctrine. But as several notable critics have shown, symbolism has a much broader aesthetic and historical base and may include works dating from 1857 (when Baudelaire's revolutionary book of poems, *The Flowers of Evil*, appeared) to the 1930s.[1] Among the symbolist writers, one could then number the four greatest French poets of the second half of the nineteenth century—Baudelaire, Rimbaud, Verlaine and Mallarmé (sometimes called pre-symbolists or precursors of symbolism); the lesser-known poets and theoreticians (e.g. Henri de Régnier, Gustave Kahn, René Ghil, Jean Moréas, Francis Vielé-Griffin, Charles

---

[1] See, for example, Anna Balakian, *The Symbolist Movement: A Critical Appraisal* (New York: Random House, 1967); James R. Lawler, *The Language of French Symbolism* (Princeton, N.J.: Princeton University Press, 1969); Henri Peyre, *Qu'est-ce que le symbolisme?* (Paris: Presses Universitaires de France, 1974); and Edmund Wilson, *Axel's Castle: A Study in the Imaginative Literature of 1870–1930* (New York: Charles Scribner's Sons, 1931).

1

Morice, Emile Verhaeren); and several of the finest writers of the first third of the twentieth century: Paul Valéry, Paul Claudel, Marcel Proust, Rainer Maria Rilke, Hugo von Hofmannsthal, William Butler Yeats, James Joyce, T. S. Eliot, Gertrude Stein and Wallace Stevens (sometimes called post-symbolists or heirs of symbolism). Symbolism would then imply a general trend, and a special attention to language.

In its largest and most interesting aesthetic sense, symbolism implies at once a rebellion and a re-creation. It is a revolt against the kind of realism that is but the description of things, feelings and people. For the symbolists do not wish merely to describe; instead, they aim to re-create through their words a state of being, a feeling, a glimmer, a vision. They want the reader to sense, and to react to, the experience itself. Seen this way, symbolism is above all an attempt to transmit by means of symbols—frequently by means of a poetic language that the poet must invent—the mysteries that palpitate beneath appearances. A symbol is something that stands for or represents something else. It calls attention to itself while also suggesting far more than it is itself. The "meaning hidden behind the appearance is not necessarily one: the symbol is not a riddle. . . . There is therefore, in the symbol, polyvalence: a multiplicity of meanings," writes Henri Peyre.[2]

And so symbolism uses a veil, and seeks to pierce a veil. It uses a veil of words to convey emotions, perceptions and visions. And it seeks to pierce the veil of nature, of sensation and of truth: of truth that is the experience of a moment, and of truth that is eternal. In its most elevated reaches, symbolism is a quasi-religious quest that seeks to capture and to convey the ephemeral, the mysterious and the transcendent. "Every thing sacred and that wishes to remain sacred envelops itself in mystery," writes Mallarmé, whose pronouncements on poetry are invaluable to an understanding of what symbolism means in its most arcane and exalted aspects.[3]

---

[2] See his excellent book *Qu'est-ce que le symbolisme?* (note 1 above), p. 17. Unless otherwise noted, all translations throughout are my own.

[3] "Hérésies artistiques: L'Art pour tous" ("Artistic Heresies: Art for Everyone") in Stéphane Mallarmé, *Oeuvres complètes* (Paris: Gallimard, Bibliothèque de la Pléiade, 1945), p. 257. For the other three poets, I quote from the following editions: Charles Baudelaire, *Oeuvres complètes* (Paris: Gallimard, Bibliothèque de la Pléiade, 1961); Arthur Rimbaud, *Oeuvres complètes* (Paris: Gallimard, Bibliothèque de la Pléiade, 1972), and Paul Verlaine, *Oeuvres poétiques complètes* (Paris: Gallimard, Bibliothèque de la Pléiade, 1962). Unless otherwise stated, all references to the four poets are to these four editions. I give English titles for poems translated in this book; for other works, I list the French titles first.

Mystery, therefore, is paramount: mystery not merely described or interpreted or explained, but mystery reenacted, by means of the word. Mystery implies secrecy, obscurity and the quality of being inexplicable. Mystery also evokes a religious experience, suggesting by its etymology a supernatural thing, a secret rite or a divine secret. In fact, poetry for some of the symbolists is at times an almost divine utterance during which the poet appears a kind of god or a medium for a god. Through the mystery of the word, which may evoke the Word—the Logos, the poet seeks to commune with and to reveal the invisible, the infinite or the unknown. In "The Beacons," for example, Baudelaire portrays art as a reaching out toward the infinite; and at the end of "The Voyage," the poet exclaims that he wishes "to plunge . . . / . . . Into / The depths of the Unknown to find something *new*!" Rimbaud, who followed Baudelaire and who went farther than Baudelaire, proclaims that the poet "arrives at the *unknown*!" (Letter of May 15, 1871 to Paul Demeny). These poets' reachings out for the infinite, the invisible, or the unknown are certainly not traditional religious experiences. Nevertheless, their strivings and their exaltations carry overtones of the religious and of the prophetic: the ecstasy of experiencing, and of transmitting through words, the mystery.

In many ways, Baudelaire, Rimbaud and Mallarmé seek to create, by means of their art, a religion of poetry. Verlaine, on the other hand, creates at times, as in some of his poems in *Sagesse* (*Wisdom*) (e.g. "My God said to me . . . "), a poetry of religion. But in his own way Verlaine, too, seeks to capture and to convey his experience of the mystery. For his lyric transpositions are glimmerings of what is most fragile and most mysterious—mysterious in all senses of the word—in life: emotions, moods, memories, and moments.

Along with mystery, the secret and sacred value of the word, several other traits are more or less characteristic of the writers one may call symbolist, and particularly of the four poets upon whom we shall concentrate. Their poetry is above all suggestive. "I think that . . . there must only be allusion," Mallarmé told Jules Huret in an interview. "*To name* an object . . . is to suppress three-quarters of the enjoyment of the poem . . . *to suggest* it, there's the dream. The perfect use of this mystery constitutes the symbol: to evoke little by little a mood, or, inversely, to choose an object and to disengage from it a mood, through a series of decipherings" (Mallarmé, *Oeuvres complètes*, p. 869).

Their sensitivity is acute. Frequently they plunge into sensations, memories and dreams. So deeply do they delve into themselves that at times they become isolated and hermetic as they re-create their inner, private worlds. Their poetry then extends and develops the Romantic image of the poet isolated from the uncomprehending and hostile crowd: Baudelaire's "The Albatross" and Mallarmé's "Edgar Poe's Tomb" explore such figures. Mallarmé's poetic language and at times Rimbaud's (e.g. in "Memory" and other poems he wrote during the spring and summer of 1872—poems included in this book under the heading of "Last Poems Written in Verse"—and throughout much of *A Season in Hell* and *The Illuminations*), draw their richnesses from the secrets of the poets' psyches that perhaps they could explain, but certainly *will not*. Instead, the artists wish to remain obscure, seemingly aloof, isolated, disdainful. It is up to the reader to pierce the veil, to approach the mystery. The lonely towers in Yeats's poems are emblematic of such involuntary—and voluntary—isolation and alienation from the world.

Often in symbolist poetry there is music: music evoked to capture the poet's mood and to epitomize his emotions (as in Baudelaire's "Music"), or music re-created in sounds that filter through the lines. "Music before anything else . . . ," Verlaine advises in his "Art of Poetry." In fact, Verlaine's book *Romances sans paroles* ([Sentimental] *Songs without Words*) takes its title from music and implies that the poet's words are superfluous or that they are the music itself. There are also Rimbaud's beautiful rhythms and rhymes in lyrics like "The Crows" and "Shame"[4] and in the "songs" (like Verlaine, Rimbaud uses the word "romances") he mentions in "Deliriums II" of *A Season in Hell*: songs like "Eternity," which appears in an earlier version in this book. For Mallarmé, poetry in its purest, most ideal form is music, created by words: "Poetry, approaching the Idea, is Music, par excellence" ("Variations sur un sujet: Le Livre, instrument spirituel" ["Variations on a Theme: The Book, Spiritual Instrument"], p. 381). His lyrical and finely sensual "A Faun's Afternoon" inspired Debussy to compose in 1894 his melodious and exuberantly sensual *Prelude to A Faun's Afternoon*. In fact, Mallarmé said that his method of poetical notation ("this naked use of

---

[4] For studies of these poems, see Enid Rhodes Peschel, "Rimbaud's 'Les Corbeaux': A Hymn of Hopelessness—and of Hope," *French Review*, Vol. LII, No. 3 (Feb. 1979), 418–22; and "Shame" in Enid Rhodes Peschel, *Flux and Reflux: Ambivalence in the Poems of Arthur Rimbaud*, Preface by Étiemble (Geneva: Droz, 1977), pp. 71–78.

thought") in "Un Coup de dés jamais n'abolira le hasard" ("A Cast of the Die Will Never Abolish Chance") would create, in that poem partaking of free verse and of the prose poem, the effect of a "musical score" (p. 455).

For these four French symbolists, poetry becomes the search for, and the shaping of, a new poetic language. In order to transmit feelings, sensations and tremors, intimations of the invisible, glimmerings of truth and explosive visions; in order to re-create the vast panoply of emotions ranging from melodious languor to suicidal depression, from ethereal exaltation to volcanic joy, each poet forges his own special language: a language clothed in mystery, to reveal the mystery.

Each writer, therefore, introduces innovations, some more daring than others. Baudelaire, the earliest and perhaps the least innovative in terms of poetic diction, breaks away at times from the traditional French alexandrine (the line of 12 syllables) and from lines with an even number of syllables to use instead the *vers impair*, the line with an uneven number of syllables that Verlaine would later find so attractive, so appropriate to his unsettled, and unsettling, psyche. ("Prefer the Uneven-Syllabled Line," he would advise in his "Art of Poetry.") Baudelaire uses the *vers impair*, for example, in one of his most beautiful and lyrically unnerving love poems, "Invitation to the Voyage." He also introduces some linguistic innovations. For example, he uses anatomical and pathological vocabulary, in order to shock the reader, of course, but also and above all in order to depict fully, in all its grotesqueness and its beauty, the human condition.[5] Also, he infuses sensuous and sensual eroticism into great lyrical poetry. Not that French literature had been lacking in eroticism until Baudelaire's day, but in Baudelaire's poetry sensuality is at once lyrical, sensuous, erotic and spiritual (and not merely lewd, or crude or ribald). Baudelaire also uses synaesthesia, the evoking of one sense impression by means of another, to produce some of his most revolutionary, most powerful and most transcendent effects. For example, touch and smell call forth taste, sight and sound—all the body, mind and soul, therefore—in "Exotic Perfume," where the poet, who inhales "the scent" of his mistress's warm breast, sees and feels a vision unfolding that includes dazzling

[5] See Robert L. Mitchell, "From Heart to Spleen: The Lyrics of Pathology in Nineteenth-Century French Poetry" in *Medicine and Literature*, ed. Enid Rhodes Peschel (New York: Neale Watson Academic Publications, 1980), pp. 153–59.

sights, "savory fruits" and the perfumed scents of exotic trees that mingle in his "soul with the bargemen's melodies."

Following Baudelaire's lead in linguistic and rhythmic innovations, Rimbaud begins his poetic career with daring uses of blasphemy and scatology (e.g. "Evening Prayer"), and with stark, often grotesque evocations of human physiology or bodily excretions (e.g. "The Seated Ones," "The Plundered Heart" and the lines in "The Drunken Boat" about "vomit," birds' "droppings," and "mucus"). Both Baudelaire and Rimbaud, in fact, create an aesthetics of ugliness—partly through a predilection for perversity and perversion, a turning away from what is conventionally accepted (from the Latin *per*, an intensive, + *vertere*, to turn); partly through a desire to scandalize; and partly through their perceiving beauty in what is traditionally regarded as repulsive. For example, in "To the Reader," the prefatory poem to *The Flowers of Evil*, Baudelaire says: "In repugnant objects we find alluring charms." And as a fat and foul-smelling woman rises from an old bathtub in Rimbaud's sonnet "Venus Anadyomene," her "broad rump" is "hideously / Beautiful with an ulcer on the anus." While the title and the first thirteen lines clearly deride the classical conception of beauty, Venus rising from the sea, the words "hideously / Beautiful" reveal that for Rimbaud there is something sensuously and intellectually pleasurable in what others consider repulsive.

In his use of rhythmic innovations, Rimbaud goes much farther than Baudelaire, for he frees himself so completely from the constraints of French versification (he begins to break away in some of his poems of the spring and summer of 1872) that he writes two of the first free verse poems in French ("Marine" ["Seascape"] and "Mouvement" ["Movement"], which were eventually published in the *Illuminations*). More, he invents in the *Illuminations* a prose poem truly his own: a poem-illumination that is a synaesthetic explosion of sound, color, emotion and perpetual movement. Baudelaire, too, had created an original type of prose poem in his book published posthumously in 1869, *Petits Poèmes en prose: Le Spleen de Paris* (*Little Prose Poems: Paris Spleen*). But Baudelaire's prose poem, more discursive than Rimbaud's, is closer to lyric prose: a musical meditation that caresses, unnerves, and thrills. Rimbaud's poem-illumination, like a flash of lightning, is fiery and concentrated: a vision that bursts into being during a moment of almost divine revelation and is gone the next, remaining only—but remaining searingly, for one does not forget such explosions—in the memory and in the awakened senses. An illumination that dazzles, before the inevitable darkness.

Verlaine's poetry is on another plane, but it too scintillates with intimations of immortality, and mortality. His language is less daring than Rimbaud's; his innovations are far more timid. But while Verlaine never abandons rhyme, at times he stretches rhyme to its farthest limits by rhyming on an unstressed syllable, as in "Autumn Song," where he uses the article "la" as a rhyme word: "Et je m'en vais / Au vent mauvais / Qui m'emporte / Deça, delà, / Pareil à la / Feuille morte." (My translation attempts to capture that unexpectedness: "And I go off in / The evil wind / That carries me ahead / To this area / And that, like the / Leaf that is dead.") Or in "Moonlight," Verlaine's rhyming on the unstressed adjective "quasi" creates an unexpected rhyme that highlights the importance of this word which questions the very nature of his description. The maskers and bergamasche, he says, are "quasi / Sad Beneath their fantastical disguises." Thus, while rhyme is present for the eye in these cases, it is not there naturally for the ear unaccustomed to hearing an unstressed syllable as a rhyme word.

Verlaine is also somewhat innovative in terms of rhythm (he prefers the *vers impair*, as we have noted) and in vocabulary. Upon occasion he introduces colloquial, even popular, expressions into his poetry, phrases that he then juxtaposes with images that are extremely lyrical or delicate. For example, in the fourth stanza of "Brussels: Merry-Go-Round," a poem in which he immerses himself in dizzying sounds and movements, he says, using rather colloquial language: "It's entrancing how drunk it makes you to go / Like this in this silly carrousel: / Well-being in the belly and in the head, aching, so / Much aching and heaps of feeling well." But in the seventh, which is the final stanza, his language is highly poetic: "Go round, go round! the sky in velvet comes / To dress itself with golden stars." In "Kaleidoscope" he combines the colloquial and vulgar with the lyrical. In the sixth stanza he evokes prostitution, disease ("scurf") and "the scents of urine," as well as the sound of firecrackers, which in French may suggest passing gas (the French word for firecracker is *le pétard*). But the last stanza is delicate, sensuously lyrical and refined in vocabulary: "It will be like when one dreams and one wakes from sleep! / And one falls asleep again and one dreams once more / Of the same enchantment and the same décor, / In the summer's grass, to the moiré noise of the flight of a bee."

Like Rimbaud, Mallarmé was a daring and inimitable inventor of a poetic language. In "Edgar Poe's Tomb," his sonnet eulogizing and epitomizing his vision of the American poet, Mallarmé writes that Poe's goal was to "give a purer meaning to the words of the tribe." This is Mallarmé's goal, as well. To achieve his ends, Mallarmé takes words away from their ordinary usage in order to set them apart and to purify them. He dislocates syntax, places words in an unconventional, yet profoundly meaningful and above all suggestive order. He uses common words in uncommon ways, or he selects strange and uncommon words. He wrote to a friend on May 3, 1868, that he hopes that the word "ptyx," which he was using in his sonnet "Her pure nails . . ." (which critics now call the "sonnet in -ix"), "does not exist in any language" because that would give him "the charm of creating it by the magic of the rhyme" (p. 1488).[6] To Mallarmé, the meaning of "ptyx"—and of the whole poem—is unimportant in comparison to the word's—and to the entire poem's—evocative, mysterious and even mystical powers. In July 1868, Mallarmé wrote Henri Cazalis that this sonnet's "meaning, if it has one (but I would console myself with the opposite thanks to the dose of poetry it includes, it seems to me) is evoked by an internal mirage of the words themselves. In murmuring it several times one experiences a rather cabalistic sensation" (p. 1489). Meaning—or its opposite—is suggested here by what is beautiful but intangible, perceptible but unattainable, alluring but evanescent: the "internal mirage of the words themselves." This mirage is a vision created by the words, contained, closed in (Mallarmé uses the word "renferme"), concealed—yet also revealed—by the words. And this mirage, like all mirages, is bound to delight, and to deceive. For Mallarmé, the experience of poetry, an experience that is filled with hope even as it struggles ceaselessly against imminent annihilation, emptiness, nothingness and despair—the mirage that may, that *will*

---

[6] In 1940, Emilie Noulet pointed out that before Mallarmé, Victor Hugo had used the word "ptyx," which has a Greek origin, in *Le Satyre*, but as a proper noun and not as a common noun. She noted that the Greek dictionary gives for "ptyx": "the sense of folds and recesses [windings, coils] of an organ and cites an example in which 'ptyx' means oyster shell" (Mallarmé, *Oeuvres complètes*, p. 1490).

vanish—is like an esoteric and spiritual ecstasy. It is mysterious, mystical, cabalistic. One is entranced and transported by the poet's words in the way that one experiences and is exalted by practicing a religious rite. One enters into, and becomes part of, the ecstasy.

Other ways in which Mallarmé shocks the reader in order to make him grasp the full and pristine, the holy value of words, include his resorting to preciosity and periphrasis, elaborate verbal imagery orchestrated through sounds to evoke sensations, impressions and visions. To imply that the woman in "The hair flight of a flame . . ." wears no rings on her fingers, Mallarmé says that she moves "no star nor fires on her finger." A suicide full of gore and glory is the way he suggests a sunset in "Victoriously the beautiful suicide fled / Firebrand of glory, blood through foam, gold, tempest!" His images call upon a military conquest, beauty, fear and flight; flames and splendor; the darkness, tumult and destruction of a storm; death and drowning; blood that is horrible, but may be holy; gold that images richness, jewelry, brightness, beauty and purity.

In Mallarmé's utterances about poetry and in his poetry itself, there are persistent overtones of the spiritual. In "Solennité" ("Solemnity"), he speaks of "the ministry of the Poet" (p. 336). Often there is a delicate balancing of the physical and emotional with the religious, what Robert Greer Cohn so aptly calls Mallarmé's "real and poetic hunger for the supremely sensuous Infinite."[7] For poetry is a religion to Mallarmé, and the poet is a kind of priest who, in performing the rites of the word/Word, serves as an intermediary between the divine and those who would commune with the Mystery.

In what is called Mallarmé's "Autobiography" (his letter of November 16, 1885 to Verlaine), Mallarmé writes that he dreamed of the "Great Work . . . a book. . . . I shall go farther, I shall say: the Book. . . . The Orphic explanation of the Earth, which is the sole duty of the poet and the literary game par excellence" (pp. 662–63). The word "Orphic" evokes poetry, entrancing music, the occult, oracular pronouncements, and the Orphic mysteries celebrating the dismemberment and rebirth of the god Dionysus. The poet for Mallarmé is both Orpheus with his lyre and Dionysus torn

---

[7] See his outstanding book *Toward the Poems of Mallarmé* (Berkeley and Los Angeles: University of California Press, 1965), p. 49.

apart—sacrificed, made sacred thereby—and reborn, in the Poem. More, the sacrificed and re-created Dionysus may be seen as the image of Mallarmé's poetic language: the word ripped from its ordinary context, the sentence torn asunder, in order to be reborn, pristine and pure—reshaped as the poem, the symbol of everlasting life. In this mystical setting, the word "game" ("le jeu") is shocking and richly suggestive. The word startles, dramatizing Mallarmé's revolutionary use of language. "Le jeu" may imply an amusement that follows rules (games that children—or adults—play); gambling, with its financial, moral and spiritual risks; a medieval play (the theater was dear to Mallarmé); or a performance, the way an actor interprets a role. For Mallarmé, the game—or Game—assumes metaphysical connotations, veiling and unveiling the nature of being, the essence of things. "A lace annuls itself totally / In the supreme Game's uncertainty," he begins one sonnet. "This mad game of writing," he says in his lecture about Villiers de L'Isle-Adam, "to arrogate to oneself by virtue of a doubt—the drop of ink related to the sublime night—the duty to re-create everything" (p. 481). Many themes are united here: madness (like the Dionysian or Orphic frenzy), the game, doubt, the poet's arrogance and duty, and his search for the sublime. Writing, that Mallarmé calls a game, a *recreation*, is also, profoundly, for him a *re-creation*: "the duty to re-create everything." In this perspective, the poet is a kind of god. His poetry is metaphysics, music and mystery; agony and exaltation; "the Orphic explanation of the Earth." His poetry is a game that torments and transcends, a religion that is sensuous, spiritual and, always, self-renewing. *"Poetry,"* writes Mallarmé, *"is the expression, by means of human language brought back again to its essential rhythm, of the mysterious meaning of the aspects of existence: it thus endows with authenticity our sojourn and constitutes the sole spiritual task."*[8]

For these four French symbolist poets—and to some extent for all the writers one may call symbolist—art is a kind of religion, a supreme aesthetic experience that seeks to penetrate and to transmit, to discover and to re-create, the mystery; the invisible, ineffable, intangible and secret; the evanescent and eternal; the sensuous that is at once bodily, mental, emotional and spiritual. Such revelations

---

[8] Letter of June 27, 1884 to Léo d'Orfer in Mallarmé, *Correspondance II: 1871–1885* (Paris: Gallimard, 1965), p. 266.

are necessarily disturbing, shocking, unnerving—and exhilarating. Often, and in different ways, these poets jolt you, arouse you, grasp you, and transport you—even Verlaine, whose poetry at first, but only at first and not upon closer examination, seems so disarmingly simple. Art for these poets is the transmission of ultimate experience: of life, or of Life. And their poetic word, through the symbol, seeks to veil—and to unveil—the Mystery.

Baudelaire and the Poet-Translator's Sensuous Quest for Transcendence

> *Shall I strew on thee rose or rue or laurel,*
> *Brother, on this that was the veil of thee?* . . .

> SWINBURNE, *"Ave atque vale: In Memory of*
> *Charles Baudelaire"*

Charles Baudelaire was born in Paris on April 9, 1821 to François Baudelaire, an ex-priest who was sixty-two years old, and his second wife, Caroline, age twenty-eight. François Baudelaire, who had been released from his priestly vows after the French Revolution, had married Caroline Dufays, an orphan with no dowry, in 1819.

When Charles was just short of six, his father died, and for the next nineteen months, the boy was very close to his mother. Then Caroline Baudelaire married (this time for love) a man just four years her senior, Jacques Aupick, a military officer. Aupick was in the midst of forging a brilliant career for himself. When he married Baudelaire's mother, he was a major; three years later he was a lieutenant colonel; and by 1839 he was "Général Commandant de la Place de Paris." He was appointed ambassador: to Turkey in 1848, and to Spain in 1851. In 1853, he was named a Senator. Aupick, who, like his wife, had been left a moneyless orphan in his youth, believed strongly in duty and in obligations; unfortunately, he had little understanding of literature.

At first, his stepson liked Aupick, but later he came to loathe him. Always, Charles craved his mother's comfort, closeness and help but, because of Aupick, and because Caroline herself could not fully understand her rebellious and seemingly undisciplined son, he was often estranged from her. Once for a whole year (during 1854–55), she even refused to read his letters and returned them unopened.[9] At other times, however, she came to his aid, financially and emotionally.

After Baudelaire passed his *baccalauréat*, he moved to the Latin Quarter where he drank, smoked opium and took hashish. (Later he would write—lyrically, but also lucidly and condemningly—of these experiences in his *Paradis artificiels* [*Artificial Paradises*]). Around this time (1839–40), he probably contracted the venereal disease that would plague him the rest of his life.

More than a little worried about his stepson's lifestyle, Aupick convinced Baudelaire to go on a year-long sea voyage to Calcutta. Baudelaire sailed from France in June 1841, but by early November he was already returning home from Réunion. He would travel no farther. Still, memories of the tropics and of travels would remain with him.

In April 1842, Baudelaire turned twenty-one and came into his inheritance from his father (75,000 francs of the time). He established himself in the Hôtel Pimodan (later renamed Hôtel Lauzun, at 17, quai d'Anjou) on the Île-Saint-Louis. There he decorated his apartment lavishly, hired a servant, and took hashish with the other members of the *Club des Haschichins*. And he accumulated enormous debts.

By the autumn of 1843, Baudelaire was in love with Jeanne Duval, a mulatto actress. His bond to her would continue, with numerous interruptions, for the rest of his life. Passion—and quarrels, cruelty and treachery characterized their liaison. The poet and his mistress were for each other both victims and torturers. One time when Jeanne left him, Baudelaire wrote his mother: "I've used her and abused her! I've taken pleasure in torturing her, and now I've been tortured myself!"[10] Still, Baudelaire felt attached to Jeanne and even responsible for her. When Jeanne was old and ill, addicted to drugs and drink, and when they were no longer lovers, Baudelaire still continued to give her a monthly allowance. And Jeanne Duval is the woman who inspired some of his most beautiful, rapturous—and tormented—erotic poetry. (See in this collection "Exotic Perfume," "Head of Hair," "The Vampire," "The Cat," "*Duellum* [War]," the

---

[9] Enid Starkie, *Baudelaire* (New York: New Directions, 1958), pp. 272–73.
[10] Letter of September 11, 1856 in Starkie, *Baudelaire* (note 9 above), p. 283.

four-sonnet sequence called "A Phantom," and "Lethe." "The Jewels," too, may be about her.[11])

During the first eighteen months of his majority, Baudelaire had spent about one half of his inheritance. A family council was called, and the lawyer Ancelle, who later became Mayor of Neuilly, was appointed *conseil judiciaire*. For the rest of Baudelaire's life, Ancelle would dole out to Baudelaire, in monthly installments, the interest on his remaining capital. Always the poet would remain in debt, because at the time of the family council the debts of the twenty-two-year-old poet were not paid off.

Baudelaire led a bohemian—but far from idle or unproductive—existence. As an artist he instinctively understood and sided with newness. He became an art critic and exalted the work of Delacroix. He was the friend of Courbet, who painted him, and of Manet, who painted him as well as Jeanne Duval. He was the first French writer to translate Poe, whose works he revealed to the French. (Later, Mallarmé, too, would revere and translate Poe.) Baudelaire wrote essays about literature, modernity and the music of Wagner. He "dreamed of the miracle of a poetic prose, musical without rhythm or rhyme, supple enough and shocking enough to adapt itself to lyrical movements of the soul, undulations of reverie, sudden leaps of conscience" (Preface to *Petits Poèmes en prose*, p. 229). And so he invented his own form of the prose poem.

New loves entered Baudelaire's life and inspired new poems, even as his liaison with Jeanne interwove between them. Two other women are especially important: Madame Sabatier and Marie Daubrun. Madame Sabatier (her real name was Aglaé-Joséphine Savatier, but she changed it to Apollonie Sabatier, and added the Madame) was a beautiful and kind-hearted demimondaine. At her Sunday parties, she received numerous writers and artists, including Théophile Gautier, Barbey d'Aurevilly, Auguste Clésinger (whose marble bust of her is now in the Louvre), Ernest Feydeau and, of course, Baudelaire. Between 1852 and 1854, Baudelaire sent her anonymous love letters and poems that often idealize or spiritualize her. At times, his poems about her mingle the sensuous with the

[11] Some critics think that the poem was inspired by Jeanne (e.g. Starkie, *Baudelaire*, p. 283 (note 9 above), and Y.-G. Le Dantec and Claude Pichois, eds. Baudelaire, *Oeuvres complètes* [Pléiade, 1961], p. 1566), but Antoine Adam disagrees (ed., Baudelaire, *Les Fleurs du mal* [Paris: Garnier Frères, 1961], pp. 432–33).

religious, as in the exquisite "Evening Harmony." But sometimes they infuse elements of cruelty or vengeance, as in "Reversibility." In 1857, when *The Flowers of Evil* came out, Baudelaire finally wrote to her in his own name. Soon after that, she offered herself to him. He, revolted that his idealized love had become real, refused. "A few days ago you were a divinity," he wrote to her on August 31, 1857, "but now you're a woman. . . ."[12]

The other woman he loved—this one passionately—was the actress Marie Daubrun, who for years was the mistress of the poet Théodore de Banville. Baudelaire composed several poems to her during 1854 and 1855. One of the most beautiful, "Invitation to the Voyage," depicts his dream of going with her to a land where they would be surrounded by nothing but "order and beauteousness / Luxury, calm and voluptuousness." But the melodious poem is not without its unnerving rhythms (the French lines all have an uneven number of syllables) and the poet's awareness that this is all a dream: that if Marie with her "treacherous" eyes is the image of the country to which they will travel, then there can be no peace in that land that "resembles" her.

In June 1857, *The Flowers of Evil* was published and created a scandal. In August, in the Palais de Justice, Baudelaire and his publisher (Poulet-Malassis and de Broise) were brought to trial before the Sixième Chambre Correctionnelle, which generally heard cases of petty larceny, burglary and vagrancy. The Imperial Prosecutor was Ernest Picard, who earlier that year, and before the same magistrates' court, had tried—and had lost—the case against *Madame Bovary*. (The novel had been accused of offending public morals.) But in Baudelaire's case, Ernest Picard won—and literature lost. *The Flowers of Evil* was judged a "crime of outrage against public morality and accepted standards of good behavior."[13] Six poems were declared obscene and were henceforth banned from the book. (Two of these, "Lethe" and "The Jewels," appear under the heading "Condemned Pieces" in this collection.) Baudelaire was fined 300 francs, and Poulet-Malassis and de Broise, 100 francs apiece. Unsold copies of the book were confiscated. Thus was the reception accorded to the birth of modern poetry.

[12] Starkie, *Baudelaire* (note 9 above), p. 332.
[13] " . . . le délit d'outrage à la morale publique et aux bonnes moeurs" in Baudelaire, *Oeuvres complètes* (Paris: Éditions du Seuil, 1968), p. 733.

Illness began to plague Baudelaire's life. Jeanne was partially paralyzed in 1859. In 1860, Baudelaire suffered a seizure. Nevertheless, he was very productive. In 1859, excerpts of his translation of Poe's "The Philosophy of Composition" appeared; 1860 saw the publication of Baudelaire's *Paradis artificiels*. The next year was an eventful one. His ecstatic appraisal of Richard Wagner was published, as well as the second edition of *The Flowers of Evil*, which contained thirty-one new poems to replace the six condemned pieces. (My translations are based on this 1861 edition.) On September 6, an enthusiastic article about *The Flowers of Evil* appeared in *The Spectator*. It was written by another poet who, in honor of Baudelaire's death, would write a melodious and mournful dirge, "Ave atque vale": Algernon Charles Swinburne. But this year, strapped for funds, Baudelaire sold to Poulet-Malassis and de Broise the rights to publish his works: those already published, and those that he would write in the future. Pitifully, too, he presented himself as a candidate for membership in the French Academy. He was cruelly rebuffed, and withdrew his name.

In 1864, Baudelaire went to Brussels to try to earn some money. The next year, two young writers accorded his works great praise in the press: Mallarmé in "Symphonie littéraire" ("Literary Symphony") printed in *L'Artiste*, and Verlaine in three articles published in *L'Art*.

Baudelaire was now quite ill. In March 1866, in Belgium, began the symptoms of hemiplegia and aphasia that were never to leave him. In July 1866, partially paralyzed and totally speechless, he was brought back to Paris. The poet could still think, but he could not form the words to utter his thoughts. He died on August 31, 1867, in his mother's arms.

The next year, the third edition of *The Flowers of Evil* was published with several new poems ("Meditation" is one of them). In 1869, his splendid book of prose poems appeared.

"The artist, the true artist, the true poet, ought to paint only according to what he sees and what he feels," wrote Baudelaire in an essay in which he describes imagination as the "queen of the faculties" (p. 1037). And "Imagination," he adds, "is positively related to the infinite" (p. 1038). For Baudelaire, then, the artist's creating according to his sense impressions also implies his creating according to his imagination: his mind, his creative power and his images. His sensuous impressions and his imagination enable him to translate into word symbols his experiences of reality, and of the infinite.

The poet is, in fact, for Baudelaire a translator, a decipherer of symbols:

> . . . we arrive at this truth that everything is hieroglyphic, and we know that symbols are obscure only in a relative way, that is to say according to the purity, the good will or the native clearsightedness of souls. Now what is a poet (I'm taking the word in its largest sense), if not a translator, a decipherer? In excellent poets, there is no metaphor, no simile or epithet that is not an exact mathematical adaptation in the actual circumstance, because these similes, these metaphors and these epithets are drawn from the inexhaustible funds of the *universal analogy.* . . .

> ("Victor Hugo," p. 705)

The poet-translator transposes and decodes the symbols he encounters everywhere, for "everything, " Baudelaire says, "is hieroglyphic." The poet-translator's central quest—which is Baudelaire's quest—is to perceive and to communicate, to reach out for and to convey the resonances between the material, sensuous world and the realm of the spiritual. For excellent poets these resonances are exact, even mathematical, according to Baudelaire, since they are drawn from what he calls the *"universal analogy"*: the essential, metaphysical and unchanging similarities that he believes exist between the realms.

Baudelaire's famous sonnet "Correspondences" is emblematic of his sensuous quest for the infinite. Nature in this poem is holy; it is called a "temple." The hieroglyphs, the "symbols," are omnipresent, waiting, watching. Here, as often in his poetry, Baudelaire uses synaesthesia. Sounds, sights and scents evoke each other and seem to respond to each other:

> Like drawn-out echoes that from afar unite
> In a unity mysterious and profound,
> As boundless as the night and as the light,
> The scents, and colors and sounds all correspond.

The "correspondences" between the "scents, and colors and

sounds" combine in a unity that contains mystery, darkness and radiant revelations: deep meaning, secret rites and sacred truths.

Next comes a startling statement. For as Baudelaire dwells on the scents and on what they suggest, he says that it is not the fresh and mellow scents, but the scents evoking evil, that enable man to commune with the infinite:

> There are scents as fresh as children's bodies,
> As mellow as oboes, as verdant as the prairies,
> —And others, corrupted, rich and triumphant, having
>
> The expansiveness of infinite things,
> Like ambergris, musk, benzoin and incense,
> That sing the transports of the spirit and the senses.

By calling the scents in the last four lines "corrupted, rich and triumphant," the poet implies that they are debased and morally unsound; yet in their perverted state they are extremely fragrant and alluring, valuable and luxurious, elated and triumphant. More, it is these fallen and victorious scents precisely that perform the same function as the poet-translator. For, like the poet who translates the hieroglyphs of the transcendent into melody, so these scents "sing" the act of translation itself: "the transports of the spirit and the senses." The word "transport," after all, like the word "translate," may be rendered by the Latin verb *transfero, transferre, transtuli, translatus,* which means "to carry over or across," "to transfer," "to transport," "to convey" and "to translate." The physical, the evil, the fallen, which are also rich and exultant, are essential elements, therefore, of Baudelaire's reaching for the infinite. The sensuous is absolutely central to his apprehension of the spiritual.

Let a few examples suffice. "The Jewels," one of the "Condemned Pieces," is frankly sensual. In it the poet's quest takes the form of a symbol: the title describes the "jewels" the woman is wearing (and they are *all* that she is wearing: "My dearly beloved was nude, and, / She had kept on only her sonorous jewelry"), but they also describe much more. At first the literal jewels enrapture the poet, changing for him from jewelry into a world of commingling sensuous impressions: "When it hurls in dancing its alive and mocking jingle, / This radiant world of metal and stone grips me / With ecstasy, and I love passionately / The things in which sound and light commingle." As the poem progresses, however, it becomes clear that the real "jewels" are the parts of the woman's naked body in all its "candor" and "lubricity":

> With her eyes fixed on me, like a tiger made tame,
> In a vague and dreamy way she tried out poses,
> And her candor combined with her lubricity
> Gave a novel charm to her metamorphoses;
>
> And her arm and her leg, and her loins and her thighs,
> As smooth as oil, as sinuous as a swan,
> Moved past before my serene and clearsighted eyes;
> And her belly and her breasts, those clusters of my vine,
>
> Advanced, more wheedling than the Angels of evil. . . .

And the poem's last line characterizes her skin in terms of a jewel, for it is "the color of amber!"

"The Jewels," therefore, is a poem of metamorphoses and of symbols translated into other symbols. It is also, superbly, a rhapsody over the physical and metaphysical richnesses—animal, human and mythic—of a naked female body. It is a sensuous poem that soars to spiritual heights. "The nakedness of woman is the work of God," says the Voice of the Devil, which is the voice of inspiration, in Blake's *Marriage of Heaven and Hell*.[14]

In "Evening Harmony," mysticism, melody and melancholy interweave to portray the poet's vision of nature as a temple (or church) in which his "memory" of Madame Sabatier becomes a "monstrance," the image of Holy Communion and of salvation. In this mystical religious context, the setting sun, described in terms of a bloody death ("The sun has drowned in its blood that is clotting yet"), evokes the blood of Christ, the wine of Holy Communion. This, along with the poem's repetitive lines, rhymes and images contributes to an ambiance of swirling and intoxicating effects. This sensuous and spiritual evening is ever so appealing to this poet who loves sadness, languor and the dizziness of intoxication.[15]

---

[14] *Poetry and Prose of William Blake*, ed. Geoffrey Keynes (London: The Nonesuch Library, 1961), p. 184.

[15] For a fuller discussion of this poem and of the following one, see Enid Rhodes Peschel, "Love, the Intoxicating Mirage: Baudelaire's Quest for Communion in 'Le Vin des amants,' 'La Chevelure,' and 'Harmonie du soir' " in *Pre-Text/Text/Context: Essays on Nineteenth-Century French Literature*, ed. Robert L. Mitchell (Columbus, Ohio: Ohio State University Press, 1980), pp. 121-33.

Intoxication—exaltation and poisoning—through love are clearly evoked in "Head of Hair," inspired by Jeanne Duval. The fifth stanza is pivotal to the poem; it is also pivotal, I believe, to an understanding of Baudelaire's quest for love. For here, speaking of Jeanne's black hair in terms of an ocean that contains the vision of another ocean upon which he will travel, the poet says: "I'll plunge my head in love with drunkenness / Into this black ocean where the other is enclosed. . . ." His plunging suggests both physical and cerebral acts: he dreams of plunging into her hair/ocean in order to pursue his own sensations and visions. His quest in this poem ostensibly occasioned by love is not at all for communion—or even for communication—with the woman loved. Rather, it is for the ecstasy of intoxication itself. His "head" (and not his "heart") is "in love," and it is "in love" not with the woman, but "with drunkenness": with the physical and emotional elation that transports, but also harms, the one intoxicated. His eloquently erotic and strangely cerebral poem translates his essentially lonely vision of love: rich in dreams and in memory; rich, also, in evoking ardor and languor; but painfilled and bitter behind all the apparent beauty. Through Jeanne's hair the poet seeks—and is granted—a vision of heaven: "Blue hair, pavilion of outstretched night, you unbar / Once more the azure of the vast round sky for me. . . ." But through the symbol of Jeanne's hair, he also reveals the terrible truth that love for him is a solitary, albeit voluptuous, intoxication.

When depression and destruction set in, along with feelings of isolation, ennui, impotence and illness, Baudelaire translates his physical, emotional and spiritual struggles by means of a poetic language that creates claustrophobic, deathlike, almost airless atmospheres. For example, in "Spleen" ("I have more memories than were I a thousand years old"), his "sorrowful brain" is "a pyramid, a huge burial vault," and he himself is "a cemetery abhorred by the moon." All living matter appears to him lifeless, nothing more than a piece of granite alone and abandoned in the Sahara: an "old sphinx . . . /. . . . . / whose sullen / Humor sings only to the rays of the setting sun." Here is language in the act of portraying and conveying physical and imaginative, bodily and spiritual contests. Here is language re-creating verbally—viscerally—the vision of the transcendent as it is being smothered by sadness, anger, isolation, decrepitude and death.

But death is not always a wholly negative presence in Baudelaire's poetry. In "The Voyage," the last poem of *The Flowers of Evil*, the poet reaches out dramatically for death, which he sees as a "poison" that is also a hope for "something *new!*" And "Meditation," which appeared in the third edition of *The Flowers of Evil*, is a lyrical waiting for and welcoming of night—the symbol of death—in an ambiance of gentle, enticing calm.

For Baudelaire, therefore, the poem itself is the sensuous and imaginative search for transcendence. It is the transposing into melody of the quest: the struggles, the longings, the despairs, the visions and the victories. By means of his poetic language and symbols, the poet-translator carries over and decodes the "correspondences" he perceives between the physical and the spiritual realms. In so doing he re-creates for the reader his unending search for beauty, love, newness, mystery and rapture, in the face of his ceaseless struggles against ennui, time, illness, damnation and death. For Baudelaire, the poet-translator, the power of the poet is to make the otherworldly palpable: to translate the hieroglyphs of the transcendent into the language of the soul, the mind, the spirit, and the senses.

Rimbaud: Violence and Vision

> *I laughed at the blond waterfall which tossed dishevelled hair across the pines: on the silvery summit I espied the goddess.*
>
> *Then, one by one, I lifted her veils. . . .*
>
> RIMBAUD, *"Dawn"*[16]

Mallarmé, in a letter to Harrison Rhodes of April 1896, called Rimbaud a "flash . . . of a meteor" (p. 512). That image is particularly apt.

Arthur Rimbaud was born on October 20, 1854 in Charleville (Ardennes, now called Charleville-Mézières), a town in northeastern France near the Belgian border. He died thirty-seven years later in Marseilles, amputated of a leg that had developed a tumor, possibly

---

[16] Arthur Rimbaud, *A Season in Hell. The Illuminations*, trans. Enid Rhodes Peschel (New York, London, Oxford: Oxford University Press, 1973), p. 147.

of syphilitic origin, and totally unaware that in Paris his works were being published and acclaimed. For Rimbaud, who had renounced writing poetry by the time he was nineteen or twenty, had spent the last sixteen or seventeen years of his life traveling across Europe, often by foot, and working as a businessman, explorer and gun-runner in Cyprus, Egypt and Africa. Yet during the three or four—at most five—years of his meteoric literary career (1870 to 1873, 1874 or 1875), he helped revolutionize and revitalize the language, style, form and visionary content of French poetry.

Rimbaud's childhood was lonely, oppressive, and extraordinary. His father, Frédéric Rimbaud, a captain who had risen from the ranks of the French army, married Vitalie Cuif, a twenty-eight-year-old of peasant stock in 1853. Within seven years, the couple had five children. Arthur was the second child and second son; three girls followed, one of whom died in infancy. Two months after Isabelle, the last baby, was born, Captain Rimbaud abandoned his family. He never returned. Arthur was six years old.

Life was not easy for Madame Rimbaud, who was left with four young children, little money, and neighbors who looked askance at her because her husband had deserted her. Nor was she an easy person. "Statements from contemporaries are unanimous. Mme Rimbaud was haughty, inflexible, severe."[17] This authoritarian woman believed firmly in "work, money, [and] religion."[18]

As a child, Arthur was dutiful, pious, and an excellent student at school. As an adolescent, however, he would scrawl "Shit on God" on the park benches of his home town.

In 1870, Georges Izambard, a young teacher who also wrote poetry, became Rimbaud's teacher. He encouraged the boy and lent him books by Villon, Rabelais, Hugo, and the Parnassian poets. Madame Rimbaud was grateful for Izambard's interest, but her literary judgments were not of the best. For example, she berated Izambard for having given her son Victor Hugo's *Les Misérables*: "it would certainly be dangerous to let him read such books," she wrote him on May 4, 1870 (p. 236).

The year 1870 marks the beginning of Rimbaud's literary career. During this year he composed twenty-two poems in which he wrote about such topics as dreaming, eroticism and the pleasures of nature

[17] Suzanne Briet, *Rimbaud notre prochain* (Paris: Nouvelles Éditions Latines, 1956), p. 11.
[18] Suzanne Briet, *Madame Rimbaud: Essai de biographie* (Paris: Minard, 1968), p. 8.

("Feeling"), revolt as well as ugliness that is repulsive and appealing ("Venus Anadyomene"), children's loneliness, hunger and suffering ("The Bewildered Ones"), and the Franco-Prussian War ("The Sleeper of the Valley").

In July 1870, the Franco-Prussian War began. Izambard left Charleville. Rimbaud wrote to him on August 24: "You, you're lucky not to live in Charleville any more!—My native town is superlatively idiotic. . . . I'm like a fish out of water, sick, furious, stupid, at the end of my wits. . . . it's death!" (p. 238). Four days later Rimbaud suddenly boarded a train for Paris. Since the fifteen-year-old did not have enough money for a ticket, he was thrown into Mazas prison when he reached the City of Light. One week later he finally wrote to Izambard, begging for help. Izambard brought Rimbaud back to Douai in the north of France, where he was living with his two unmarried aunts, the Gindre sisters. A poem Rimbaud wrote some time after, "The Women Who Seek for Lice," probably evokes how he felt, and how he imagined these women felt, as they deloused him following his sojourn in Mazas. A current of eroticism—gentle, fearful, sad and dreamy—runs through this poem that depicts on the surface the rather repulsive act of plucking lice from a boy's head.

Izambard returned Rimbaud to Charleville on September 26, but after only a few days at home, Rimbaud ran away again. This time he walked for two weeks: from Charleville to Belgium and back to Izambard's. "My Bohemian Life," composed in 1870, evokes the intoxicating freedom he felt as he wandered alone in his tattered clothes on those fine "September nights."

Rimbaud ran off a third time. Between February 25 and March 10, 1871, he was in Paris again, but he was back home before the "bloody week" ("la semaine sanglante") of the Paris Commune.

Because of the war, schools did not reopen in the fall of 1870. And when classes finally began again in April 1871, the sixteen-year-old Rimbaud refused to return to the classroom. He had new ideas and projects. These were nothing more—and nothing less—than the revision of the nature, the perceptions and the provinces of poetry.

On May 15, 1871, Rimbaud described his new poetic theories to his friend Paul Demeny (in a letter that critics now call the "Lettre du voyant"): how he would make himself a poet-prophet-visionary—a *voyant*, Rimbaud calls it—by means of "a long, immense and reasoned *deranging* of *all his senses*" (p. 251). The oxymoron "reasoned *deranging*" stresses his dual impulses for order and anarchy; it highlights as well the fact that his sensuous deranging is both systematic and intentional. The poet who makes himself a *voyant* (I use the French word because Rimbaud's term incorporates—along with the notions of poet, prophet and seer—the revolutionary process of derangement he describes), must seek out and experience "all the forms of love, of suffering, of madness. . . ." This will be "unutterable torture in which he needs all his faith, all his superhuman strength." For the *voyant* becomes, Rimbaud proclaims, "the great invalid, the great criminal, the great accursèd one,—and the supreme Savant!—Because he arrives at the *unknown!*"

Right after these exultant words, however, Rimbaud reveals how his poetic method bears within it the seeds of its own destruction. "He arrives at the unknown, and when, crazed, he would end up by losing the understanding of his visions, he has seen them! Let him die in his leaping through unheard-of and unnameable things: other horrible workers will come; they will begin on the horizons where the other collapsed!" The statements seem a cry of joy: but the bravado cannot belie the impact of these words which foretell, in fact, the *voyant*'s fated dementia and demise. For he will become "crazed" and unable to understand his visions; and he may "die." That death may imply the death of the man, or the death of the poet in the man.

Speculation abounds as to why Rimbaud abandoned writing poetry at the age of twenty or thereabouts to begin a life of wandering and commercial enterprising so far removed from the poetic terrain. Yet a possible explanation presents itself right here, in Rimbaud's own words. For Rimbaud reveals, even as he euphorically brings forth his poetic plans, that his method of poetic creation itself, that "long, immense and reasoned *deranging* of *all his senses*," would help create, and then kill, his poetic genius.

The pattern outlined in this truly prophetic letter—exaltation followed by imminent, inevitable defeat—recurs often in Rimbaud's poetry.[19] For instance, "The Drunken Boat," written shortly after the letter, is a stunning illustration of the poet's dazzling visions and intimations of the unknown, followed by his lyrical and lucid

[19] For a more detailed discussion of this, see "Evolution of a Revolutionary Poet: Part Two" in Peschel, *Flux and Reflux* (note 4 above), pp. 33–52.

awareness of the fated and fatal outcome of his unprecedented adventure.

In 1871, Rimbaud was again smoldering in Charleville. That September he wrote to Paul Verlaine, a poet of twenty-seven who was already the author of two published volumes. Rimbaud told Verlaine that he had no money and that he wanted to go to Paris. He sent Verlaine several poems, including "The Seated Ones" (which satirizes the Charleville librarians who invariably complained when they had to get up to get books for Rimbaud) and "The Plundered Heart." This poem, evoking soldiers and a boat, drunkenness and nausea, transmits, in a playful meter whose tripping rhythm marches counter to the words' meaning, the adolescent's anguish, his feelings of filthiness and impurity, and his longings to be magically cleansed. Verlaine answered right away: "Come, dear great soul, we call you, we wait for you" (p. 261).

And so on September 10, 1871, Rimbaud went to Paris. At first he lived in Montmartre (at 14, rue Nicolet) with Verlaine and his young wife, Mathilde Mauté de Fleurville, at the home of her well-to-do parents. Immediately, however, Rimbaud's unkempt manner, unruly behavior and foul language scandalized Mathilde and her parents. By the end of the month, Rimbaud left their home. Verlaine and Rimbaud were now lovers. Their liaison would last nearly two years.

In Paris, Verlaine introduced Rimbaud to the literati of the capital, including José-Maria de Heredia, François Coppée, Charles Cros, Albert Mérat and Théodore de Banville. Rimbaud and Verlaine drank a lot. They attended meetings of the Vilains Bonshommes. After one of those meetings, however, Rimbaud was no longer allowed to return. He had been drunk and bored, and as Jean Aicard was reading his poems, Rimbaud had punctuated every line with "Shit!" When the photographer Carjat had finally tried to silence Rimbaud, Rimbaud had lunged at him with Verlaine's sword stick.

"A sort of sweetness shone and smiled in those cruel blue eyes and on that strong red mouth with its bitter pucker: what mysticism and what sensuality!" Verlaine would write years later about Rimbaud.[20] During their time in Paris, the two poets often went to talk,

---

[20] "Arthur Rimbaud" in *Hommes d'aujourd'hui* in Henri Peyre, *Rimbaud vu par Verlaine* (Paris: Nizet, 1975), p. 93.

drink and smoke with the other artists and writers who rented a room together in the Hôtel des Étrangers (rue Racine). Ernest Delahaye describes how Verlaine and he once found Rimbaud there after Rimbaud had taken some hashish. The poet who wanted to make himself a *voyant* was asleep on a bench in the large room. When his friends arrived, he woke up, "rubbed his eyes while making a face," and told them that "he had taken some hashish. —Well? . . . asked Verlaine. —Well, nothing at all . . . some white moons, some black moons, that were chasing each other . . . ." And Delahaye concludes: "In other words the famous drug had muddled up his stomach, given him dizziness, prostration: an 'artificial paradise' totally bungled."[21]

In July 1872, Rimbaud and Verlaine left Paris for Belgium and England. During their years together and shortly thereafter, Rimbaud composed most of his greatest works, including his lyrical poems of the spring and summer of 1872, *A Season in Hell* and the *Illuminations*.[22]

On July 10, 1873, the poets were in a hotel room in Brussels (Belgium). They had been quarreling for some time. Just one week before, Verlaine had abandoned Rimbaud penniless in London; then from the boat, he had written to Rimbaud, telling him that he "loved him immensely (Honni soit qui mal y pense)" (At sea, [July 3, 1873], p. 270). Verlaine had added that if his wife did not join him within three days, he planned to commit suicide. And he had begged Rimbaud to write to him. Rimbaud had answered immediately. On July 4 and July 5, he had written to Verlaine that he missed him and loved him: "The only true word, is: come back, I want to be with you, I love you" (London, July 5, 1873, p. 272). Verlaine had then called Rimbaud to Brussels, and Rimbaud had gone there. So, too, had Verlaine's mother, because Verlaine had also sent her a letter announcing his intention to kill himself if his wife did not come. (Mathilde Verlaine never came.)

It was early afternoon on July 10, and this time Rimbaud was threatening to leave Verlaine. Verlaine, who had been drinking all

---

[21]*Delahaye témoin de Rimbaud*, eds. Frédéric Eigeldinger and André Gendre (Neuchâtel, Suisse: Éditions de la Baconnière, 1974), p. 141.

[22] No one knows exactly when the *Illuminations* were composed. Verlaine claims that they were written between 1873 and 1875 ("Preface," Arthur Rimbaud, *Poèmes, Les Illuminations, Une Saison en enfer* [Paris: Vanier, 1891], p. v), but Delahaye says that they preceded *A Season in Hell* (*Souvenirs familiers à propos de Rimbaud, Verlaine, Germain Nouveau* [Paris: Albert Messein, 1925], p. 146).

morning, went out several times for a few more drinks, even as he argued with Rimbaud. All at once, Verlaine locked the door of their room and barricaded it with a chair. He grabbed a revolver that he had bought earlier that day and fired two shots. One bullet entered Rimbaud's left wrist; the other went towards the floor.[23] When Verlaine realized what he had done, he ran next door to his mother's room and threw himself, "almost crazed," on the bed (p. 281). Putting the revolver into Rimbaud's hands, he told the eighteen-year-old to shoot him in the temple.

Somehow, Rimbaud and Madame Verlaine were able to calm Verlaine down and to bandage Rimbaud's wrist. Next they went to a hospital, where they were told that the bullet could not be extracted that day. Rimbaud, who did not consider the wound very serious, then insisted that he would take the train back to France that evening. "That news threw Verlaine into despair once again" (p. 281). As Verlaine and his mother accompanied Rimbaud to the train station, Verlaine kept his hand in his pocket, where Rimbaud believed the revolver was. Suddenly, Verlaine walked ahead of Rimbaud, turned, and came back towards him in what seemed to Rimbaud like a threatening manner. Terrified, Rimbaud ran away and found a policeman. "I saw . . . [Verlaine] put his hand into his pocket to seize his revolver," Rimbaud told the Police Superintendent at about eight o'clock that night (p. 277). And so Verlaine was arrested.

Rimbaud, who had developed a fever by then, was admitted to the hospital. Two days later, because the doctor said that Rimbaud was too ill to testify in the courtroom, a judge interrogated him in the hospital. The bullet was finally extracted on July 17. On July 18, Rimbaud tried to have all charges dropped against Verlaine. In a signed statement, he said that "Verlaine was in such a state of drunkenness that he was not at all conscious of his action" ("Acte de Renonciation de Rimbaud," p. 284). But the legal processes had begun and could not be stopped. Mathilde's lawyer had come from Paris to garner incriminating material for her divorce suit.

There was a trial. The poets' homosexuality aroused prurient curiosity and censure. An incriminating letter from Verlaine, dated

---

[23] This information and what follows comes from "Déclaration de Rimbaud au Commissaire de Police, 10 juillet 1873 (vers 8 heures du soir)" and "Déposition de Rimbaud devant le Juge d'Instruction, 12 juillet 1873" in *Oeuvres complétes*, pp. 276–77 and 279–82.

May 18, 1873, had been found on Rimbaud. "I'm your *old cunt ever open* or *opened*," Verlaine, who was "a little drunk," had written.[24] (The italics mark his use of English. Earlier in the letter, he had complained about the difficulties of translating French into English.)

On August 8, Verlaine received the maximum sentence for criminal assault: a fine of 200 francs and two years in prison. (He would be freed after eighteen months.) Rimbaud was not present at the proceedings. On July 20, he had returned to his mother's farm in Roche (in the Attigny district) to complete *A Season in Hell.* "Deliriums I" of this masterwork is clearly a transposition of his life with Verlaine, a dramatization and analysis of their search for a new love. In it, the "Infernal Bridegroom," a self-characterization of Rimbaud, who is married to the "Foolish Virgin," a stylization of Verlaine, says: " 'I don't like women. Love has to be invented over again. . . .' "[25]

Rimbaud published *A Season in Hell* in Brussels (Alliance typographique, Poot et Cie) in 1873, at his own expense. He gave some copies to his friends: Verlaine, Delahaye, perhaps some others. But since he could not afford to pay for the rest of the books, they remained, forgotten, at the publisher's until 1901, when they were rediscovered.

In 1874, Rimbaud returned to London, this time with the poet Germain Nouveau. He may have been working on some of the *Illuminations* at this time.

In 1875, after his release from prison, Verlaine went to see Rimbaud in Stuttgart, where Rimbaud had gone to learn German. During this time, Rimbaud may have given Verlaine the manuscript of the *Illuminations*, which Verlaine later had published. Rimbaud described their meeting to Delahaye: "Verlaine arrived here the other day, a rosary in his paws . . . Three hours later one had denied his god and made the 98 wounds of O[ur] L[ord] bleed. He stayed for two and a half days and was quite rational . . . " (March 5, 1875, p. 296). The two poets never saw each other again.

After Rimbaud's adventures in poetry—his visionary voyages into the unknown—he began his life of real travels and of lived, instead of literary, adventures. Some writers have romanticized his life of

---

[24] In Peyre, *Rimbaud vu par Verlaine* (note 20 above), p. 28.
[25] Rimbaud, *A Season in Hell. The Illuminations* (note 16 above), p. 69. For an analysis of this astonishing and moving text, see Peschel, *Flux and Reflux* (note 4 above), pp. 87–102.

wandering and traveling in Europe and Africa.[26] But his letters to
his mother and sister in France reveal how difficult, how prosaic and
how boring his life often was as he tried to earn and to accumulate
money. For example, he wrote from Aden (in present Southern
Yemen) on April 14, 1885. "I'm suffering from a gastric fever, I can't
digest anything. . . . Life here is horribly bad . . . one leads the
world's most atrocious life here. . . . Business has become very
difficult here, and I live as penuriously as possible, to try to get out of
here with something. Every day, I'm busy from 7 till 5, and I never
have a day off. When will this life end?" (pp. 398–99). Two years
later, he wrote again from Aden: " . . . for two years, my business
has been very bad, I tire myself out pointlessly, I have a lot of trouble
keeping the little that I have. I'd really like to have done with all
these confounded countries . . . " (October 8, 1887, pp. 449–50).
Boredom ("ennui") runs like a leitmotif through his letters. "I'm
very busy, very bored," he wrote from Harar (Abyssinia, modern
Ethiopia) on July 4, 1888 (p. 497). "I'm very bored, always," he
repeated one month later (p. 501).

Still, the events of Rimbaud's nonliterary life are noteworthy,
intriguing as incidents in themselves and as part of the pattern of his
life. In 1876, Rimbaud joined the Dutch colonial army because he
wanted to go to Java, but he deserted in Batavia. The next year he
wrote to the American consul in Bremen to inquire about enlisting
in the United States Navy, but he apparently neglected to include a
return address. In 1879, he left France and did not return until twelve
years later, when he was dying. During those years, he worked in
Aden and Harar, dealing in skins and in coffee. He was the first
European to explore the Ogaden area of Ethiopia. In 1887, he tried
to make a fortune by carrying and selling guns to King Ménélik II of
Shoa (the province in modern Ethiopia whose capital is Addis
Ababa). But during this perilous five-month expedition, Rimbaud
lost sixty percent of his capital.

Rimbaud returned to France in May 1891 and died in Marseilles
on November 10. He never knew that in Paris the "symbolists" were
reading his works. For Verlaine, like the "Foolish Virgin" of *A
Season in Hell* who was "never . . . jealous" of her lover,[27] had

---

[26] For some excellent criticism of this, see "Rimbaud l'aventurier" in Etiemble, *Le Mythe de
Rimbaud*, Vol. II, *Structure du mythe* (Paris: Gallimard, 1961), pp. 235–41.
[27] Rimbaud, *A Season in Hell. The Illuminations* (note 16 above), p. 73.

introduced Rimbaud's writing to the public. Verlaine had devoted a chapter to Rimbaud in *Les Poètes maudits* (*The Accursèd Poets*) in 1884, and he had edited the first edition of the *Illuminations*, published in 1886. In the year of Rimbaud's death, *A Season in Hell* was republished, along with his poems and the *Illuminations*, with a "notice" by Verlaine.

Violence and vision inhere equally in Rimbaud's art. Even before the "Lettre du voyant," his poetry is full of visceral fury, anger and the desire to shock, even as he seeks to create his own poetic language and vision (e.g. "Venus Anadyomene," "The Bewildered Ones," "The Sleeper of the Valley"). Violence signals Rimbaud's rebellion against bourgeois values (e.g. work, religion, and material rather than spiritual concerns), against suffering caused by poverty and by tyranny, and against accepted aesthetic doctrines. Further, violence signals his method of creation itself: a personal and total, physical and psychic deranging that, although ultimately destructive—and one can never forget that it is destructive—will lead the poet to illuminating rearrangements: of perceptions, of language, and of knowledge. Because, exults Rimbaud, the *voyant* becomes "the supreme Savant!" A dynamic tension pulsates, therefore, throughout Rimbaud's poetry, reflecting his antithetical urges for destruction and creation, anarchy and order, torture and transcendence. Along with ambivalent longings, rapidly modulating moods and images become emblems of his search and of his art. He must destroy in order to create, and he must create before he himself is overcome. For like rebellion, vision and loss of vision are central to Rimbaud's art.

While Rimbaud's poems present many different stages of his quest, "The Drunken Boat," which he brought to Paris in September 1871 to show Verlaine his new kind of poetry, may be read as a symbolical illustration of the fateful poetic pattern Rimbaud outlined in the "Lettre du voyant."[28] This one-hundred-line poem, which has become a classic of French literature, retells—really re-creates—the experiences and results of Rimbaud's "long, immense and reasoned *deranging* of *all his senses.*" The narrator of the poem

[28] The discussion that follows is a development of part of my essay " 'To Plunge into the Bottom of the Abyss': Rimbaud's Search for the Unknown in 'The Drunken Boat' and 'Memory' " in *French Symbolist Poetry: Sou'wester* (Southern Illinois University), ed. Enid Rhodes Peschel, Special Issue, Vol. 6, No. 1 (Winter 1978), 73–85.

is the poet-boat who, by the second stanza, proclaims that he has become an active agent in his own adventure: "The Rivers let me sail down where I desired." Now "heedless" of others, he pursues wholly his own sensuous, emotional and visionary experiences.

The poet-boat's search is a tumultuous one, reflected in the ever-changing images of the poem. Stanza 4, for example, balances and blends opposing figures: a storm and a blessing, sea and land, intoxicated dancing on the waves and death in the sea. Opposites contrast and conjoin. The beauty of "the Poem / Of the Sea, infused with stars, and lactescent"—evoking art and water, heaven and a mother figure—is immediately juxtaposed with the horror of a drowned man sinking into the sea in stanza 6. But this drowned man is appealing, even extremely alluring to the narrator, who depicts him as "a pale flotsam in ecstasy." Toward the end of the poem, in fact, in stanza 23, the narrator, too, will want to merge with the sea.

Beauty and ugliness seem to call for each other in "The Drunken Boat." Thus, stanzas 12–14 shift rapidly back and forth from the beautiful to the repulsive: from "Rainbows / Stretched like bridles beneath the horizon / Of the seas, to glaucous droves!" to fermenting fens and a rotting Leviathan; and then to "Glaciers, silver suns, skies of embers, pearly waves," just before "Hideous runnings aground," "voracious bugs" and odors that are "black!"

The poem, therefore, does not progress in a linear structure; instead, it develops through a clash of changing images that reflect the disturbances inherent in the *voyant*'s voyage and his encounters with the unknown. Still, an overall pattern, the one sketched in the "Lettre du voyant," does emerge: rebellion and sensuous derangements prepare the way for a momentary, ecstatic vision, which then vanishes, or vanquishes the poet.

Stanzas 1–5 develop the tale of how the narrator achieved his liberation. Images of sourness and pleasure, cleansing water (suggestive of a baptism) and vomit, intoxication and sickness, control and loss of control mingle in stanza 5. After this initiation, the poet-boat, who has lost his "rudder and grappling," is finally free to pursue—unfettered, for better and for worse, for now he cannot really steer or restrain himself—his quest for the unknown.

"And since then, I have bathed in the Poem/Of the Sea," he begins stanza 6, as he immerses himself in the spiritual and physical elements, the Poem/Sea, of his intoxicating voyage. Through a constant counterpoint of figures and tensions, stanzas 6–22 re-create the poet's ecstasy and agony in his all-consuming quest for the unknown. Nothing here is static. The search is relentless and incessant; the vision sought, illuminating and evanescent. A momentary climax is reached in stanza 8. First, the poet juxtaposes violence ("skies bursting into lightnings, and waterspouts / And undertows and currents") with the vision—ecstatic, uplifting and suggesting the sacred—of "Dawn/Exalted like a flock of doves." Then he erupts with the words: "And I have seen sometimes what man believed he saw!" This exclamation is as extraordinary in what it reveals, as it is disappointing in what it conceals.

The poet's overall pattern of vision that leads to loss of vision begins to emerge clearly in stanzas 16–18, where figures of depression, martyrdom, sobbing, helplessness and death predominate. Stanzas 19–20 counter this to some degree with images evoking liberty, power and the conquest of "the reddening heavens." But by now the poet-boat, a "crazy plank" (stanza 20), feels descending upon him the madness that Rimbaud predicted would destroy the *voyant* ("when, crazed, he would lose the understanding of his visions," as he wrote in the "Lettre du voyant," p. 251). Stanza 21 returns to the theme of depression, darkening its image now with fear ("I who quaked") and with the startling revelation that the poet-boat now longs for what he had rejected at the beginning of his adventure: tradition, restraints, land and country. For here he exclaims: "I have regrets: / I miss Europe with its ancient parapets!"

The last three stanzas (23–25) portray the voyager sinking deeper and deeper into defeat. Amid figures of destruction and depression in stanzas 23 and 24, there are still some elements of lyricism, if not of hope. The narrator envisions a merging with the sea in stanza 23, and a fragile beauty in stanza 24. But stanza 25, constructed entirely around the negative phrase "I can no longer," is an admission of impotence, exhaustion and failure.

Let us look a little closer at these three stanzas. In stanza 23, the narrator is disgusted with himself. He finds each new day and each new night hateful or bitter. He wants to be destroyed as a boat and to merge with the sea:

> But, really, I've wept too much! The Dawns are distressing.
> Each moon is atrocious and each sun depressing.
> With intoxicating torpors bitter love swelled me.
> O let my keel burst! O let me go into the sea!

He blames "bitter love"—erotic or spiritual—for causing his "intoxicating torpors," those exaltations that are also ruinations. "Torpors" suggest sensuous and amorous exhaustions, the loss of the power of sensation, the forgetting of oneself and of the physical. But "torpors" also imply inaction due to dullness, lethargy and apathy: dead weight. The narrator's desire to burst apart and to be embraced and subsumed by a larger force suggests a destruction that is a joining with nature. But this joining is longed for out of despair, and not out of hope. It is a merging with oblivion and unconsciousness, and not a rebirth as a thinking or feeling or spiritual entity.

Stanza 24 evokes a childlike—but very sad—innocence and purity.

> If there is a water in Europe that I desire,
> It's the black, cold puddle where in the embalmed air of twilight
> A crouching child filled with sadnesses, releases
> A boat as frail as a Maytime butterfly.

The sounds and words first seem lyrical, caressing. The frail boat, like the butterfly, suggests something delicate and lovely. But an anger wells up behind those words, for the poet-boat who has traveled on the spectacular seas of the unknown now says that "if" he desires a water in Europe—and the "if" is important, for perhaps he no longer wishes to travel at all, or to be in Europe—the water he would wish for would be an image of coldness and constraint: a "black, cold puddle." He has traveled from the sublime to the pathetic: from the oceans of the unknown to a mud puddle. And on that muddy puddle, a "child filled with sadnesses" (one thinks of the child that Rimbaud himself was, perhaps, a child so filled with sadness that the word must be used in the plural) would release a beautiful but "frail" boat: one doomed to travel little (on a mud puddle) and to last but a short time ("like a Maytime butterfly"). The ambiance also predicts impending darkness and doom, for the twilight is scented (it is "embaumé," not "parfumé") with the air of death: it is "embalmed."

The final stanza portrays the poet-boat's despair, his inability to move, to act or to hope. Still, the words maintain the ambivalent balancings of emotion and language that pervade Rimbaud's poetry. The *voyant* is defeated here, yet in his fallen state he also condemns and attacks the things that now seem to overwhelm him: the "pride" around him, and "the horrible eyes of prison ships."

The oppositions and continual contrasts in "The Drunken Boat" highlight the fact that violence, which is central to Rimbaud's search for the unknown, is also at the heart of his visionary poetry. Rimbaud seeks to burst through all barriers in order to discover the unknown. His visionary voyage—wonderful and terrible, creative and destructive, rapturous and ruinous—is founded on what Hart Crane calls "the rapturous and explosive destructivism of Rimbaud."[29] Other figures of fire also epitomize Rimbaud and his poetry. One thinks, for example, of a "flash of lightning," which is the title of one chapter of *A Season in Hell*, and of Mallarmé's shooting star, the "flash . . . of a meteor"—a blaze of light before the certain blackness and the cold. And one thinks of the flame-etched poems that are the vision, and the struggle.

Verlaine: Soulscapes of Quiet and Disquiet

> *It's beautiful eyes behind veils,*
> *It's the full noon's trembling light,*
> *It's the blue jumble of bright*
> *Stars in a tepid autumn sky!*
> VERLAINE, *"Art of Poetry"*

Rimbaud used to say about Verlaine, "He's a charming child, violent and dangerous when he's drunk."[30] These clashing qualities permeate Verlaine's troubled and tormented life and poetry. On the one hand, there is charm—gentle, attractive and captivating; and there are the innocent strengths and lovable weaknesses one associates with childhood—like purity, spontaneity, vulnerability and naïveté.[31] On the other hand, however, there are anger, passion and viciousness, and a depression so devastating that it seeks relief in drunkenness. The tale of the contradictions in Verlaine's life is like a prelude that prepares one to understand, to accept—and to listen for—the contradictions in his poetry. For beneath the musical

[29] Letter to Waldo Frank, June 20, 1926 in *The Complete Poems and Selected Letters and Prose of Hart Crane*, ed. Brom Weber (New York: Doubleday, Anchor Books, 1966), p. 231.
[30] According to their mutual friend Ernest Delahaye, in *Delahaye témoin de Rimbaud* (note 21 above), p. 187, n. 52.
[31] For an excellent study of naïveté in Verlaine's art, see James R. Lawler, *The Language of French Symbolism* (note 1 above), pp. 21–70.

charm of his melodies, an anger and an anguish seep, or rend their way through.

Paul Verlaine was born in Metz on March 30, 1844. His father, Nicolas-Auguste, an adjutant battalion captain, was forty-six. His mother, Élisa, was thirty-five. She had had three miscarriages before Paul was born. He would be their only child.

In 1851, Captain Verlaine resigned his military commission and moved his family to Paris. Paul grew up adored by his mother and by his cousin whose name, like his mother's, was Élisa. Élisa Moncomble, an orphan eight years older than Paul, was being reared by Paul's mother.

When Verlaine was nine, he began attending boarding schools. Although he was a good student at first, by the time of his *baccalauréat* he had dropped to the bottom of the class.

At eighteen or nineteen, he began drinking. Around this time, in 1863, his first poem was published and he became friends with other writers in Paris, including Théodore de Banville, Villiers de l'Isle-Adam, Louis-Xavier de Ricard, Léon Valade, Albert Mérat, Catulle Mendès, Charles Cros and Sully Prudhomme.

During the next few years, two events deeply upset Verlaine: his father's death in 1865 (Captain Verlaine had been quite sick since 1862), and his cousin Élisa's unexpected death in February 1867, after a difficult childbirth. When Verlaine arrived for her funeral in Lécluse, where she had been living with her husband, the funeral procession was just leaving her house. Verlaine got so drunk for three days after this that he scandalized his entire family and the town. This pattern of grief followed by obstreperous drunkenness would recur.

Verlaine's first book, *Poèmes saturniens* (*Saturnine Poems*), was published in 1866. The press, Verlaine would later say, accorded it "a fine *succès d'hostilité*."[32] Although strongly influenced by the Parnassians, the book shows that Verlaine was already beginning to find his own voice. Thus, landscapes in several of these poems are already soulscapes. For example, "Nevermore," which takes its title from Poe's "The Raven," blends ideas of love and loss, harmony and discord, happiness and nostalgic sadness, health and sickness, perfumed flowers and their inevitable demise: the beginning of love,

---

[32] *Les Poètes maudits* in *Oeuvres complètes de Paul Verlaine*, Vol. IV (Paris: Vanier, 1910), p. 79.

therefore, and its end. And the melodious "Autumn Song" is a sad and sensuous merging with nature, with evil and with death.

Verlaine's next book, *Fêtes galantes (Gallant Festivals)*, "whose title belies the deep sadness often found in the verses," as Diana Festa-McCormick notes,[33] appeared three years later, in 1869. This lyrical and disturbing medley of poems inspired by love and its loss takes its inspiration from the gallant festivals depicted in eighteenth-century painting (one thinks, for example, of Watteau's "The Embarcation for Cythera"). In the poems, maskers and figures from French pantomime and Italian comedy, phantoms and phantomlike people act out the gallantries that live and die beneath the moon's bewitching, but often less than beneficent, gaze.

Off and on around this time, Verlaine was drinking. Twice in July 1869, he tried to kill his mother. His relatives thought that married life might calm him down, and they proposed one of his cousins for his mate. Instead, Verlaine asked his friend Charles de Sivry if he could marry Sivry's half-sister, the sixteen-year-old Mathilde Mauté de Fleurville. Verlaine courted Mathilde with poems that he composed for her (e.g. "Before you depart, / Pale morning star . . . " and "The moon shines white . . . "). These lyrics would go into his next book, *La Bonne Chanson (The Good Song)*, which was printed in 1870 but not distributed until 1872, because of the Franco-Prussian War.

On August 11, 1870, when Mathilde was seventeen (she was a year and a half older than Rimbaud) and Verlaine was twenty-six, they were married. At first, they lived in their own apartment and Verlaine was a clerk in the Hôtel de Ville (Town Hall). But a few months later, Verlaine participated in the Paris Commune of 1871; and when the Commune was overthrown, he lost his job. Since they could no longer afford their own apartment, Verlaine and his pregnant wife moved in with her parents at 14, rue Nicolet in August 1871. Rimbaud would arrive there one month later. (Details of that saga are recounted in the Rimbaud section of this book.)

On October 30, 1871, Verlaine's son, Georges, was born. Verlaine was drinking again. He would come home late at night, horribly intoxicated. He fought with Mathilde, at times would hit her, and in January 1872, almost strangled her.

[33] "Verlaine: Meditation within Shimmering Sketches" in *French Symbolist Poetry: Sou'wester* (note 28 above), p. 93.

On July 7, 1872, Mathilde was feeling ill. Her husband said that he would go out to find Dr. Cros. Verlaine did go out . . . and found Rimbaud. And on that day the poets began their travels together that would terminate one year later with two pistol shots in Brussels. During all this time of cruelty and callousness towards Mathilde, of drunkenness and of impassioned seeking for a "new love" with Rimbaud, Verlaine was writing one of his most beautiful and lyrical, and original, collections of poetry, *Romances sans paroles* ([Sentimental] *Songs without Words*). It would be published in 1874, when the poet was in prison.

After the events in Brussels on July 10, 1873, Verlaine spent a year and a half in prison. There, he wrote many memorable and moving poems, including "My God said to me . . . ," "Hope shines like a blade of straw . . . ," "A great dark drowsiness . . . " (composed on August 8, 1873, the day on which he was sentenced), "Kaleidoscope," "Art of Poetry," and his vision of Rimbaud and of their "crime of love," "*Crimen amoris*." In *Mes Prisons* (*My Prisons*), Verlaine evokes the atmosphere of "The sky is, above the roof . . . ": "Above the front wall my window (I had a window, a real one! provided, the idea! with bars that were side by side . . . and I used to see, it was in August, the top swaying, with its voluptuously shivering leaves, of some tall poplar of a nearby boulevard or square. At the same time faraway noises, softened, would reach me, of a festival . . . " (p. 1131). These poems would be included in his next two books: *Sagesse* (*Wisdom*), published at Verlaine's expense, in 1881; and *Jadis et naguère* (*Long Ago and A Short While Ago*), published by Vanier in 1885.

In the spring of 1874, when Verlaine was in prison, Mathilde received an official separation from him and custody of their child. The court also ordered Verlaine to pay 100 francs per month for child support. The poet was distraught. In June he reconverted to Catholicism, the religion of his youth, and in August he received communion. *Sagesse* is imbued with religious inspiration and symbols, sometimes explicit and sometimes extremely delicate and subtle. Verlaine's faith—and this is scarcely surprising to anyone who knows his life—is not simple, nor is it exuberantly joyous. Instead, it is a constant struggle, a full acceptance of man's fallen state, sufferings and weaknesses with all of which, the poet believes, Christ empathizes and, through the crucifixion, embodies. Thus, "God" tells the "pitiable friend" in "My God said to me . . . ": "Haven't I sobbed your utmost anguish, and haven't / I sweated the sweat of your nighttimes, pitiable friend / Who seeks for me where I am?"

Upon his release from prison in January 1875, Verlaine was expelled from Belgium. In late February, in Stuttgart, he saw Rimbaud for the last time. For some months after that, he corresponded with his former lover. But Rimbaud was now importuning him for money. On December 12, 1875, Verlaine sent Rimbaud a final letter: he said that he would not send him any money and also that he did not want Rimbaud to have his address. But he added that Rimbaud could write to him at Ernest Delahaye's. And over the years, when Verlaine no longer heard from Rimbaud, he would continue to ask Delahaye about the man whose poetry he would begin to reveal to the public in 1883 and 1884, in *Les Poètes maudits* (*The Accursèd Poets*), ten and more years after their liaison had ended.

From 1875 to 1879, Verlaine found teaching jobs: first in England—at a grammar school in Stickney (Lincolnshire), where he taught French and drawing, and then at a secondary school in Bournemouth. He taught French, English and history in France, from October 1877 to June 1879, at the Institution Notre-Dame de Rethel. The students and staff there thought him strange. "He kept his arms crossed on his chest, his hands spread out. The ecclesiastical staff thought this layman was overdoing it, and the students, with their lively sense of ridiculous, called him Jesus Christ."[34] Verlaine was drinking again and was finally dismissed from the school.

One of his pupils in Rethel was a nineteen-year-old peasant named Lucien Létinois. Verlaine became closely attached to him, and they traveled to England together. When they returned to France, Verlaine bought a farm in Juniville and lived on it with Lucien and Lucien's parents. Farming, however, proved a financial disaster for them, and so in 1882, Verlaine tried to get his job back at the Hôtel de Ville, from which he had been dismissed after the Paris Commune of 1871. But records of his trial, prison term and impending divorce arrived, and he was denied reinstatement in April 1883. It was a devastating blow. So was another event that occurred that month. For on April 7, Lucien died suddenly of typhoid fever. From

[34] Antoine Adam, *The Art of Paul Verlaine*, trans. Carl Morse (New York: New York University Press, 1963), p. 39.

this time on, although Verlaine's literary fame and acclaim were increasing, his style of living was becoming more and more degraded and desperate.

In September 1883, Verlaine moved with his mother onto a farm in Coulommes. Not only was farming a failure for him once more, but this time he led such a debt-plagued, drunken and degenerate life that he horrified the inhabitants of the environs. He spent a month in jail from April 13 to May 13, 1885, for having nearly strangled his mother when he was in a drunken rage. The month of his release from jail, Mathilde obtained her official divorce from him.

Destitute, Verlaine returned to Paris, and his mother moved into the building where he was living. He was suffering at this time from hydrarthrosis of the knee. Often he could not even get out of bed. When his mother died in January 1886, his hydrarthrosis prevented him from attending her funeral.

Four days after Verlaine's mother died, Mathilde's family insisted on getting money from him for his son, Georges, because Verlaine had never paid the child support required by the separation decree. "When the sheriff arrived, Verlaine handed over to him the bundle of twenty thousand francs worth of bonds that his mother had left, and which had been concealed under a mattress. A gesture at once noble and insane. For when he had paid Madame Verlaine's burial expenses and settled his bills, the poor man was left with exactly eight hundred francs."[35]

From 1886 until his death almost ten years later, Verlaine was constantly in and out of hospitals. Among his ailments were complete ankylosis of the left knee, ulcers that would not heal, rheumatism, heart murmurs, diabetes, infectious erysipelas of the leg, and the final stages of syphilis. Often he was in great pain. In September 1887, he nearly died of hunger, and he contemplated suicide.

But his literary fame was growing. In 1888, the Decadents considered him a leader, but he soon disassociated himself from their doctrines. Every Wednesday, his admirers came to his room. Among them were Villiers de l'Isle–Adam, Maurice Barrès, Jean Moréas and Paterne Berrichon (who would later marry Rimbaud's youngest sister, Isabelle). In 1888, Verlaine's collection *Amour (Love)* was published, and in 1889, *Parallèlment (In a Parallel Direction)*.

[35] *Ibid.*, p. 47.

All this time, Verlaine was drinking a lot. He frequented homosexual prostitutes (his collection *Hombres* [*Men*] was published posthumously). "I'm a feminine gender [un féminin], which would explain a great many things," Verlaine wrote F.A. Cazals on August 26, 1889.[36] Verlaine also frequented female prostitutes. Until the end of his life, two women alternately lived with him and abandoned him, robbed him and took care of him: Philomène Boudin, a prostitute; and Eugénie Krantz, who had been a prostitute in vogue at the end of the Empire but who, when Verlaine met her, was a dressmaker who worked at home. One time when Philomène left Verlaine in 1894, she took everything of his, including the only picture he had of his mother. In great anger, he wrote to her: "I demand, by this post card, my mother's portrait before my other things and in spite of what your fancy man or your filthy pimp demands. / Shit / P.V." But he ended the message pitifully, almost imploringly: "And, seriously, without threats, *quick*, my mother's portrait, before anything else, as fast as possible c/o the publisher Vanier."[37]

In 1891, Verlaine was living at 15, rue Descartes, in a hotel frequented by prostitutes and pimps. Over the next years, he would be earning money both from his books, which were selling well, and from the lectures he was invited to give (e.g. in Nancy, London, Oxford, Manchester, Holland and Belgium). But whenever he had some money, he spent it wildly, inviting his friends on drunken sprees. Or he surrendered it to Philomène or Eugénie.

Respect for Verlaine's poetry kept growing. He was elected "Prince of Poets" in 1894, succeeding Leconte de Lisle. The poet who would succeed him would be Mallarmé.

Just before Verlaine died, on January 8, 1896, he lived in some kind of quiet with Eugénie Krantz. At his graveside, speeches were given by several literary luminaries of the day, including François Coppée, Maurice Barrès, Gustave Kahn, Catulle Mendès, Jean Moréas and Stéphane Mallarmé.

"Your soul is a selected landscape," Verlaine begins "Moonlight," the first of the lovely and unsettling, happy and sad, populated and lonely poems of his *Fêtes galantes*. This poem, which sets

---

[36] In Henri Peyre, *Rimbaud vu par Verlaine* (note 20 above), p. 186.
[37] Paul Verlaine, *Lettres inédits à divers correspondants*, ed. Georges Zayed (Genève: Droz, 1976), pp. 38–39.

the ambiguous scene for that entire book, is emblematic of much of Verlaine's other poetry as well:

> Your soul is a selected landscape that maskers
> And bergamasche go about beguiling
> Playing the lute and dancing and quasi
> Sad beneath their fantastical disguises.
>
> While singing in the minor mood
> Triumphant love and life that is opportune,
> They do not seem to believe in their good fortune
> And their song mingles with the moonlight,
>
> With the calm moonlight sad and beautiful,
> That makes the birds dream in the trees
> And the fountains weep with ecstasy,
> The great svelte fountains amid the marble statues.

Here, a landscape and a soulscape are equated. Perceptions in Verlaine's poetry are paramount, for just as a person's soul reflects or incorporates a "selected landscape," so a landscape will reflect or incorporate the person perceiving it. The soul in the first stanza is another person's soul (a woman's soul, perhaps, or perhaps *your* soul, the reader's soul, as you enter this world of gallant festivals). But that soul also reflects, in some profound and important ways, the poet's soul, for it is he who is depicting its inner depths. In that soul, the site of a masked ball, people are actors and dancers, "maskers and bergamasche." Their masks, which both conceal what they are and reveal what they might like to be or what they play at being, suggest theater and artifice, charm and disguise, enchantment and deceit. Are these phantomlike figures only acting the roles of lovers, or do they—or can they—love in reality? The word "bergamasche" is richly suggestive. While Verlaine seems to imply dancers by it, the word actually means some fast dances (or the music for those dances) similar to the tarantella, the rapid, whirling southern Italian dance for couples. "Bergamasche" therefore evoke exoticism, eroticism, and a whirling, swirling frenzy: the kind of dizzy, intoxicating and disequilibriating motion in which Verlaine so often delights (e.g. see "Mandolin" and "Brussels: Merry-Go-Round").

Subtly now, indications of malaise are insinuated. The actors, dancers and musicians "go about beguiling" the soul they inhabit, enchanting, captivating and charming it for good—but perhaps for evil. Suddenly a chill ripples through. For the end of the first stanza reveals that amid all the charm and gaiety of the masked ball, the gallant figures are "quasi / Sad beneath their fantastical disguises." Words about seeming, that by their nature question the existence and very essence of what is seen and what is said, are one of the hallmarks of Verlaine's poetry. For him, things rarely *are*; instead, they *seem to be*, which means that they almost always suggest the lurking presence of something else, of something alien perhaps, or even opposite. These figures, clothed in their "disguises," seem sad, almost sad. What are they disguising? Are they really sad, or is that the poet's projection of himself onto the scene? In any case, a note of melancholy is sounded here. Too, the word "fantastical" insinuates a disturbing tone, for while it means fantastic—of the mind or the imagination—it also may imply something strange, or weird or grotesque.

In the second stanza, the poet continues his impressionistic medley of sights that are both precise and hazy, and of sounds that are simultaneously soothing and unsettling. Now the nature of everything evoked is questioned, for although the figures sing what would seem to be victorious, favorable and timely ("Triumphant love and life that is opportune"), still they sing these "in the minor mood," suggesting the melancholy and plaintive sounds associated with the minor key. Once again, a motif of seeming questions everything. Phrased now in a negative way ("They do not seem to believe in their good fortune"), the words cast doubt not only on the singers' feelings, but also on the nature of their fortune.

Finally, their song mingles with the moonlight: the microcosm of this soul inhabited by people and a landscape mingles fully with the macrocosm—with the universe, with "the calm moonlight sad and beautiful." The word "calm," like motifs of seeming, is a key word for Verlaine, a word that almost invariably veils an underlying malaise or frenzy, at times even a feeling of despair. "Calm" is often a mask or veil that Verlaine uses to cover, or to try to cover, a face of anguish. "Calm in the twilight that / The high branches make above, / With this profound silence let's / Completely imbue our love," he begins "With Muted Strings," another of the *Fêtes galantes* which, like several poems in that collection, proceeds from ostensible calm to a cry of anguish: "And when the solemn evening / Falls from the black oaks, / Voice of our hopelessness, / The nightingale will sing."

The moonlight in "Moonlight" is at once "sad and beautiful": beauty for Verlaine implies the presence of sadness. So, too, does his notion of "ecstasy," for the very intensity of this emotional rapture leads inevitably to its loss (see, for example, "Mandolin," "With Muted Strings" and "Sentimental Colloquy"). In "Moonlight," where "the fountains weep with ecstasy," the trancelike state is so overpowering that the joy expresses itself in tears: tears of rapture that recall sorrow and pain.

This brief examination of "Moonlight" suggests that Verlaine's poetry, which might appear calm or simple on the surface, is actually much more complex, extremely rich in underlying tensions and implications. Even such an apparently carefree piece as "Streets" (a poem inspired by Verlaine's and Rimbaud's stay in London) contains an inner anguish, despite its exclamatory refrain sounded five times, "Let's dance the jig!" For, from the poet's evocation of the woman's "mischievous eyes," to his exclaiming that the way she had of "making a poor lover grieve" was "really . . . charming indeed!", to his recalling in the last stanza that the times and talks they had had together were the "best" of his "possessions," certain impressions of pain and of melancholy have filtered through. When the refrain is sounded a final time after the last stanza, the poet's call to dance the jig seems like an attempt to shake off, by means of this fast, gay and springy dance, the loneliness, nostalgia and sadness that have been welling within him. "The desired lightness of motion and emotion is there; but almost inadvertently, the presence of thought, tinged by regret, has been insinuated. 'Let's dance the jig' contains at the end an echo of remembrance more than an invitation to joy," writes Henri Peyre.[38]

The incessant interplay between quiet and disquiet continues throughout Verlaine's poetry, contributing to its uniqueness and its melancholy beauty, and to its powers to enchant and to disturb. Thus, *Crimen amoris*," one of Verlaine's most fascinating and ambitious poems, modulates from a swirling and violently agitated vision into a melodious and peaceful soulscape at the end. It is

[38] "Verlaine: Symbolism and Popular Poetry" in *French Symbolist Poetry: Sou'wester* (note 28 above), p. 24.

almost as though for Verlaine the excess of one emotion calls for, and must be balanced by, its opposite. But for the reader well-attuned to the ceaseless struggles going on in Verlaine's tortured psyche, the calm vision at the end of *"Crimen amoris"* contains echoes of the agitations that preceded and—we know from Verlaine's life—would follow.

"Crimen amoris" is Verlaine's one-hundred-line vision of Rimbaud as a sixteen-year-old prophet, an "evil" angel, a "Satan," who also, in certain ways, resembles Jesus. It is written in lines of eleven syllables, a rhythm that is somewhat jarring to the French reader reared on classical alexandrines. But just because of the line's unevenness and its sense of imbalance, the *vers impair* is so well suited to this poem and to Verlaine's equivocal nature.

The "crime" takes place in Persia, in Ecbatana (the ancient name of Hamadan in present-day Iran). The location adds exotic, mythical and religious dimensions to the tale. As the poem opens, "Beautiful demons, adolescent Satans," celebrate "the festival of the Seven Sins." Their glorification of sensuous and sensual pleasures ("ô how beautiful / It is! All desires beamed in brutal fires") is, of course, a rebellion against the church. Their festival, as described lyrically, excitedly—delightedly—by the poet, is melodious, amorous, luxurious, and filled with "Goodness." Verlaine's words capture its splendor, rapture, fierceness and excitement, its tender erotic ecstasies that bring on tears, its cosmic proportions and powers of enchantment:

> Dances to the rhythms of epithalamiums
> Were swooning in long sobs quite tenderly
> And beautiful choirs of men's and women's voices
> Were rolling in, palpitating like waves of the sea,
>
> And the Goodness that issued from these things was so potent
> And so charming that the countryside
> Around adorned itself with roses
> And night appeared in diamond.

In stanza 5, Rimbaud, "the handsomest of all those evil angels," appears. Because he is deeply distressed, the other Satans try to cheer him. Finally, in stanzas 10–14, he addresses them, proclaiming a "gospel of blasphemy" that is at the same time a "metaphysical rebellion."[39] " 'Oh! I will be the one who will create God!' " he begins his scandalous and prophetic pronouncements. He then delineates his dream of abolishing the concept of sin, for sins, he says, will henceforth be rejoined to virtues. And he announces that he will sacrifice himself—make himself sacred thereby—for the sake of others, and for the sake of "universal Love": " 'through me now hell/Whose lair is here sacrifices itself to universal love!' " This, therefore, is his "Crime of Love": his vision of a new and revolutionary Love, of a total and completely unrestricted Love, of a Love that is universal, all-embracing, erotic, emotional and spiritual. But this Love is also a rebellion that implies, among other things, Verlaine's and Rimbaud's homosexual love. It is a physical and metaphysical revolt against the teachings of Catholicism, and so is a "crime" in the eyes of society and the church. The title is, therefore, an indictment against Rimbaud (and Verlaine). But it may also be interpreted as an indictment against the church and state that condemn a complete and free and universal Love.

The sacrifice, flame-licked, tortured, but exalted, begins in stanzas 15–18, with repeated intimations that death and destruction are imminent as the other Satans follow their visionary prophet:

> And the dying Satans were singing in the flames . . .
> . . . .
> And he, with his arms crossed in a haughty air,
> With his eyes on the sky where the licking fire climbs along,
> He recites in a whisper a kind of prayer,
> That will die in the gaiety of the song.

Suddenly, the song ends, for "Someone had not accepted the sacrifice." Everything is then destroyed, and all becomes "but a vain and vanished dream . . . " (stanza 21). But does that dream really disappear?

The four last stanzas are lyrical and calm, a gentle song after the exploding visions in the twenty-one that preceded. Yet calmness in Verlaine's poetry is so often a veil cast over an inner agitation that one cannot but wish to look more closely here. In stanza 22, the entire ambiance is veiled, wavering, almost palpitating; something seems to be rising from just below the surface. One senses a soul

---

[39] Henri Peyre, *Rimbaud vu par Verlaine* (note 20 above), pp. 172–73.

behind the scene. The plain is "evangelical," "severe and peaceful." The word "severe" might indicate an underlying strain. The tree branches, "vague like veils," suggest angels—or ghosts. They also "look like wings waving about," intimating angels' wings perhaps, or perhaps wings of birds that wish to fly—to flee.

In the next stanza, all seems calm. "The gentle owls float vaguely in the air / Quite embalmed with mystery and with prayer." But the word "embalmed" (as we pointed out at the end of Rimbaud's "Drunken Boat") suggests, along with sweet scents, intimations of death. "At times a wave that leaps hurls a flash of lightning." This sentence at the end of the stanza startles: its fire is reminiscent of the flames of the Satanic festival.

In stanza 24, a "soft shape" rises from the hills "Like a love defined unclearly still, / And the mists that from the ravines ascend / Seem an effort towards some reconciled end." In the context of Verlaine's other poetry, the word "seem" is somewhat troubling. While here it seeks to define nature in terms of the divine, still the word does raise a question, for it is certainly possible that the mists might not *be* "an effort towards some reconciled end."

The last stanza is clearly an invocation to Christ—a "heart," and a "soul," and a "word" (the Word), and a "virginal love":

> And all that like a heart and like a soul,
> And like a word, and with a virginal love,
> Adores, expands in an ecstasy and beseeches
> The merciful God who will keep us from evil.

The word "ecstasy" is used here in its religious sense, but for Verlaine, as we saw earlier, the notion of ecstasy leads almost invariably to feelings of loss, or pain or sadness. Two other words clearly inject some uneasiness into the apparently serene soulscape of this last stanza: "beseeches" ("réclame") and "evil" ("[le] mal"). The word "beseeches" stresses urgency and need. It means "to ask for earnestly," "to implore" and "to beg for." This is a heartfelt and a pressing prayer. One senses at this point the poet's profoundest longings for peace and for a pure love: for a "virginal love" that would counter the "crime of love," and for a "virginal love" that would be free from sexuality. The poet's calling upon God to help him in his distress is typical of Verlaine's religious poetry. It is also significant, I believe, that he does not beseech a "God who will lead us to good" but rather a "God who will keep us from evil." This is, in the closing quiet of *"Crimen amoris,"* a muffled cry of anguish. The fact that Verlaine ends his poem on the word "evil" suggests that "evil" will continue to torment—and to attract—him. In fact, judging from the length of the poem, and from the beauty and power of the description of the Satanic festival, that "evil" undoubtedly continued to allure Verlaine, even as he wrote the poem and sought to condemn the "Crime of Love."

Verlaine's poems mediate ceaselessly, therefore, between gaiety and sadness, hope and fear, quiet and disquiet. It is as though just below their melodious and apparently simple surfaces, a silent scream is waiting to be released. In his poetry, as Festa-McCormick notes, "The tragic shows through the surface, as it shows through the surface in certain impressionist paintings or in Watteau's so melancholy picture ["The Embarkation for Cythera"] in which the voyagers seem sadly satiated or disenchanted with the pleasure for which they are embarking."[40] Verlaine's moods and language, his mysterious music "with muted strings," his choice of rhythms, rhymes and words that continually question the scene's—and therefore the soul's—serenity, combine to create a state of uneasy calm, a vision of happiness or pleasure that may be undermined at any moment. One can sense in Verlaine's poetry, as in his life, both control and loss of control. For his soulscapes are permeated with a kind of restless repose and with tremors of the ephemeral or otherworldly which seek to convey calm or hope or joy, but which almost invariably insinuate hidden presences of pain or sorrow, as well. And always in Verlaine's poetry there is "Music before anything else. . . ." Never overpowering or thunderous in its orchestration, his music, lute-like, or like the music of other stringed instruments, is melodious, lyrical and seductive, an integral part of his poetry of moods and sensations. Through its sounds and its rhythms, his poetry filters into you, caresses you, possesses you, lulls you and disturbs you, subtly. You are taken into its beauty and its uneasiness, almost unawares. Verlaine's malaise, through his music, becomes your own disquietude. And his poetry, that "One wants to think caressing . . . both delights / And distresses simultaneously."[41]

[40] Diana Festa-McCormick, "Y a-t-il un impressionnisme littéraire: Le cas Verlaine," *Nineteenth-Century French Studies*, Vol. II, Nos. 3 & 4 (Spring-Summer 1974), 152–53.
[41] See Verlaine's sonnet beginning "The hunting horn grieves towards the forest. . . ."

Mallarmé and the Poetry of "Purer Meaning"

> *I have found in an old diary a saying from Stéphane Mallarmé,*
> *that his epoch was troubled by the trembling of the veil of the*
> *Temple.*
>
> YEATS, *The Trembling of the Veil*[42]

Poetry "consists of *creating* . . . : it is, in sum, the sole human creation possible," Mallarmé said in an interview (p. 870). The word creation suggests art, birth, and the Creation itself. The poet for Mallarmé is at once a man and a god figure, or a medium for the divine. And his poetic word—an image of the Word—participates both in present reality and earthiness, and in eternal reality or the "real real":[43] the elemental, essential, or Ideal. Almost incessantly, Mallarmé pondered about the problems of purity, perfection and essential meaning. "Quench your thirst on the Ideal. The happiness of here below is ignoble," he wrote, when he was twenty-two, to his friend Henri Cazalis (who became a doctor and published poetry under the name of Jean Lahor).[44] But although Mallarmé always set his sights upon the "Ideal," he did not neglect the richnesses of reality and "life here below." His language, in fact, which is often charged with erotic undertones, combines the sensuous and sensual with intimations of the infinite. His poetry—like his life—is at once of the body and of the mind and spirit; of the earth and of the beyond.

Stéphane Mallarmé was born in Paris on March 18, 1842. His family on both sides, he later wrote Verlaine, had been "since the [French] Revolution, an uninterrupted succession of civil servants ["fonctionnaires"] in Administration and Teaching" (p. 661). By becoming an English teacher at the lycée level, Mallarmé would break with that tradition.

[42] *The Autobiography of William Butler Yeats* (New York: The Macmillan Company, 1965), p. 74. I am grateful to Robert Greer Cohn for pointing out Mallarmé's phrase "a disquietude in the veil in the temple with meaningful folds and somewhat its rending," to which Yeats might have been referring ("Crise de vers" ["Verse Crisis"], p. 360). I am grateful to Richard Ellmann for writing me that there is no proof that Yeats went to Mallarmé's "mardis" and that he, too, believes that "Crise de vers" is the source for Yeats's quotation. Both Cohn and Ellmann remarked upon the New Testament source—the moment when Christ died—for the Mallarmé quotation: "And, behold, the veil of the temple was rent in twain from the top to the bottom . . ." (Matthew 27:51).

[43] Robert Greer Cohn, "Stevens and Mallarmé," *Comparative Literature Studies*, Vol. XVI, No. 4 (December 1979), p. 349.

[44] June 3, 1864, in Henri Mondor, *Vie de Mallarmé*, Vol. I (Paris: Gallimard, 1941), p. 92. Future references to the two volumes of Mondor's biography will be given as Mondor I and Mondor II.

Mallarmé's youth was haunted by death, which would become a major symbol in his poetry. When he was six, his mother died, and when he was fifteen, his beloved sister, Maria, died at the age of thirteen.

After his mother's death, Mallarmé was reared by his maternal grandmother, who adored him. By the time he was ten, he began attending boarding schools, first in Paris and then in Sens. He was a mediocre student. In fact, he failed his *baccalauréat* examination the first time he took it, in August 1860. But he passed the second time, three months later.

In 1862, Mallarmé met and began courting Maria Gerhard, a German who was a teaching governess for a French family in Sens. That autumn they lived together in London. After some happiness, several ruptures and separate trips back to France, they were married in London, in the Catholic church, on August 10, 1863. Even before his marriage, Mallarmé no longer sought great joy from this union. "I'm marrying Marie. . . . I'm not acting for myself, but for her only," he wrote Cazalis on April 27, 1863.[45] Around this time, Mallarmé was writing poems and translating Poe's poetry into French prose. He would later say that he had "learned English simply in order to read Poe better" (p. 662).

From 1863 to 1866, Mallarmé was an English teacher at the lycée in Tournon. His life there was hard, lonely and exhausting. His students and colleagues did not understand him and often scorned him; and although his wife was completely devoted to him, she could not comprehend his poetry. In fact, aside from his correspondence with friends and fellow poets, Mallarmé was virtually isolated in Tournon. He hated the peasant mentality of the town as well as the climate, which he found too hot in summer and too cold in winter. He also hated his job, which he called "this hideous work of a pedagogue."[46] His classes were a torture for him: he could neither please nor control his students. To Cazalis, he wrote in April 1866: "to tell you how much my classes, full of hoots and of stones that are flung, shatter me, would be to cause you pain. I return home dazed."[47]

[45] Mondor I, p. 87.
[46] March 1865, to Cazalis, in Mondor I, p. 160.
[47] Mallarmé, *Correspondance I: 1862–1871* (Paris: Gallimard, 1959), p. 207. Future references to this volume will be given as *Correspondance* I.

To compound Mallarmé's misery, his long hours of teaching brought little financial remuneration. When the Mallarmés' daughter, Geneviève, was born on November 19, 1864, their apartment was so small that the infant's cradle could be located only a few steps away from the poet's writing table. At that time Mallarmé was working on "Hérodiade," a poem-"mystery" which he thought and talked about throughout his life but was never able to complete. "With her cries, this naughty *baby* [Mallarmé used the English word] has made Hérodiade flee," he wrote the Provençal poet Aubanel, one of the *félibres* he had met in Avignon that summer.[48]

Although physically and emotionally drained by his teaching, Mallarmé forced himself to stay up late into the night in order to pursue his ceaseless poetic meditations and to write. Slowly, he was developing his philosophy of poetry that would equate art with religion, beauty, purity, birth and re-creation. "There is nothing true, immutable, great and sacred other than art," he wrote Cazalis on July 24, 1863.[49] In fact, Mallarmé saw himself engaged in a physical and spiritual struggle from which—like Jacob after his nightlong battle with the angel—he would emerge changed: wounded, but blessed. Poetry was becoming for him an act of transformation, a symbolic *rite de passage*. Like Jacob renamed Israel after his victorious struggle with the angel, Mallarmé believed that he, too, would be reidentified as a result of *his* victorious struggle: re-created, in a sense, and sanctified through the Poem. Mallarmé saw himself battling not with God in the form of the biblical angel, but with the Ideal. In a letter lamenting his exhaustion to Cazalis, Mallarmé described his struggle to write in these quasi-biblical terms: "When, after a day of waiting and thirst, arrives the holy hour of Jacob, the struggle with the Ideal, I do not have the power to align two words. And it will be the same the next day!"[50]

Always Mallarmé would continue the struggle. He believed, in fact, that all the reality emanating in the world from the Ideal, which he intuited at the source of his poetry, could be expressed in a lacy network that he, as a "sacred spider," would spend his life weaving. "I have . . . found," he wrote Aubanel in July 1866, "the center of myself, where I hold fast like a sacred spider, on the principal

[48] November 27, 1864 in Mondor I, p. 149.
[49] Mondor I, p. 95.
[50] February 1865 in Mondor I, p. 157.

threads already issued from my mind/spirit [the French word "esprit" means both "mind" and "spirit"; sometimes one word is called for, sometimes both are implied] and with the help of which I shall weave *at the meeting points,* marvelous laceworks, that I divine, and that exist already in the bosom of Beauty."[51] Mallarmé's veil of words is simultaneously physical, intellectual and spiritual, for the poem/lacework seeks to re-create the artist's vision both of this world and of the ideal. The poet as a spider who must weave his web of words calls to mind a condemnation (one thinks of the myth of Arachne) that is also a consecration. The spider's web is fragile but silken, a labor that is also a creation issuing directly, and formed directly, from the substance and essence of its maker. Indeed, all through his life, Mallarmé would continue to feel upon him the burden and the blessing of artistic creation.[52] And by weaving, spider-like, his lacy networks of words, he would try to capture and to create his vision of the relations of everything in the universe: "the Book," or the "Great Work" (p. 662).

During his three years in Tournon, Mallarmé was also writing some of his finest and most memorable poems. Among them are, in this collection: "A Faun's Afternoon" (the first draft of which he completed in less than four months), "The Chastened Clown," "Sea Breeze," "Gift of the Poem" and "Saint." Ten of his poems (including "Sea Breeze") were published in May 1866 in the first *Parnasse contemporain,* which also published poems by Baudelaire and Verlaine. But this accomplishment did not increase Mallarmé's prestige at the lycée: on the contrary. Instead of being proud, or at least respectful of their teacher, Mallarmé's pupils mocked him by quoting lines from his poetry in a derisory way.

His goal in poetry, Mallarmé wrote to Cazalis in October 1864, in an expression that has now become famous, emblematic in fact of his art, is *"To paint, not the thing, but the effect that it produces."*[53] The poem "Saint" is an excellent illustration of these words. Its first title, "Saint Cecilia Playing on a Cherub's Wing," describes more explicitly what the poem now evokes mysteriously: a stained-glass

---

[51] *Correspondance* I, pp. 224–25.
[52] For a symbolic treatment of this, see "The Chastened Clown," written around 1864, in which the poet-clown is "chastened"—punished and made purer—by his clownish (i.e. artistic) state, from which he tries to escape. In the poem, as in the spider image, are the burden and the blessing, and the irony of a condemnation that is also a consecration.
[53] *Correspondance* I, p. 137.

window with the image of the patron saint of music, Saint Cecelia, whose finger seems to be playing a harp, which is actually an angel's wing. In "Saint" there is a continual interplay between absence and presence, reality and vision, the real and the ideal, music and silence (in the last line, the Saint Cecelia in the window is called the "musician of silence"). In other words, *"the thing"* for Mallarmé *is "the effect that it produces"*—physical, visual, auditory, intellectual and spiritual. This type of poetic creation thrives on enigma or obscurity. "There must always be enigma in poetry, and that is the goal of literature,—there are no others—to *evoke* objects," Mallarmé said to Jules Huret in an interview (p. 869).

After Tournon, Mallarmé taught English for a year (1866–1867) in Besançon. Shortly after he arrived there, he received his first letter from a twenty-two-year-old poet who had admired his poems in *Le Parnasse contemporain*: Paul Verlaine. Along with his letter, Verlaine sent Mallarmé his newly-published *Poèmes saturniens*.

In Besançon, Mallarmé pursued his meditations in the realms of mystery and of meaning. More and more he was probing the world of his mind. An astonishing letter to Cazalis, dated May 14, 1867, reveals how wholly he was involved in his spiritual struggles. "I have just spent a terrifying year; my Thought thought about itself, and reached a pure Conception," he wrote.[54] The expression "pure Conception" suggests both a philosophical Idea or Notion, and a birth—human and/or divine—that is perfect and free from sin or guilt. Mallarmé believed, in fact, that during this "terrifying year" he had undergone a physical and spiritual death after which he had been reborn as a Mind/Spirit freed from all Occidental, terrestrial and human limitations. "Everything . . . that my being has suffered, during this long death agony, is untellable, but luckily, I am perfectly dead, and the most impure region where my Mind/Spirit may venture, is Eternity, my Mind/Spirit, this habitual recluse of its own Thought, that is no longer even darkened by the reflection of Time." The fact that Mallarmé says the Eternity is only "the most impure region" where his Mind/Spirit may venture, reveals that for him there are realms more virgin and more absolute than the spheres envisioned by Western thinking and belief. His Thought, intense and solitary, and oblivious now even of Time, transports him to

---

[54] *Correspondance* I, pp. 240–43.

newer and higher realms. Spiritually dead to the outer world, Mallarmé is wholly alive to the inner, vaster universe of his Thought. There, in infinite spatial and spiritual expansiveness, he reaches out not for mere Eternity, but for "pure Conception," which is the Eternity of the Poetic Mind.

The letter continues. The "terrifying" *rite de passage* described above, Mallarmé reveals, has taken place as a result of his "terrible struggle" with God, whom he has rejected now and whom he characterizes in this letter as a wicked old bird. Mallarmé says that he is now incapable of enjoying himself, but he adds: "Yet how much more so, I was, a few months ago, at first in my terrible struggle with that old and wicked plumage, vanquished, luckily, God! But since that struggle had taken place on his bony wing that, through a death agony more vigorous than I would have suspected in him, carried me into Darkness, I fell, victorious—frantically and infinitely— until finally I saw myself again in my Venetian mirror, such as I had forgotten myself several months previously." During that struggle, he reveals, in the universe suddenly devoid of God's divinity, he came to know Darkness and Nothingness, and he believes that he must continue to fight against them. Even now, he admits to Cazalis, he still finds that he must look at himself in his Venetian mirror, in order to be able to think and in order not to lose himself once more in Nothingness.

Mallarmé's images in this letter recall his "holy hour of Jacob, the struggle with the Ideal." For here he describes himself as wounded but blessed and, in a way, renamed. "This is to inform you that I am now impersonal, and no longer Stéphane whom you knew,—but an aptitude that the spiritual Universe has for seeing itself and for developing, across that which was I." His image of himself as a medium for the divine, a concrete entity through which the spiritual Universe manifests itself, is also an apt image of what a poem is for him: a revelation—in and through the physical—of the otherworldly.

Poetry is, therefore, for Mallarmé a vital coming together of three necessary components: the physical, the intellectual, and the divine. His poetry is a reaching out for, and a re-creation of, "pure Conception." This phrase epitomizes the triple nature of his vision: the physical (conception of life in the womb), the intellectual (conception which is an abstract notion or idea), and the divine (a virgin birth). Poetry for Mallarmé is the embodiment of the Ideal in the real.

After his year in Besançon, Mallarmé taught English at the lycée in Avignon from 1867 to 1871. Unceasingly he was oppressed by poverty; unceasingly he gave himself to his sleepless nights and poetic pursuits. In 1869, he sent a fragment of his "Hérodiade" to the second *Parnasse contemporain*, in which it was eventually published. In 1869, also, he experienced an attack of hysteria ("une crise nerveuse," Mondor writes[55]) that had been building up to its climax since his years in Tournon. "I felt very disquieting symptoms caused by the sole act of writing and hysteria was going to begin to disturb my utterance." Mallarmé wrote to Cazalis on February 4, 1869.[56] Unable even to perform the physical act of writing for a time, Mallarmé dictated his letters to his wife. Once again, he believed that he had undergone a death and rebirth. "My brain, invaded by the Dream, [and] shunning its external functions that no longer solicited it, was going to perish in its permanent insomnia; I implored the great Night that granted my prayer and stretched out its darkness. The first phase of my life was finished. Consciousness, worn out with shadows, is awakening slowly, forming a new man, and should find my Dream again. . . ."[57]

Until May 1871, Mallarmé continued teaching in Avignon. Finally he decided that he could stand the provinces no longer. And so, although he did not have a job there yet, he moved his family to Paris in September. Just two months before, his son, Anatole, had been born in Sens. The boy would die at the age of eight.

A month after his arrival in Paris, Mallarmé was appointed to the lycée Fontanes (now called Condorcet). Always he would find teaching tedious, but now at least he was able to mingle with the poets, musicians and artists of the French capital. In 1873 he met Manet (who would later paint his portrait), and "for ten years," until the painter's death, he saw him "every day" (p. 664). In 1875, Mallarmé's rendition of Poe's "The Raven" was published with illustrations by Manet. Since the book did not sell well, the publisher decided not to put out another book by them. In 1876, Mallarmé and Manet collaborated once more, this time on an edition of Mallarmé's "A Faun's

[55] Mondor I, p. 277.
[56] *Correspondance* I, p. 299.
[57] February 18, 1869, to Cazalis, in *Correspondance* I, p. 301.

Afternoon." Two years earlier, that poem had been rejected by the third *Parnasse contemporain*, which had also rejected work by Verlaine. Among the judges who objected to Mallarmé's masterpiece were Anatole France and François Coppée.

In 1876, at a private exposition in Manet's studio of his paintings that had been turned down by the Salon, Mallarmé met Méry Laurent, who would become his mistress. (At one time, too, she was Coppée's mistress, and she was also kept by a rich American dentist who lived in France, Thomas W. Evans.) Méry, who was the model for several of Manet's paintings (including "Lady in the Maroon Hat," "Lady in the Fur-Collared Coat" and "Veiled Lady"), inspired, among other Mallarmé poems, "The hair, flight of a flame. . . ."

Although Mallarmé was appreciated by members of the literary avant-garde, he was scarcely appreciated at his school. In 1876, the headmaster of the lycée Fontanes complained about him in these terms: "This teacher is busy with something other than teaching and his students. He seeks notoriety, and, undoubtedly, a certain profit, in his publications that have no relation whatsoever to the nature of his functions at the lycée Fontanes: *insane productions*, in prose and in verse. Those who read these strange lucubrations of M. Mallarmé's brain should be astonished that he occupies a teacher's chair at the lycée Fontanes."[58] These criticisms of Mallarmé's writings are, of course, vicious and unenlightened, but one must admit that Mallarmé was certainly not the most diligent teacher imaginable. The poet Léon-Paul Fargue, who was one of Mallarmé's pupils at the lycée, describes how Mallarmé would come to class. The teacher's body "delineated discreetly, according . . . to the seasons, the profile . . . of a kiosk, a demijohn, or a kangaroo: it's that the pockets of his overcoat were stuffed enough to split apart with newspapers, reviews, old books and small thin books." These, Mallarmé would arrange neatly on his table. He would then sit down and tell his students to do their lessons. And he would try to read.[59]

Around 1880 began "les mardis," the famous Tuesday evening gatherings at Mallarmé's apartment at 89, rue de Rome. They continued until 1897 and were attended, at one time or another, by many of the foremost literary and artistic figures of the day, as well as by

[58] Mondor II, p. 377.
[59] Mondor II, p. 562.

the writers who would become the celebrities of the next generation. Among the "mardistes" were: Maurice Barrès, Catulle Mendès, Paul Verlaine, Jean Moréas, Villiers de L'Isle-Adam, Leconte de Lisle, Gustave Kahn, Charles Morice, Henri de Régnier, Francis Vielé-Griffin, José-Maria de Heredia, Jules Laforgue, Paterne Berrichon, Pierre Louÿs, André Gide, Paul Valéry, Paul Claudel, Léon-Paul Fargue, James McNeill Whistler, George Moore, Arthur Symons, Oscar Wilde, Maurice Maeterlinck, Émile Verhaeren, Claude Debussy, Odilon Redon, Édouard Vuillard and Paul Gauguin.

Over the years the setting for these gatherings was essentially the same. In the small room—a living room with a dining area—was a round table with some chairs. On the table was an "old china pot full of tobacco" for the guests, some cigarette paper, and a bouquet of flowers arranged by Mme Mallarmé and Geneviève.[60] The ambiance assumed a sacred air. Almost invariably, Mallarmé stood in front of the white earthenware stove, smoked his pipe, and spoke. Almost never did the others talk, for they came to this chapel-like sanctuary in order to listen to Mallarmé, who uttered his thoughts like a High Priest of Poetry. In fact, anyone who did talk, or who dared to criticize Mallarmé, was scorned by the others. Each year, more and more artworks appeared on the walls. Eventually there were two paintings by Manet (including his portrait of Mallarmé), and art by Redon, Whistler, Monet, Berthe Morisot and Gauguin. There was also a Constantin Guys picture that had been Baudelaire's. Starting from the winter of 1892, Mallarmé wore some "thick wool slippers and . . . on his shoulders a Scotch plaid or a plaid with black and white squares."[61] (See the photo in this book.)

During his years in Paris, Mallarmé continued to teach in order to eke out his meager living. In addition, he wrote poems and prose poems, and translated Poe; he also composed articles on theater, music and ballet. Under different male, female and mythological pseudonyms—e.g. Marasquin, Marguerite de Ponty and Ixion (the ancestor of the centaurs who was punished by Zeus for having dared to love Hera; he was bound on a flaming and eternally revolving wheel in Tartarus)—Mallarmé wrote and edited eight issues of a womens' fashion magazine, *La Dernière Mode* (*The Latest Fashion*). Even if Mallarmé did hope to make some money in this

[60] Mondor II, p. 425.
[61] Mondor II, p. 643.

venture, he also wished to educate the public, for he published in the magazine some poems and stories by writers he liked, including Théodore de Banville, Sully Prudhomme and Alphonse Daudet. Mallarmé also tried to earn some money by publishing two books: *Les Mots anglais* (*English Words*), a "Little Philology" intended for students and others, which actually contains some illuminating insights into his ideas about language (e.g. "the Word presents in its vowels and diphthongs, a sort of flesh; and, in its consonants, a sort of delicate skeleton to be dissected [p. 901]); and *Les Dieux antiques* (*The Ancient Gods*), an illustrated mythology based on a book by George W. Cox.

During 1883 and 1884, Mallarmé became better known to the public because of Verlaine's essay about him in *Les Poètes maudits* (published in a journal in 1883, and a year later in book form), and because Des Esseintes, the protagonist of Joris-Karl Huysmans's novel *A Rebours* (*Against the Grain*), quoted and praised Mallarmé's work. Mallarmé reciprocated the generous gesture by entitling one of his poems "Prose for Des Esseintes."

Not until 1887 did a complete book of Mallarmé's poems appear, and when it did, it was printed in an elegant edition by *La Revue Indépendante* that was too expensive for most poets to afford. And so several of them copied it by hand.[62]

After he was finally able to retire from teaching in January 1894, Mallarmé often went alone to think and to write in Valvins, a little town on the Seine near Fontainbleau where, for the past twenty years, he and his family had been renting a small peasant house a few feet from the river. Often he went sailing there and meditated in his yawl about poetry and "the white page of the sail."[63]

Mallarmé was elected Prince of Poets in 1896, succeeding Verlaine. The next year, "Un Coup de dés . . ." was published in the review *Cosmopolis*. With its words—"prismatic subdivisions of the Idea—arranged like a "musical score" or the stars of a constellation "in some exact spiritual mise en scène" (p. 455), this poem found appreciative readers in the young André Gide and Paul Valéry.

On September 8, 1891, Mallarmé was in Valvins with his wife and daughter. He had been ill during the day, and he wrote them a note saying that if he died, they were to burn all his papers. He wanted

[62] Mondor II, p. 518.
[63] August 1898, to L. Dauphin, in Mondor II, p. 797.

others to see only what he himself believed was finished. The next morning, while his doctor was examining him, Mallarmé had a throat spasm and died.

Conflicts between the real and the ideal, the physical and the intellectual or spiritual permeate Mallarmé's poetry, contributing to its richness and to its uniquely sensuous intellectuality. Always, through the physical, Mallarmé reaches out for something beyond. "In the poetic universe of Stéphane Mallarmé, the poet has the power to create with words, to go beyond the object by making an absolute out of language. . . . [In his] poetry, the object becomes a word which dissolves its material reference points and reveals a permanence beyond words. . . . This transformation of the real permits us to describe him as a 'pure' poet," writes Virginia A. La Charité.[64] In fact, by means of what he called "the game of the word," Mallarmé dreamed of going from the real or physical—a "fact of nature"—to the essential or Ideal—the "pure notion" ("Crise de vers," p. 368). Invariably, his poetic words seek to span and to incorporate the tensions between the real and the "real real": "the double state of the word, rough or immediate here, there essential" (p. 368).

Epitomizing the "double state of the word," the image of the tomb becomes a monumental symbol in, and of, Mallarmé's work. For death and rebirth, which so often preoccupied Mallarmé's early letters, also came to haunt his poetry. "Edgar Poe's Tomb" is one of his finest tomb-poems:

> Such as into Himself eternity changes him finally,
> The Poet rouses with a naked sword his century terrified
> At not having recognized
> That in that strange voice death reigned triumphantly.

These opening words of the sonnet celebrate Mallarmé's vision of the "poet" who, through his death and his poetry, is transformed into his essential and eternal Self: the "Poet." For two reasons death "reigned triumphantly" in Poe's "strange voice." First, in Poe's writings (as in Mallarmé's), death is an important symbol; and second, just because the man Poe died, his essence, which is his

---

[64] See her fascinating essay "Mallarmé and the Elasticity of the Text" in *French Symbolist Poetry: Sou'wester* (note 28 above), p. 1.

Poetic Word, remains, and reigns. His physical absence transforms him into pure and poetic, and everlasting presence. The phrase "naked sword" startles. It suggests at once sensuality, brutality, and purity: an erotic stance, a military assault, or a symbol of spiritual warfare against the forces of evil. By means of this image, Mallarmé insinuates physical, even erotic, feelings into this otherwise highly intellectual and spiritual sonnet. Such a mixing is typical of his poetry, in which the corporeal and the spiritual—nature and the Notion—continually contend, or blend.

After evoking what he envisions as Poe's triumphant spiritual reign, Mallarmé returns immediately to the crudities of reality, describing them now in sensuous and ugly terms. For during his lifetime, Poe was regarded with distrust, fear and hatred by those who could not understand his acts or his word. The people who maligned Poe, who proclaimed him a drunk and a sort of sorcerer (it is known that Poe drank and that alcohol had disastrous effects on him; he was also accused of being a drug addict), Mallarmé compares to the loathsome twitching of a hydra: a symbol of repulsive and proliferating evil. For the hydra is the mythological nine-headed water serpent that, if one head were cut off, would grow back two in its place. But Poe—Mallarmé's symbol of the isolated, alienated and divine poet, he whose gaze is fixed on the infinite—Mallarmé compares to an "angel":

> They, like a vile start of a hydra hearing of yore
> The angel give a purer meaning to the words of the tribe
> Proclaimed on high the sortilege imbibed
> In the dishonorable wave of some black mixture.

The phrase about the angel's act portrays, I believe, Mallarmé's understanding of his own poetic search, its sublime longings and ironic limitations. The "angel" is, of course, a symbol of the poet who is divine, or at least a medium for the divine: a poet-priest. The angel's giving a "purer meaning to the words of the tribe" suggests at once the linguistic, sociological,[65] metaphysical and religious ideals that Mallarmé set for himself in writing poetry. "Purer"

---

[65] Mallarmé "saw art as the initial stimulus towards an ideal mankind and society. . . . [He] often referred to the creation of poetry as a form of action," writes Paula Gilbert Lewis in "Stéphane Mallarmé: Literature as Social Action," *Romance Notes*, Vol. 17, No. 1 (Fall 1976), 15–17.

implies what is made clearer, cleaner and holier—spiritually, morally and physically (one thinks of Mallarmé's unorthodox arrangements of the words on the page, his dislocation of traditional syntax, etc.). And "meaning," akin to the German *meinen* (to have in mind, to have as an opinion) suggests, along with the mind and its intentions, both sense and significance. "Purer meaning" evokes, therefore, a better intent, purpose or design that exists in the mind and approaches the Idea. It is significant that the phrase is a comparative and not a superlative. By describing a relative degree rather than an absolute, the comparative simultaneously lessens—and heightens—the impact of Mallarmé's words. Just because "purer meaning" implies an imperfect state that can be surpassed, it suggests a process, dynamic and ongoing, rather than an end, closed and final. The angel-poet's quest will go on and on. More, it must go on and on: for him there can be no repose. His search is a sublime one, therefore, since it is a mental, artistic and divinely-inspired quest for what is clearer, cleaner and holier. But it is an ironic quest as well, because it can never truly end. Implying infinite and uplifting longing, along with perpetual unease and dissatisfaction, the search for "purer meaning" describes perforce a quest that is both a conquest—and a never-ending quest.

The tercets of the Poe sonnet evoke two types of tombs: the one Ideal, the other real:

> Of the hostile earth and the cloud, ô grievance!
> If our idea with it does not sculpt a bas-relief
> With which Poe's dazzling tomb may be adorned,
>
> Calm block fallen here below from an obscure
> Disaster, let this granite at least show forever its boundary to
> The black flights of Blasphemy dispersed into the future.

The antagonism between the real and the Ideal, the "earth and the cloud" that are hostile to each other, is a major theme of this poem and of Mallarmé's entire work. Like a battle cry, the exclamation "ô grievance!" voices the poet's complaint about injuries and injustices seen and suffered. With this "grievance" and with his "idea," Mallarmé says that he must try to "sculpt" a "dazzling [poem]-tomb": an eternal monument in words. The symbol of the poem-tomb, a refuge that both conceals and reveals—that shrouds and protects the physical, but displays and proclaims the spiritual and eternal—is dear to Mallarmé's heart. "For me," he told Jules Huret, "the case of a poet, in this society that does not permit him to live, is the case of a man who isolates himself in order to sculpt his own tomb" (p. 869).

After evoking the "dazzling [poem]-tomb" in the Poe sonnet, Mallarmé then calls forth Poe's real tomb. Let the real tomb, he says, mark the limit destined for the vituperative words of people who will malign Poe in the future. That limit, the "boundary" to their "Blasphemy," is death: lifelessness like an inert block of stone, a "granite." The "Calm block fallen here below from an obscure / Disaster" refers ambiguously both to the real tomb (the "granite") and to the poet. For the "obscure / Disaster" suggests both a literal and a symbolical star (from the Latin *dis* + *astrum*) that has fallen to the earth, a disaster not easily perceived amid the vastness of the universe: the fall of a meteoroid, or the death of a poet. In fact, in his sketch of Poe, Mallarmé described Poe "like an aerolith; stellar" (p. 531). And so, Mallarmé says, may the tomb marking Poe's physical death "at least show forever" its limit to the blasphemies to come. "Forever" will Poe's Word endure, Mallarmé implies; nevermore will the "black flights of Blasphemy" be able to harm the poet who, changed "into Himself," has become the Poet.

Thus, while Poe's real death and real tomb (the "granite") symbolize his physical lifelessness, his tomb also evokes his transfiguration through his words—and through Mallarmé's—into eternal life in the "dazzling tomb" that is the Poem.

Mallarmé's search for perfection and "purer meaning," it must be noted, is dangerously close to an encounter with Nothingness. Emptiness, after all, is untouched and untainted; but it is also the void. During his struggle with God, whom he had rejected, Mallarmé had come to know and to fear Nothingness and annihilation. These were not the only dangers that he faced in his search: he also recognized the perils of inaction or immobility, another kind of nothingness—dangers evoked stunningly in the sonnet beginning "Will the virgin, hardy and beautiful present time . . .":

> Will the virgin, hardy and beautiful present time
> With one stroke of an intoxicated wing tear free
> For us this hard, forgotten lake haunted under the rime
> By the transparent glacier of flights that did not flee!

Here life battles against perfection, motion against stillness. Whiteness may suggest unsullied presence or total absence; virginity may evoke loveliness and holiness, or inaction and frigidity. The conflict is expressed in both spiritual and erotic terms as this first stanza highlights the irony inherent in Mallarmé's search for "purer meaning." Will the swan, a symbol of the poet and of the "virgin . . . present time," burst forth wildly as though inebriated or in an erotic ecstasy ("With one stroke of an intoxicated wing") and tear open the icy lake of the past and of memory "haunted" by inaction, the "flights that did not flee!" The flights embedded in the "transparent glacier" are beautiful and perfect, in a sense, since nothing has marred them: they are the Idea of flights. But they are also flights that were not taken: they are the negation of flights. As such they are symbols of stillness, immobility and frigidity, of sexual, poetical and spiritual sterility. Because of their dual nature, to Mallarmé they are at once terrible and wonderful.

As the poem progresses, it becomes clear that the poet-swan's sublime longings have caused his undoing: his icy, almost deathlike rigidity. In the last tercet, in fact, the Swan is portrayed as a ghost, a "Phantom":

> Phantom assigned to this place by his pure radiancy,
> He immobilizes himself in the cold dream of scorn put on
> Amid his useless exile by the Swan.

Despite his immobility, the Swan/Poet who scorns the real world stands as a sign of the otherworldly for those who contemplate him, even though he himself, frozen into his frigid lake, cannot fly to the ideal realm he envisions. The Swan in this poem symbolizes at once the dream of the eternal and the impossibility of reaching it. He is a figure of the sublime longings and ironic consequences of Mallarmé's cravings for "purer meaning."

Even though Mallarmé always sought the "real real," he did not deny corporeal life. At times, in fact, he even delighted in it. But his delectation of the physical and the erotic invariably merges in his poetry with his grasping for the intellectual or the spiritual. In fact, his sensuous intellectuality is, I believe, one of the most fascinating hallmarks of his poetry and one of the most powerful forces motivating his poetic creation. For example, it permeates the magnificent music of "A Faun's Afternoon," a symphony to delight—and to tease—the senses, the mind and the spirit.

This poem, which inspired art by Manet and music by Debussy, is a splendid illustration of how Mallarmé attempts in his poetry to go from a "fact of nature" to the "pure notion." It illustrates as well how the struggle to do so is a sublime quest that is filled with ironic overtones. Already, the title suggests the mythical, the grotesque, and the divine, for the faun—a popular figure in late nineteenth-century French poetry (see, for example, Rimbaud's "Faun's Head" and Verlaine's "The Faun")—is at once repulsive and pruriently appealing. An ancient rustic Roman deity, the faun is traditionally depicted with a man's body and a goat's hind legs, with a tail, beard, pointed ears and horns. Historically, fauns derive from the fertility god Faunus; they are also associated with the god Pan. One of the tales about Pan implicitly invoked in Mallarmé's poem is about the nymph Syrinx who, when fleeing from the lascivious Pan, was transformed into a reed by her father, upon whom she had called for help. Pan, who was foiled in his attempted rape, then plucked the reed that Syrinx became and made it into the musical instrument that would become his emblem: his panpipes or syrinx. Thus, the faun of Mallarmé's title suggests at once the animal, the human, the artistic, and the divine. Mallarmé's lecherous and intellectual faun, divine in his origin and in his artistic desires, but grotesque in appearance, lewd in his longings, and stymied in his cravings (to possess two nymphs and later the goddess Venus) is, of course, a metaphor for the poet: the poet who continually reaches for, and is mocked or wounded—yet also blessed—by his vision of the eternal.

The "Eclogue" takes place in a marsh in Sicily and in the faun's mind and reveries. It begins with his lustful and artistic proclamation: "These nymphs, these I want to perpetuate." As Robert Greer Cohn remarks, the "opening line has the joint possibilities of pro-creation and creation; to perpetuate in the flesh or in the spirit . . . . *Perpétuer*, in sum, is of the essence of art." The words imply, therefore, that the faun wants to bring the nymphs "back in the flesh, prolong them in his memory, perpetuate them in art, perpetu-ate them in off-spring."[66] From the faun and the nymphs, one has leaped to ideas about physical, artistic and primeval creation.

[66] Cohn, *Toward the Poems of Mallarmé* (note 7 above), pp. 13–14. See also his illuminating discussion of the whole poem on pages 13–32.

Immediately, the faun-poet's senses and intellect focus on the nymphs' flesh, which merges and all but vanishes in the air, making the faun wonder if the nymphs were but a dream. Here is an excellent example of Mallarmé's sensuous intellectuality:

> So clear,
> Their light flesh color, that it hovers in the air
> Made drowsy with tufted sleeps.
>
> Did I love a dream?

Even as the nymphs become airy and spiritualized, the air becomes as though incarnate: there is an intermingling between the realms, real and dreamed, sensual and spiritual. Now the air is sensuous, heavy, tired, "Made drowsy with tufted sleeps" that seem at once physical and insubstantial. And so the faun begins to wonder: did he love a dream? And we begin to wonder: does the dream symbolize the ideal that the poet seeks to attain? A double problem arises immediately. If the faun wants to possess real, and not dreamed-of nymphs, then his mere dream of the nymphs cannot be his ideal. Still, dreamed-of nymphs can be more perfect than any real nymphs. And so the faun-poet's dream, like the eternal, is both exalting and disappointing: it is perfect and yet ultimately unsatisfying, because unattainable. The faun-poet's goal—like the angel-poet's goal—must not be the final conquest, but the continuing quest. Since the dream is no more perfect a fulfillment than a real possession would be, the faun-poet will continue to be delighted and deceived, and to yearn for something beyond. Throughout the poem, the faun will portray sensuously, intellectually and spiritually Mallarmé's unceasing search, stymied and sublime, for "purer meaning."

One beautiful passage from "A Faun's Afternoon" will illustrate the exaltations and limitations of the poet's quest. After the faun-poet ponders about the nymphs (were they real or imagined: "Let us reflect . . .," he says, implying "Let us think" as well as "Let us make an image"), he plays his syrinx. The syrinx is, of course, reminiscent of another love longed-for and lost, but in a way possessed, through Pan's shaping and playing the reed that was the nymph. As Mallarmé's faun plays his panpipes, he meditates on the nature of art and of inspiration. In the sensuous and heavy heat of the day, there is no breath of air, he says, no water but the air that he blows through his syrinx which sprinkles the thicket "with harmonies." The only wind in that place is, therefore, beautiful (it is his music), but also deceptive, dry and barren, for it is an "arid rain" (it is music and not liquid water.) While characterizing the lack of liquid, the word "arid" also casts subtle aspersions on the music and, therefore, on the nature of art:

> And the only wind outside of the two reeds
> Prompt to be exhaled before in an arid rain it spreads
> Forth sound, is, on the horizon where no wrinkle moves by,
> The visible and serene artificial breath
> Of inspiration, which regains the sky.

Like "arid," the term "artificial" both describes and disparages what it modifies. The "artificial breath / Of inspiration," the motivation behind the faun's music, is by definition "artificial" (from the Latin *ars*, art + *facere*, to make). But "artificial" also means made by human work or art; hence something that is not natural, an imitation. In these lines, the faun's inspiration (his blowing into his panpipes, as well as his stimulus to creative thought or action) appears visually as a "serene and artificial breath" that regains the divine source of his creative impulse: "the sky." Here is art merging again with (it "regains") the divine. Precisely because the faun-poet's music is "artificial," that is, made by art, it is at once both exalted and limited. His art implies a continuing dialogue between presence and absence: a conquest that is, at the same time, a continuing quest.

Thus, the struggle between the real and the ideal, "the earth and the cloud," presence and absence, the body and the mind/spirit, carries on in Mallarmé's poetry a vital, ironic, and essential interchange. For even in his role as poet-angel or poet-priest, Mallarmé never deceives himself into thinking that he has completely captured, or that he *can* completely capture, his vision of the otherworldly which is present in, and beyond, the physical. Still, always, with the complete conviction of a prophet, he believes that through the lacy network of his art—of his "artifice"—he is able to transmit the essence and existence of the "real real" that he envisions, and that he ceaselessly seeks to attain.

The web of words that Mallarmé weaves is at once sensuous,

intellectual and spiritual. It is an artistic creation that contains both the words and their essences: a "fact of nature" *and* "the pure notion." It is a continual quest for "purer meaning." As a "sacred spider," poet-angel, poet-priest or poet-faun, Mallarmé seeks to lift the veil of mystery and to confront the naked vision; and to transmit the transcendent by means of the lacework woven by his poetic word. For the written word is, according to him, a combination of darkness, grace, and illumination—a veil and a vision—a "fold of dark lace, that holds within it the infinite."[67]

[67] "Quant au livre" ("As Regards the Book"), p. 370.

A NOTE ON TRANSLATION

> *Now what is a poet (I'm taking the word in its largest sense), if not a translator . . . ?*
>
> BAUDELAIRE

Translating is, in a way, like an act of love. It is a reaching out toward something that is different from, but profoundly appealing to, the self. It is a pleasure-filled encounter that is sensuous, emotional and spiritual, exhilarating, broadening and deepening. The translator of poetry merges with the original poet, thinks his thoughts, feels his feelings, sees his visions, experiences and comprehends his images, perceptions and points of view. Then, through an empathy so strong that it might seem at times like self-identification, the translator re-creates, in another tongue and form, the original artist's creation. For translation is at its best a re-creation of art, by means of art. The translator of a poem "must be a poet as well as an interpreter," writes Dudley Fitts, and "his interpretation must be an act of poetry."[1]

I do not believe that any one translator can translate every type of poet; nor do I believe that any one person can appreciate or love every other type of person. The translator, like the one who loves, must be finely attuned to the original poet's psyche and feelings, his

[1] "The Poetic Nuance" in *On Translation*, ed. Reuben A. Brower (New York: Oxford University Press, 1966), p. 34.

mind and his music, his moral and his spiritual concerns, his insights and his outward views, his turn of mind and his turn of phrase. The translator must be moved by an "elective affinity" for the poet he is translating, writes Renato Poggioli, who feels that the word *"Einfühlung* or 'Empathy' " is "best suited to define the activity and the experience of the translator."[2] What I have described in terms of love, and what Poggioli calls "elective affinity," *"Einfühlung* or Empathy" are all attempts to epitomize the intense, intimate and essential closeness—the native and natural liking or sympathy—that the translator feels for the poem he is translating.

For me, the original poem, like a person loved, deserves to be respected, accepted and understood on its own terms. The original poem becomes for me, therefore, an almost sacred text to be appreciated, revered and re-created as faithfully as possible. Perhaps that is why I find so illuminating the essay by Eugene A. Nida called "Bible Translating" in which he discusses the difficulties—and the delights—of trying to transpose the Judeo-Christian sacred texts into other languages and cultural contexts. A "definition of translating which is in accord with the best traditions of Biblical scholarship could be stated as follows: 'Translating consists in producing in the receptor language [the language *into which* one is translating] the closest natural equivalent to the message of the source language [the language *from which* one is translating], *first in meaning and secondly in style,*' " Nida writes. "It is recognized that equivalence in both meaning and style cannot always be retained. . . . When, therefore, one must be abandoned for the sake of the other, *the meaning must have priority over the stylistic forms"* (italics mine).[3] These are my precepts as well.

If poetry is, as Coleridge says it is, "the best words in their best order," then in translating poetry—especially lyric poetry, as exemplified by the four French poets in this book—one must respect as much as possible the original poet's "best words." And transposing those "best words" into another tongue, time setting and cultural context requires finding a "best order" for them appropriate to a new poem that seeks to transmit in English the power, import and impact of the original text.

[2] "The Added Artificer" in *On Translation* (note 1 above), p. 141. Future references to Poggioli are to this essay and are included in my text.

[3] In *On Translation* (note 1 above), p. 19.

Faithfulness to the meanings of the original poet's "best words" implies interpreting each word in itself and also in its context in the poem. Translating is, therefore, both a supremely critical and a supremely creative act. It encompasses both the critic's act of reading, interpreting and understanding, and the poet's act of creating. For these reasons, translating is one of the finest ways of coming closer to a text. For translating permits—more, it forces—one to explore, experience and re-create the multiple meanings, mystery and magic of the original poem.

Translating is re-creation, therefore: but it is more than that. On another plane, translation is an image of the act of communication, or of creative expression itself. Communication means that something is carried over or across from one realm or medium into another. Communication with others entails the transmitting or conveying of information: one must transfer or translate one's feelings, ideas and visions, etc. into sounds, signs or gestures that can be interpreted and shared. Essentially, then, all communication is translation; and translation is at the heart of all communication.

On an artistic plane, translation is not just communication: it is also the image of the original poet's act. For isn't the art of poetry, in a certain sense, the art of translation itself, the art of *carrying over* the poet's feelings, thoughts, images, imaginings, impressions and visions into another medium: the foreign medium of words? "There is a sense . . . in which [*The Odyssey*] was itself a translation," writes Robert Fitzgerald in the "Postscript" to his outstanding translation of the epic. "It was a translation into Homer's metered language, into his narrative and dramatic style, of an action invented and elaborated in the imagination."[4] And Baudelaire asks rhetorically in his essay on Victor Hugo: "Now what is a poet (I'm taking the word in its largest sense), if not a translator . . . ?"[5]

The poet, the creator, the "one who makes" (as derived from the Greek poiētēs) is actually, then, for Baudelaire a poet-translator who creates with words, a sketch pad or paint, or music. All original artists are, for him, poet-translators. Several times, in fact, he praises other creative geniuses by characterizing their productions as trans-

[4] Homer, *The Odyssey*, trans. Robert Fitzgerald (New York: Doubleday & Company, Inc., Anchor Books, 1963), p. 506.
[5] "Victor Hugo" in Charles Baudelaire, *Oeuvres complètes* (Paris: Gallimard, Bibliothèque de la Pléiade, 1961), p. 705. All future page references to Baudelaire are to this edition and are included in my text.

lations. For example, he writes, "Victor Hugo's verses know how to translate for the human soul not only the most immediate pleasures that it gathers from visible nature, but also the most fleeting, the most complicated sensations . . ." (p. 704). Because the concept of the poet-translator is very dear to him, Baudelaire summarily dismisses readers who cannot understand it: "Those who are not poets do not understand these things" (p. 704).

Elsewhere, Baudelaire describes other "poets" as translators. About Constantin Guys, the artist whose work he praises so lovingly in "Le Peintre de la vie moderne" ("The Painter of Modern Life"), he writes, "Thus, M. G[uys], translating faithfully his own impressions, marks with an instinctive energy the culminating or luminous points of an object" (p. 1166). Guys's work, Baudelaire adds, is the "*legendary* translation of external life." In his essay "Richard Wagner and 'Tannhaüser' in Paris," Baudelaire describes how Berlioz, Liszt, Théophile Gautier, and he himself "translated"—in this case, wrote words about—their reactions to Wagner's music. And Wagner, too, is described as a translator: he "possesses the art of translating, by subtle gradations, everything that is excessive, immense, ambitious, in spiritual and natural man" (p. 1214).

And so, translation, which implies communication and re-creation, is also an image of original artistic creation: not an image of the original *Fiat* that no mortal can reproduce, a creation out of nothingness—but an image of the sublimely mortal desire to share and to shape something, to *make* something with art. And the poet's translation, which is actually his original creation—the re-creation in an artistic medium of his inner feelings and visions—seeks not only to communicate, but to communicate eternally through art.

An understanding of the nature of translation is helpful—one might even say essential—to an understanding of poetry. For all poetry is, in a sense, a translation.

When I translate poetry, I immerse myself in the sounds, images and tones of the original poem, while always keeping in mind the literal and symbolical meanings both of the French words and of the English words I wish to use. Then I let the poet's images, ideas and evocations flow musically, sensuously and spiritually. Translating, for me at least, is an intellectual and emotional, visceral and visionary merging with the original poet. I also find that translating is a way of refreshing and renewing myself as a thinker, writer, critic, poet and feeling person.

I believe that one must love and appreciate both the language from which one is translating, as well as the language into which one is translating. More, just as we understand best those whom we love best for themselves, so a translator can translate best the poets whose works he loves best. The four poets I have translated here have fascinated me, haunted me, possessed me ever since I first read their works seventeen years ago when I was a junior at Brown University. Baudelaire, Rimbaud, Verlaine and Mallarmé have become over the years the focus of much of my reading and writing. I began to translate Rimbaud when I was writing my doctoral dissertation on him at Harvard; my translations of *A Season in Hell* and *The Illuminations* were published in 1973 by Oxford University Press. Soon after that, I discovered that I could not stop translating! Something drove me on, inspired me, compelled me to try to render in an English worthy of them the works of the four poets whose writings and aesthetics, whose music, images and visions, whose bravadoes and anxieties, joys and sorrows, loathings and longings had become, in a way, a part of me. This book is the result of that need, and of that desire.

In translating these four poets who are so different from each other but who are linked by certain similarities (e.g. they all participated, more or less, in a certain era, and they may all be considered under the broad rubric of "symbolist"), I followed a few general principles. Let me lay these forth first, before discussing some specific problems—and pleasures—I encountered in translating each poet.

First and always, I tried to remain as close, as faithful as possible to the original poet's meanings and intentions. Always, I aimed to reproduce the original poet's words and tones, including his obscurities, when he is obscure, and his stylistic or linguistic levels of discourse (e.g. lyrical, colloquial or vulgar language, use of neologisms, etc.). Whenever possible, I also sought to re-create the flow of the French word order. For example, in Verlaine's "The hunting horn grieves towards the forest . . .," I was able to reproduce Verlaine's line "Et l'air a l'air d'être un soupir d'automne" as: "And the air has the air of being an autumn sigh. . . ." I also wanted to reproduce the flow of the poet's ideas, and so I tried to place a word located at a climactic point in the original poem at a similarly climactic point in the translation. For example, in Mallarmé's "Victoriously the beautiful suicide fled . . . ," I ended the poem, as Mallarmé does, on the word "roses" so that the image of the flower, stimulating both the visual and the olfactory senses, lingers in the mind as the poem closes.

Because music is fundamental to the poetry of these four poets, I used rhyme whenever possible, when the rhyme did not interfere with the poet's meaning(s). But I refused to let a rigid adherence either to English metrics or to English verse forms dominate or dictate my translating. I do not like to alter the meaning of the original text—either by taking away from it, or by adding to it—just for the sake of a metric foot or a rhyme. My renditions often do not scan as "regular" English lines or verse forms, therefore; but my translations always seek to create rhythms and sounds that are pleasing to a person attuned to English poetry. For me, the essential thing in translating poetry is to capture *both* the meaning and the aesthetic pleasure of the original poem: its lyricism (or antilyricism, as in the case of some poems by Baudelaire and Rimbaud), its sensuous appeal, its musicality and its spirituality. When I could not use rhyme naturally in English, then I used assonance or consonance in order to suggest the original poet's musicality. For instance, I used assonance and consonance in the closing lines of Mallarmé's "Gift of the Poem": " . . . will you press / With your faded finger the breast / Through which flows in sibylline whiteness the woman for / The lips starving for the air of the virgin azure?"

Rhymes and rhythms alone do not make these four French poets great, or unique. Rather, it is the interplay between their metrics and their music on the one hand, and their meanings on the other hand, that makes them what they are, and different from all other poets. Countless other poets use rhyme; but only a Baudelaire, a Rimbaud, a Verlaine or a Mallarmé transmits through rhyme and rhythm the message that is uniquely his own. My translations, therefore, seek to mediate between the poet's message and his metrics.

Sometimes, to suggest rhyme or assonance, I put an unaccented syllable at the end of a line. I did this, for example, in stanza two of Rimbaud's "Memory," where "She" at the end of line two reproduces Rimbaud's "Elle" at the end of his second line, and suggests in English the effect of a rhyme with "canopy" in line three:

l'ébat des anges;—Non . . . le courant d'or en marche,
meut ses bras, noirs, et lourds, et frais surtout, d'herbe. Elle
sombre, ayant le Ciel bleu pour ciel-de-lit, appelle
pour rideaux l'ombre de la colline et de l'arche.

the frolic of angels;—No . . . the gold tide on the march,
moves its arms black, and heavy, and blooming above all,
    with grass. She
sinks, having the blue Sky for her canopy,
calls as curtains the shade of the hill and the arch.

I have chosen a few examples from each poet to illustrate what I have tried to do in my translations. Each poet presented me with new melodies, new challenges, new problems—and new delights.

Baudelaire's sensuousness and sensuality are, for me, among the most salient and distinguishing characteristics of his poetry. In my translations of Baudelaire, therefore, I tried to capture his commingling sense impressions by choosing words that create synaesthetic effects. I also tried to use rhythms and rhymes that would reproduce the amplitude and the tone of his poems. For example, in the seventh stanza of "The Jewels," I used iambic pentameter, rhyme and assonance to try to capture the richness and the symbolical importance of these lines. For "The Jewels," a celebration of the naked body of the poet's mistress, is, on another level, a poem about metamorphoses that are physical, mythical and spiritual. Here is how I render Baudelaire's alexandrines: "I thought I saw the hips of Antiope / Joined with a boy's bust in a new design, / Her waist set off her pelvis to such a degree. / On that fawnlike and dusky complexion the rouge was sublime!"

When Baudelaire uses octosyllabic lines, my lines, too, are shorter. In "Lovers' Wine" and "Parisian Dream," I attempted to convey the poet's experiences of intoxication and disorientation caused by wine and love in the first poem, and by a drug-induced dream in the second. In "Lovers' Wine," I found that a tetrameter generally suited my translation. Here are the last six lines: "Softly balanced in equilibrium / Upon the intelligent whirlwind, in / A parallel delirium, / / My sister, as side by side we swim, / We'll flee without rest unceasingly / Towards the paradise of my reveries!" In the airier and eerier atmosphere of "Parisian Dream," I found that a trimeter generally captured the "terrible landscape" of the poet's dream, as well as the terrible landscape of his awakening after it: "The clock with funereal tones / Tolled noon brutally, and there swirled / Down darkness from heaven upon / The sorrowful, torpid world."

At times, Baudelaire's sensuous language creates an antiaesthetic effect, as in his "Spleen" poems. The lines in the poem beginning "When the low, heavy sky weighs like a lid . . ." pound upon the reader with words, sounds and images that immure him in the prison of the poet's mind. By means of his sensuous language, which my translation seeks to reproduce, Baudelaire makes us see, feel, battle against, and succumb to that imprisonment and that despair. In stanza two, for instance, my repeated dental and plosive sounds (d,t and p,b), and the huffing h sounds try to re-create the oppressive, foul atmosphere of the dungeon where Hope is at once frantic and vanquished, repulsive ("like a bat") and pitiable (with its "timorous wings"): "When the earth is changed into a humid dungeon, / Where Hope, like a bat, goes plunging / Against the walls with its timorous wings / And hitting its head against the rotted ceilings. . . ."

In several of Baudelaire's most beautiful poems, form was a particular challenge. In "Head of Hair"—a poem that re-creates the erotic and languorous intoxication of love—Baudelaire's alexandrines are arranged in five-line stanzas with two rhymes per stanza (Baudelaire's rhyme scheme is abaab). I also used two rhymes (or assonance plus rhyme) per stanza, in order to try to capture some of Baudelaire's effects. Thus, here is my rendition of stanza one: "O fleece, foaming down upon the neck! O curly / Locks! O scent filled with nonchalance! Ecstasy! / To people tonight the alcove's obscurity / With memories sleeping in this hair I wish / To wave it in the air like a handkerchief!"

"Evening Harmony" was an even greater challenge. This splendid poem is based on the Malayan pantoum form: the second and fourth lines of each stanza become the first and third lines of the following stanza. The poem, therefore, has only two rhymes throughout. (Baudelaire's rhymes are on /ar/ as in "soir,"and /iʒ / as in "vertige"). Since lines are repeated, each line must be phrased so that it is meaningful in two different contexts. I felt that it was essential to try to reproduce the poem's pattern because the limited number of echoing lines and rhymes contributes to the poem's dizzy and intoxicating effects. The two rhymes I selected for my translation are on -ess and -ē, but I found that I had to use assonance as well. Here is how I rendered the first stanza: "Here come the times when swaying on its stem's crest / Each flower like a censer exhales its fragrancy; / Sounds and scents revolve in the evening's obscurity; / Melancholy waltz and languid dizziness!" I used "s" and "v" sounds to help suggest the /v/, /f/ and /s/ sounds Baudelaire used to create the vertiginous atmosphere in which he evokes his sensuous, spiritual, languorous, melancholy and intoxicated feelings about love.

Another great challenge in form was the dreamy and yet unnerving "Invitation to the Voyage," inspired by Baudelaire's mistress Marie Daubrun. Since the poem is composed in *vers impairs* (Baudelaire uses five or seven syllables per line), I felt that my translation had to try to mirror Baudelaire's somewhat jarring rhythms, his inner uneasiness portrayed by his uneven-syllabled lines. I did not want my translation to be too evenly rhythmic, too eloquent, too full. After all, Baudelaire's asking his mistress to travel to a land that resembles her with her "treacherous" eyes is a rather disturbing idea. For these reasons, I sought to create a slight rhythmic disequilibrium in my translation. Thus, when Baudelaire used two five-syllable lines one after the other, I tried, whenever I could without altering his meaning, to use one line of trimeter and one line of dimeter. For instance, I rendered "Mon enfant, ma soeur, / Songe à la douceur" as: "My child, my sister, imagine / The sweetness in. . . ." I wanted my rhythms to disturb the reader, because that is what Baudelaire's rhythms do. Where Baudelaire used seven-syllable lines, I used a tetrameter, but for his two-line septisyllabic refrain: "Là, tout n'est qu'ordre et beauté, / Luxe, calme et volupté," I used the slightly uneven: "There all is but order and beauteousness, / Luxury, calm and voluptuousness." Nowhere did I think that the translation could bear the weight of an English pentameter.

Baudelaire's rhyme scheme in "Invitation to the Voyage" was also a tremendous challenge. Throughout my translation, I used rhyme or assonance and I always tried to reproduce or give the effect of Baudelaire's rhyme pattern (which is aabccbddeffe). Here is my rendition of the first stanza:

> My child, my sister, imagine
> The sweetness in
> Our going to live together there!

To love as time slowly goes by,
To love and to die
In the land that resembles you everywhere!
The wet suns that rise
And set in those murky skies
For my spirit have the charm that inheres
So mysterious
Within your treacherous
Eyes glistening across their tears.

Rimbaud's poetic universe offered other challenges. Translating his poetry often necessitated finding words, tones and rhythms to reproduce his particular combinations of violence and vision, the conflicts between his antiaesthetic stances and his underlying lyricism. These contrasts are evident, for example, in "The Sleeper of the Valley" in which a lyrical tone lulls the reader into a false serenity, until the last line. Then, the realization that the young soldier "sleeping" in the grass is actually dead makes all the lyricism that preceded appear cruel, indifferent and ironic: "It's a gap of greenness where a singing river / Madly hooks upon the grasses silver / Shreds; where the sun from the lofty mountain's height, / Shines down: it's a valley that froths with rays of light."

In translating Rimbaud's poems, my language had to try to capture his almost ceaseless dialogues between beauty and ugliness. In "The Crows," for instance, Rimbaud calls upon these birds of carrion with ambivalent emotions ranging from loathing to love, and including sensuous, even erotic longings, fear, awe and reverence. In the depressing, distressing atmosphere of the first stanza depicting a landscape wracked by winter and wracked by war, the poet calls upon God for help. His call is at once full of violence, and full of hope. For he asks God to send down, like an invading army, the crows—those fear-inspiring, glossy black birds that by feeding on carrion will help purify both the earth and the air. My language attempts to capture Rimbaud's antithetical emotions. His octosyllabic lines seemed to call for an English tetrameter. Although I could not reproduce his exact rhyme scheme (abbacc), I was able to use rhyme and assonance throughout, as in my rendition of the first stanza: "Lord, when the meadowland is chilled, / When in the demolished hamlets' gloom, / The lengthy angelus bells are stilled . . . / Upon nature that has lost its bloom / Make sweep down from the vast skies those / Belovèd and delicious crows."

The subtle and incessant dialogue, ambivalent and intimate, between beauty and ugliness is, for me, one of the most fascinating aspects of Rimbaud's poetry. In "Vowels" I tried to capture the appealing and repulsive flies and smells that the poet associates with the letter A: "A, black hairy corset of dazzling flies that bombinate / Around cruel and foul / / Smells. . . ." I used "foul" to create an assonance with "vowels," which I use (as Rimbaud does) at the end of line one, because Rimbaud rhymed "voyelles" with "cruelles," the word he uses to characterize the smells ("des puanteurs cruelles"). Rimbaud's rhyme suggested to me some hidden relationship between the vowels and the smells. The word "bombinate" is English and is as close as one can get, I think, to the meaning of Rimbaud's neologism "bombiner" ("Qui bombinent autour des puanteurs cruelles").

Not infrequently, the dialogue between beauty and ugliness in Rimbaud's poetry juxtaposes the antiaesthetic or repulsive with the spiritual. The repulsive then simultaneously contradicts and complements, denigrates and suggests—even calls for—the transcendent. For instance, in stanza five of "The Drunken Boat," my language attempts to capture the caressing but disturbing sounds and rhythms of the waves and of the poet's ideas and images: "Sweeter than the flesh of sour apples / To children, green water penetrated my hull of pine / And washed from me the stains left by blue wines / And vomit, while scattering my rudder and grappling."

The intense and nervous waiting for an epiphany that Rimbaud depicts in pentasyllabic lines in "Song of the Highest Tower," I tried to capture through rhyme, assonance, and short, uneven lines that give an impression of his *vers impairs*. For instance, in stanza four the poet compares his own condition to that of an abandoned Meadow buzzing with "a hundred filthy flies": "Thus the Meadow given / Over to oblivion, / Grown taller, and flowering with / Frankincense and rye / Grass amid the fierce bourdon of / A hundred filthy flies."

"Shame," another poem in *vers impairs*, seeks to mediate ceaselessly between the repulsive (in sights, smells, experience, behavior, character, etc.) and the heavenly. My language and rhythms attempt to re-create the anger and pain, the sadistic and masochistic turn of mind, the self-abasement and the shame of the poet, who is undoubtedly the "pesterous / Child" of stanza four. I also try to transmit the poet-child's anguished hope that despite his foul life— or perhaps because of it, and because of his "shame"—someone, even perhaps God himself, will pray for him when he dies. The last two lines of the poem establish a dramatic change in tone. Here is how I tried to convey that shift. Until the child has been destroyed (by murder, lapidation or burning at the stake, or by means of his own masochistic acts), the poet says,

> . . . the pesterous
> Child, the so silly beast,
> Should not for an instant cease
> From using ruses and from being treacherous,
>
> Like a cat from the mountains of Roche,
> From polluting spheres everywhere!
> At his death however, ô
> My God! let there arise some prayer!

Two Rimbaud poems offered particular challenges in form. The French of "The Bewildered Ones" is composed of three-line stanzas: two octosyllabic lines are followed by one tetrasyllabic line. Rimbaud's rhyme scheme joins two successive stanzas in this way: aab, ccb, dde, ffe. Whenever possible, I maintained his rhyme scheme by using rhyme or assonance, because I felt that its singsong simplicity was important to the poem's mood—a simplicity that is undercut by the pathos of the poem's ending.

The other challenge in form, "The Plundered Heart," is a triolet, a poem with eight-line stanzas: line one is repeated as line four, and lines one and two are repeated as lines seven and eight. My translation preserves the triolet form with rhyme or assonance, and it transposes Rimbaud's octosyllabic lines into a tetrameter. It also seeks to maintain Rimbaud's tone that balances visceral descriptions and clinical details with an adolescent's cry of anguish. This poem, Rimbaud wrote to his former teacher Georges Izambard on May 13, 1871, "does not mean nothing."

The greatest challenge for me in translating Verlaine's poetry was to try to re-create his pervasive, insistent musicality, his lyricism composed of demitones and shadings, while also being as faithful as possible to the many subtle gradations of his meanings and insinuations. Just because Verlaine's poetry seems so simple (it is not really simple at all), it is extremely difficult—and extremely thrilling—to translate.

To try to capture the contrast between the apparent simplicity and the underlying tension in some of Verlaine's most melodious poems, I used several different techniques. To transcribe the four-syllable lines of "The moon shines white . . ." ("La lune blanche . . ."), which is composed of three six-line stanzas with the rhyme scheme ababcc (the sixth line of each stanza is set off from the others), I used rhyme, assonance, and lines that have a dimeter (except for two lines, where I used a trimeter): "The moon shines white / In the forest tonight; / From every bough / A voice calls out / Beneath the arbor . . . / / O my darling." To render the octosyllables of "The Faun," I found that alternating lines of tetrameter and trimeter were able to carry over into English Verlaine's rhythmic simplicity that veils a sense of sadness and impending evil.

Often, of course, Verlaine uses the *vers impair*, which he recommends to other poets in his "Art of Poetry." I used various methods to try to replicate its sense of imbalance, uneasiness and disruption. In "Autumn Song," Verlaine's mingling of lines with an even number of syllables with lines that have an odd number of syllables is particularly and melodically remarkable. (His six-line stanzas contain the following number of syllables: 4,4,3,4,4,3). One at first seems caressed, and then jolted, by the rhythms. In my translation, I used as much rhyme and assonance as possible without really adding to, or taking away from Verlaine's meaning. I created lines of monometer, dimeter or trimeter. For example, here is my rendition of stanza two: "Quite choking / And pallid, when / The hour is tolling, / I remember / The days gone by / And I cry."

"With Muted Strings," another poem in *vers impairs* (Verlaine's lines are pentasyllabic), I transposed, basically, in a trimeter, as in the third stanza: "Now close your eyes halfway, / Cross your arms upon your breast, / And all schemes from your heart at rest / Forever chase away." Not only did Verlaine's words and ideas fit nicely into this English rhythm, but it also seemed to me that a rhymed poem in English trimeter might create the disquieting effect of Verlaine's *vers impairs*, because in English we are so often used to hearing alternating lines of tetrameter and trimeter.

"Sentimental Colloquy," Verlaine's famous and ironic dialogue between former lovers, was a marvelous challenge. Several translators have transposed Verlaine's decasyllabic couplets into heroic couplets. But I felt that the tone and meaning of Verlaine's lines could not bear the weight of iambic pentameter throughout. For the most part, therefore, I re-created his dialogue in tetrameter (except in the fourth couplet, and in line ten). Thus, the first speaker's hope-filled question that lingers on the pronounced mute e of "rêve" (the mute e is pronounced in French poetry before a consonant) until the other speaker's rejection ("—Ton coeur bat-il toujours à mon seul nom? / Toujours vois-tu mon âme en rêve?—Non."), I rendered as: "—Does your heart still hearing my name throb so? / Does my soul still appear in your reveries?—No." In this way, the fourth accent of the tetrameter, falling on "No," cuts off the lingering dactyl of the word "reveries" and tries to reproduce the effect of Verlaine's mute e suspended in the air before the brutal rejection.

A dizzy eroticism pervades some of Verlaine's poems. In "Brussels: Merry-Go-Round," I used many echoes and repetitions in order to capture Verlaine's sensuous, swirling scene. For example, stanza one reads: "Go round, go round, good merry-go-round, / Go round a hundred turns, go round a thousand / Turns, go round often and forever go round, / Go round, go round to the oboes' sound." In "Kaleidoscope," I used many rhymes or assonances with the -ē sound and I repeated other sounds at the ends of lines (g, -ôr, and z) in order to try to re-create Verlaine's spinning, ever-changing focuses that shape his visions composed of the same bits of material. My translation tried to reproduce his colored and colorful glimpses that commingle reality with dream and fantasy, body with soul, the present with the past and the future.

In sonnets such as "Hope shines like a blade of straw . . .," "Allegory" and "The hunting horn grieves towards the forest . . .," Verlaine's lyricism combines music with a seriousness of tone and an amplitude of phrase (the first two are composed in alexandrines, the third, in decasyllables). They mingle a simplicity or naïveté with a veiled, but decidedly present, intellectual sophistication; a kind of down-to-earth realism with a certain and pervasive spiritual aspiration; and anxiety with hope. In my rendition of "Hope shines like a blade of straw . . .," I used lines of iambic pentameter, basically, as well as rhyme and assonance. In the first stanza, I tried to replicate the different linguistic levels of Verlaine's discourse evoking the earthy and earthly, as well as intimations of the otherworldly: "Hope shines like a blade of straw in the cattle stable. / What do you fear from the wasp drunk with its mad flight? / See, at some hole the sun always rises in motes of light. / Why wouldn't you sleep, with your elbow on the table?"

In "The hunting horn grieves towards the forest . . .," I tried to capture through word choice, rhyme and assonance the surging and dying of the poet's anxiety, as well as his melancholy languor. "The wolf's soul is weeping in this voice that rises / With the sun that wanes in a death agony / One wants to think caressing that both delights / And distresses simultaneously." And in "Allegory," I sought to convey the heat, heaviness and torpor that the poet finds so torturesome and so melodiously appealing, so luminous and so ominous. I ended the poem, as Verlaine did, on the word "black," for I wished to insinuate the ebb and flow of Verlaine's feelings, his intimations of hope and of despair:

> Bitter torpor has overtaken the cicadas and over
> Their narrow bed of uneven stones
> The half dried up brooks do not leap any more.
>
> An incessant rotation of luminous moires
> Extends its flowings and its flowings back . . .
> Wasps, here and there, are flying, yellow and black.

My last line follows Verlaine's model: "Des guêpes, ça et là, volent, jaunes et noires."

Translating Mallarmé's poetry requires a fundamental fidelity to the "purer meaning" of words: a devotion not only to the words' meanings, but also to their etymologies and to their sounds that evoke other sounds (e.g. rhymes, homonyms and puns). In addition, in a poet who weighs words so carefully, one must be attentive to implicit ironies.

In several ways, I tried to capture the multiple meanings and implications of Mallarmé's words. Each word presented a different challenge, and each challenge required a separate solution. In the opening sonnet of his collection, *Poésies*, the title "Salut" (from the Latin *salus*, *salutis*, meaning health, safety, well-being, greeting) is at once a greeting, a toast, and a prescription for the poet's salvation. I therefore used "Salutation," which echoes the Latin root, as the English title. In lines four, five and eight, Mallarmé puns on various forms of the word "vers" (meaning "verse" or "line of poetry"), which he uses in line one. (His wordplays are on "envers," "divers" and "d'hivers.") I tried to re-create the effect of his puns by using as rhyme words various forms of the word "verse," which I used in line one: "inversely," "diverse" and "traverses."

To try to capture the irony of the title denoting the clown's condition in "Le Pitre châtié"—his punishment that is also the means of his purification (from the verb "châtier," which means "to punish" and figuratively, "to purify"), I chose the title "The Chastened Clown" because chastened, derived from the same Latin root as "châtié" (*castigo, castigare*), also implies punishment and purification.

Sometimes, of course, I could not find just one English word to grasp Mallarmé's dual, often ironic, meanings. In two cases I used two words that I joined by a slash to indicate that both meanings were implied, and essential. In line seven of "Sea Breeze," to render the notion of a military defense and also the sacred terror of a taboo implied by Mallarmé's "le vide papier que la blancheur défend," I used the phrase "the blank paper defended/forbidden by its whiteness." And I translated the opening of "Saint" ("À la fenêtre recelant / Le santal vieux qui se dédore") as: "At the window containing /concealing / The old santal whose gilt is peeling" because I did not want to lose the antithetical richness implied by "receler."

Two poems in particular presented some great technical challenges. The famous sonnet beginning "Will the virgin, hardy and beautiful present time . . ." is constructed in French around the /i/ sound. Throughout this splendid sonnet filled with tensions and anxieties, with scorn and with suffering, Mallarmé's rhymes on /i/ (e.g. "fui"), /ivr/ (e.g. "ivre") and /iɲ/ (e.g. "Cygne") add an icy, frigid and high-pitched sound to the atmosphere. My rhymes on -īm, -ē and -īz try to capture the same. For example, here is my rendition of the second stanza: "A swan of old remembers that it is he / Magnificent but who without hope sets himself free / For not having sung the region in which to live when the ennui / Of sterile winter glittered resplendently."

The "sonnet in -ix" ("Her pure nails consecrating on high their

onyx . . .") presented the challenge of creating rhymes (or asso-
nances) on the -iks sound (the French /iks/). Although I could not
preserve Mallarmé's rhymes in toto while also being faithful to his
words (he uses only two rhymes in the poem on /ɔr/ and /iks/), I was
able to use assonance to approximate those rhymes in stanza one:
"Her pure nails consecrating on high their onyx, / Anguish, this
midnight, torchbearer, supports / Many a vespertine dream burned
by the Phoenix / That no cinerary amphora stores. . . ." In the first
tercet, I used the assonance of "north" and "décor" to suggest
Mallarmé's /ɔr/ rhymes. In the second stanza, I rhymed "ptyx" with
"Styx," as Mallarmé does, and in the tercets, I approximated Mal-
larmé's rhyme on /iks/ (nixe/fixe) with nixie/fixes. I felt that it was
important to try to preserve as much as possible Mallarmé's use of
the letter x which adds an aura of strangeness and mystery to the
poem.

"A Faun's Afternoon" was one of the greatest and most exciting
challenges. To help me translate the poem, I reread the poem over
and over. I immersed myself in the sounds, rhythms and words. I
also listened to Debussy's *Prelude to A Faun's Afternoon* again and
again. I let the music—Mallarmé's, and Debussy's—flood me and
flow through me. I tried to find a language that would interweave
the faun's insistent intellectuality with his mischievous and perva-
sive sensuality. For instance, I tried to capture the animal, intellec-
tual, artistic and spiritual atmosphere of the following lines charac-
terized by stillness, heat, ardor and intensity: " . . . Inerte, tout
brûle dans l'heure fauve / Sans marquer par quel art ensemble détala
/ Trop d'hymen souhaité de qui cherche le *la*. . . ." My repeated r, s
and z sounds, and the rhyme on -ā sought to reproduce the sensa-
tions that the faun feels both within and outside of himself. Too,
they aimed to transmit his desires to seize what is fleeing from him:
the perfect note *A*, the Ideal. " . . . Inert, all burns in the tawny /
Hour without marking by what art at the same time ran away / Too
much marriage desired by him who seeks the note *A*. . . ."

Elsewhere, I try to reproduce the sounds of the rush as it plays its
sorrowful music mediating between reality and dreams, life and art,
this world and the divine. Mallarmé creates these effects through his
words and his sounds: the /y/ (e.g. "j*u*meau") and /u/ (e.g. "j*ou*e")
that seem to hurtle against each other, and the melodic repetition of
/ʒ/ sounds (e.g. "*j*onc") and the liquid /l/s that seem to let the

music flow. Finally, he adds a humorous touch, not without irony, by rhyming "amusions" with "confusions," which he also calls "fausses." The word "confusions" is derived from the Latin *confusio*, which means (a) a mixing, blending or union (a meaning retained, for example, in the French juridical phrase "avec confusion des peines," the two sentences to run concurrently), and (b) confusion or disorder. The word suggests, therefore, both the smoothness of a blending and the disorder of a jumbling. Further, both these mixings together and these mixings-up, Mallarmé says, are "false": " . . . arcane tel élut pour confidant / Le jonc vaste et jumeau dont sous l'azur on joue: / Qui, détournant à soi le trouble de la joue, / Rêve, dans un solo long, que nous amusions / La beauté d'alentour par des confusions / Fausses entre elle-même et notre chant crédule. . . ." My s, sh, p, b and l sounds try to suggest the air being blown into the rush as it makes its music, and the assonance between "amusing" and "confusions" attempts to suggest Mallarmé's humorous and ironic rhyme: " . . . such a secret chose for its confidant / The vast twin rush on which one plays beneath the blueness: / Which rush, turning to itself the cheek's distress, / Dreams, in a lengthy solo, that we were amusing / The surrounding beauty by false confusions / Between itself and our credulous song. . . ."

The French of "A Faun's Afternoon" is composed in couplets (what the French call *rimes plates*: aa,bb,cc, etc.). Rarely are Mallarmé's lines in this poem end-stopped. Whenever I could, I used rhyme, assonance or consonance at the ends of my lines to try to create the effect of Mallarmé's couplets. In the few cases when I could not do that, I used rhyme, assonance or consonance in the pattern that the French call *une rime croisée* (abab) or so picturesquely, *une rime embrassée* (abba).

Literature "cannot afford to do without good translators," writes Renato Poggioli. "Translators are after all the most cosmopolitan among the citizens of the Republic of Letters; their absence from the scene, or their presence in too limited number, may mean that the literary tradition will rest all too easily within the Chinese wall it has erected around itself. By denying itself a look beyond that wall, a literature is bound to die of slow exhaustion, or, as Goethe said, of self-boredom" (p. 147).

Because foreign language teaching has been de-emphasized, so unfortunately, in this country at the present time, good translations become more important than ever. Translations, after all, enable a reader to encounter writers whose language and culture he knows but little, or not at all. I hope that my translations may help readers who know no French or little French to experience the beauty, power and passion of Baudelaire, Rimbaud, Verlaine and Mallarmé, who are four of the greatest poets of nineteenth-century France—and anywhere. Their work has left a lasting impact not only on French letters, but on modern world literature, as well. In addition, I hope that for serious students of French poetry my translations may serve as interpretations and commentaries on the original texts, which they seek to capture and to re-create. For translation is for me at once interpretation and re-creation, and a way of participating, intimately, in the experience of poetry itself.

Baudelaire (photograph by Carjat)

BAUDELAIRE

AU LECTEUR

La sottise, l'erreur, le péché, la lésine,
Occupent nos esprits et travaillent nos corps,
Et nous alimentons nos aimables remords,
Comme les mendiants nourrissent leur vermine.

Nos péchés sont têtus, nos repentirs sont lâches;
Nous nous faisons payer grassement nos aveux,
Et nous rentrons gaiement dans le chemin bourbeux,
Croyant par de vils pleurs laver toutes nos taches.

Sur l'oreiller du mal c'est Satan Trismégiste
Qui berce longuement notre esprit enchanté,
Et le riche métal de notre volonté
Est tout vaporisé par ce savant chimiste.

C'est le Diable qui tient les fils qui nous remuent!
Aux objets répugnants nous trouvons des appas;
Chaque jour vers l'Enfer nous descendons d'un pas,
Sans horreur, à travers des ténèbres qui puent.

Ainsi qu'un débauché pauvre qui baise et mange
Le sein martyrisé d'une antique catin,
Nous volons au passage un plaisir clandestin
Que nous pressons bien fort comme une vieille orange.

Serré, fourmillant, comme un million d'helminthes,
Dans nos cerveaux ribote un peuple de Démons,
Et, quand nous respirons, la Mort dans nos poumons
Descend, fleuve invisible, avec de sourdes plaintes.

Si le viol, le poison, le poignard, l'incendie,
N'ont pas encor brodé de leurs plaisants dessins
Le canevas banal de nos piteux destins,
C'est que notre âme, hélas! n'est pas assez hardie.

Mais parmi les chacals, les panthères, les lices,
Les singes, les scorpions, les vautours, les serpents,
Les monstres glapissants, hurlants, grognants, rampants,
Dans la ménagerie infâme de nos vices,

Il en est un plus laid, plus méchant, plus immonde!
Quoiqu'il ne pousse ni grands gestes ni grands cris,
Il ferait volontiers de la terre un débris
Et dans un bâillement avalerait le monde;

TO THE READER

Stupidity, error, stinginess, sin,
Occupy our minds and wrack our bodies with torment,
And we nourish our obliging remorse,
Like beggars nurturing their vermin.

Our sins are stubborn, our repentances are cowardly;
We make sure our confessions earn us generous gains,
And we return gaily to the miry path,
Thinking by vile tears to cleanse all our stains.

On the pillow of evil there's Satan Trismegistus
Who slowly lulls our enchanted minds to sleep,
And the rich metal of our will is completely
Vaporized by this master chemist.

It's the Devil who holds the strings that propel
Us! In repugnant objects we find alluring charms;
Each day we descend another step towards Hell,
Without horror, across the reeking darkness.

Like a poor debauchee who kisses and eats
The martyrized breast of an ancient whore,
We steal on our way a clandestine pleasure
Which we press very hard like an old orange.

Squeezed, swarming, like a million helminths, a crowd of Demons
Carouses in our brains, and, when we take a breath,
Into our lungs Death
Descends, invisible river, with muffled moans.

If fire, the dagger, poison, rape,
Still haven't embroidered with their droll
Designs the banal canvases of our woeful fates,
It's that our souls, alas! are not sufficiently bold.

But among the jackals, panthers, bitch-hounds, monkeys,
Scorpions, vultures, serpents, the screaming,
Howling, growling, creeping
Monsters in our vices' infamous menagerie,

There is one more ugly, more evil, more filthy!
Although he neither gesticulates nor hurls
Great cries, he'd willingly make of the earth a debris
And in a yawn would swallow the world;

C'est l'Ennui!—l'œil chargé d'un pleur involontaire,
Il rêve d'échafauds en fumant son houka.
Tu le connais, lecteur, ce monstre délicat,
—Hypocrite lecteur, —mon semblable, —mon frère!

It's Ennui!—his eye filled with an involuntary
Tear, he dreams of scaffolds while he
Smokes his hookah. You know him, reader, this delicate monster
—Hypocritical reader,—my fellowman,—my brother!

L'ALBATROS

Souvent, pour s'amuser, les hommes d'équipage
Prennent des albatros, vastes oiseaux des mers,
Que suivent, indolents compagnons de voyage,
Le navire glissant sur les gouffres amers.

A peine les ont-ils déposés sur les planches,
Que ces rois de l'azur, maladroits et honteux,
Laissent piteusement leurs grandes ailes blanches
Comme des avirons traîner à côté d'eux.

Ce voyageur ailé, comme il est gauche et veule!
Lui, naguère si beau, qu'il est comique et laid!
L'un agace son bec avec un brûle-gueule,
L'autre mime, en boitant, l'infirme qui volait!

Le Poëte est semblable au prince des nuées
Qui hante la tempête et se rit de l'archer;
Exilé sur le sol au milieu des huées,
Ses ailes de géant l'empêchent de marcher.

THE ALBATROSS

Often, for their amusement, crewmen seize
Upon albatrosses, vast birds of the seas,
That follow, indolent travel companions,
The ship gliding over the briny chasms.

Scarcely have they put them down, when these kings
Of the azure, ashamed and awkward,
Piteously allow their great white wings
To trail along their sides like oars.

This wingèd traveler, how he is clumsy and weak!
How funny and ugly he is, he who, but a short time by,
Was so beautiful! With a pipe, one man annoys his beak,
Another mimes, by limping, the cripple who used to fly!

The Poet is like the prince of the storm clouds
Who haunts the tempest and taunts the archer; when he
Is exiled on earth amid the crowd's scornful squawking,
His wings of a giant prevent him from walking.

CORRESPONDANCES

La Nature est un temple où de vivants piliers
Laissent parfois sortir de confuses paroles;
L'homme y passe à travers des forêts de symboles
Qui l'observent avec des regards familiers.

Comme de longs échos qui de loin se confondent
Dans une ténébreuse et profonde unité,
Vaste comme la nuit et comme la clarté,
Les parfums, les couleurs et les sons se répondent.

Il est des parfums frais comme des chairs d'enfants,
Doux comme les hautbois, verts comme les prairies,
—Et d'autres, corrompus, riches et triomphants,

Ayant l'expansion des choses infinies,
Comme l'ambre, le musc, le benjoin et l'encens,
Qui chantent les transports de l'esprit et des sens.

CORRESPONDENCES

Nature is a temple where living pillars
At times allow confused words to arise;
Man moves along within through forests of symbols
Which observe him with familiar eyes.

Like drawn-out echoes that from afar unite
In a unity mysterious and profound,
As boundless as the night and as the light,
The scents, and colors and sounds all correspond.

There are scents as fresh as children's bodies,
As mellow as oboes, as verdant as the prairies,
—And others, corrupted, rich and triumphant, having

The expansiveness of infinite things,
Like ambergris, musk, benzoin and incense,
That sing the transports of the spirit and the senses.

LES PHARES

Rubens, fleuve d'oubli, jardin de la paresse,
Oreiller de chair fraîche où l'on ne peut aimer,
Mais où la vie afflue et s'agite sans cesse,
Comme l'air dans le ciel et la mer dans la mer;

Léonard de Vinci, miroir profond et sombre,
Où des anges charmants, avec un doux souris
Tout chargé de mystère, apparaissent à l'ombre
Des glaciers et des pins qui ferment leur pays;

Rembrandt, triste hôpital tout rempli de murmures,
Et d'un grand crucifix décoré seulement,
Où la prière en pleurs s'exhale des ordures,
Et d'un rayon d'hiver traversé brusquement;

Michel-Ange, lieu vague où l'on voit des Hercules
Se mêler à des Christs, et se lever tout droits
Des fantômes puissants qui dans les crépuscules
Déchirent leur suaire en étirant leurs doigts;

Colères de boxeur, impudences de faune,
Toi qui sus ramasser la beauté des goujats,
Grand cœur gonflé d'orgueil, homme débile et jaune,
Puget, mélancolique empereur des forçats;

Watteau, ce carnaval où bien des cœurs illustres,
Comme des papillons, errent en flamboyant,
Décors frais et légers éclairés par des lustres
Qui versent la folie à ce bal tournoyant;

Goya, cauchemar plein de choses inconnues,
De fœtus qu'on fait cuire au milieu des sabbats,
De vieilles au miroir et d'enfants toutes nues,
Pour tenter les démons ajustant bien leurs bas;

Delacroix, lac de sang hanté des mauvais anges,
Ombragé par un bois de sapins toujours vert,
Où, sous un ciel chagrin, des fanfares étranges
Passent, comme un soupir étouffé de Weber;

Ces malédictions, ces blasphèmes, ces plaintes,
Ces extases, ces cris, ces pleurs, ces *Te Deum*,
Sont un écho redit par mille labyrinthes;
C'est pour les cœurs mortels un divin opium!

THE BEACONS

Rubens, river of oblivion, garden of idleness,
Pillow of cool flesh where one cannot love,
But where life flows and tosses endlessly,
Like the air in the sky and the sea in the sea;

Leonardo da Vinci, mirror somber and deep,
Where charming angels, with gentle smiles completely
Charged with mystery, appear in the shade
Of glaciers and pine trees that enclose their country;

Rembrandt, sad hospital wholly filled with murmurs,
Which only one large crucifix decorates,
Where tearful prayer is exhaled from the refuse,
And suddenly traversed by a wintry ray;

Michelangelo, wasteland where one sees Christs commingling
With Hercules, and rising upright,
Powerful specters who in the twilights
Rend their shrouds by stretching out their fingers;

Angers of a boxer, a faun's impudencies,
You who knew how to pick up the beauty
Of boors, great heart swelled with pride, weak and sickly
Man, Puget, melancholy emperor of convicts;

Watteau, that carnival where many hearts of renown,
Like butterflies, wander by in radiance,
Cool and airy scenery lit by chandeliers that pour down
Madness on that swirling dance;

Goya, nightmare filled with unknown things, with fetuses
Cooked in the midst of witches' sabbaths, with completely
Naked girls and old women at the mirror, neatly
Adjusting their stockings to tempt the demons;

Delacroix, lake of blood haunted by evil angels
And shaded by a forest of evergreens, where,
Beneath a fretful sky, strange fanfares
Pass by, like a stifled sigh of Weber;

These lamentations, these blasphemies, these maledictions,
These ecstasies, these cries, these tears, these *Te Deums*,
Are reechoed through a thousand labyrinths;
This is for mortal hearts a heavenly opium!

C'est un cri répété par mille sentinelles,
Un ordre renvoyé par mille porte-voix;
C'est un phare allumé sur mille citadelles,
Un appel de chasseurs perdus dans les grands bois!

Car c'est vraiment, Seigneur, le meilleur témoignage
Que nous puissions donner de notre dignité
Que cet ardent sanglot qui roule d'âge en âge
Et vient mourir au bord de votre éternité!

This is a cry repeated by a thousand sentinels,
Through a thousand megaphones, an order sent again;
This is a beacon blazing on a thousand citadels,
In the great forests, a summons from lost huntsmen!

For this is truly, Lord, the finest testimony
That we can give of our dignity
This ardent sob that rolls from age to age
And comes to die on the shore of your eternity!

LA VIE ANTÉRIEURE

J'ai longtemps habité sous de vastes portiques
Que les soleils marins teignaient de mille feux,
Et que leurs grands piliers, droits et majestueux,
Rendaient pareils, le soir, aux grottes basaltiques.

Les houles, en roulant les images des cieux,
Mêlaient d'une façon solennelle et mystique
Les tout-puissants accords de leur riche musique
Aux couleurs du couchant reflété par mes yeux.

C'est là que j'ai vécu dans les voluptés calmes,
Au milieu de l'azur, des vagues, des splendeurs
Et des esclaves nus, tout imprégnés d'odeurs,

Qui me rafraîchissaient le front avec des palmes,
Et dont l'unique soin était d'approfondir
Le secret douloureux qui me faisait languir.

THE FORMER LIFE

For a long time I lived beneath vast porticoes
That the seaside suns would tinge with a thousand flames,
And their tall columns, erect and majestic, made
Them seem, in the evenings, like basaltic grottoes.

The swells, while tossing reflections of the skies,
Mingled in a solemn and mystical manner
The omnipotent harmonies of their rich music
With the sunset's colors reflected by my eyes.

It's there that I lived in voluptuous calms,
Amid the azure, the waves, the splendors
And the naked slaves, quite saturated with scents,

Who refreshed my forehead with branches of palms,
And whose only concern was to divine
The painful secret that was making me pine.

PARFUM EXOTIQUE

Quand, les deux yeux fermés, en un soir chaud d'automne,
Je respire l'odeur de ton sein chaleureux,
Je vois se dérouler des rivages heureux
Qu'éblouissent les feux d'un soleil monotone;

Une île paresseuse où la nature donne
Des arbres singuliers et des fruits savoureux;
Des hommes dont le corps est mince et vigoureux,
Et des femmes dont l'œil par sa franchise étonne.

Guidé par ton odeur vers de charmants climats,
Je vois un port rempli de voiles et de mâts
Encor tout fatigués par la vague marine,

Pendant que le parfum des verts tamariniers,
Qui circule dans l'air et m'enfle la narine,
Se mêle dans mon âme au chant des mariniers.

EXOTIC PERFUME

When, with both eyes closed, on a glowing autumn
Evening, I inhale the scent of your warm
Breast, I see happy shores unfolding
Dazzled by the fires of a monotonous sun;

A lazy island upon which nature produces
Singular trees and savory fruits;
Men whose bodies are lean and full of vigor,
And women whose eyes astonish by their candor.

Guided by your scent toward enchanting climates,
I see a harbor filled with sails and with masts
Still wholly wearied by the ocean wave,

While the perfume of the verdant tamarind trees,
That circulates in the air and distends my nostrils,
Mingles in my soul with the bargemen's melodies.

LA CHEVELURE

O toison, moutonnant jusque sur l'encolure!
O boucles! O parfum chargé de nonchaloir!
Extase! Pour peupler ce soir l'alcôve obscure
Des souvenirs dormant dans cette chevelure,
Je la veux agiter dans l'air comme un mouchoir!

La langoureuse Asie et la brûlante Afrique,
Tout un monde lointain, absent, presque défunt,
Vit dans tes profondeurs, forêt aromatique!
Comme d'autres esprits voguent sur la musique,
Le mien, ô mon amour! nage sur ton parfum.

J'irai là-bas où l'arbre et l'homme, pleins de sève,
Se pâment longuement sous l'ardeur des climats;
Fortes tresses, soyez la houle qui m'enlève!
Tu contiens, mer d'ébène, un éblouissant rêve
De voiles, de rameurs, de flammes et de mâts:

Un port retentissant où mon âme peut boire
A grands flots le parfum, le son et la couleur;
Où les vaisseaux, glissant dans l'or et dans la moire,
Ouvrent leurs vastes bras pour embrasser la gloire
D'un ciel pur où frémit l'éternelle chaleur.

Je plongerai ma tête amoureuse d'ivresse
Dans ce noir océan où l'autre est enfermé;
Et mon esprit subtil que le roulis caresse
Saura vous retrouver, ô féconde paresse!
Infinis bercements du loisir embaumé!

Cheveux bleus, pavillon de ténèbres tendues,
Vous me rendez l'azur du ciel immense et rond;
Sur les bords duvetés de vos mèches tordues
Je m'enivre ardemment des senteurs confondues
De l'huile de coco, du musc et du goudron.

Longtemps! toujours! ma main dans ta crinière lourde
Sèmera le rubis, la perle et le saphir,
Afin qu'à mon désir tu ne sois jamais sourde!
N'es-tu pas l'oasis où je rêve, et la gourde
Où je hume à longs traits le vin du souvenir?

HEAD OF HAIR

O fleece, foaming down upon the neck! O curly
Locks! O scent filled with nonchalance! Ecstasy!
To people tonight the alcove's obscurity
With memories sleeping in this hair I wish
To wave it in the air like a handkerchief!

Languorous Asia and ardent
Africa, a whole world distant, absent, almost dead,
Is alive, aromatic forest, blent
In your depths! Just as other spirits scud ahead
On music, mine, ô my love! swims on your scent.

I'll go over there where, full of sap, man and tree
Slowly swoon beneath the climates' ardor; be,
Strong tresses, the surge that carries me off. You contain
A dazzling dream, sea of ebony,
Of sails and rowers, pennants, masts and flames:

A resounding port where my soul can drink the sweet
Scents, sound and color in great streams;
Where the large ships, gliding into the gold and the moire,
Open their vast arms to embrace the glory
Of a pure sky quivering with eternal heat.

I'll plunge my head in love with drunkenness
Into this black ocean where the other is enclosed;
And my subtle spirit that the rollings caress
Will know how to find you again, ô fecund laziness!
Infinite rockings of leisure, embalmed, composed!

Blue hair, pavilion of outstretched night, you unbar
Once more the azure of the vast round sky for me;
On the downy shores of your hair coiled twistingly
I become intoxicated ardently
With mingled scents of musk, and coconut oil and tar.

A long time! forever! My hand in your heavy
Mane will sow ruby, pearl and sapphire,
So that you may never be deaf to my desire!
Aren't you the oasis where I pursue my reverie,
And the gourd where I suck in long drafts the wine of memory?

LE VAMPIRE

Toi qui, comme un coup de couteau,
Dans mon cœur plaintif es entrée;
Toi qui, forte comme un troupeau
De démons, vins, folle et parée,

De mon esprit humilié
Faire ton lit et ton domaine;
—Infâme à qui je suis lié
Comme le forçat à la chaîne,

Comme au jeu le joueur têtu,
Comme à la bouteille l'ivrogne,
Comme aux vermines la charogne,
—Maudite, maudite sois-tu!

J'ai prié le glaive rapide
De conquérir ma liberté,
Et j'ai dit au poison perfide
De secourir ma lâcheté.

Hélas! le poison et le glaive
M'ont pris en dédain et m'ont dit:
« Tu n'es pas digne qu'on t'enlève
A ton esclavage maudit,

Imbécile!—de son empire
Si nos efforts te délivraient,
Tes baisers ressusciteraient
Le cadavre de ton vampire! »

THE VAMPIRE

You that, like the stab of a knife,
Have entered my heart that moans mournfully;
You that, strong as a drove of demons, came
There, crazy and decked in finery,

To make my humiliated mind
And spirit into your bed and your domain;
—Infamous one to whom I'm tied
Fast like the convict to the chain,

Like the stubborn gambler to the game,
Like the drunkard to
The bottle, like carrion to vermin,
—A curse, a curse upon you!

I have begged the speedy
Blade to conquer my liberty,
And I have told perfidious poison to assist
My cowardice.

Alas! the poison and the blade
Began to scorn me and said to me:
"You aren't worthy of being freed
From your accursèd slavery,

You imbecile!—if our efforts did liberate
You from her empire,
Your kisses would resuscitate
The cadaver of your vampire!"

LE CHAT

Viens, mon beau chat, sur mon coeur amoureux;
   Retiens les griffes de ta patte,
Et laisse-moi plonger dans tes beaux yeux,
   Mêlés de métal et d'agate.

Lorsque mes doigts caressent à loisir
   Ta tête et ton dos élastique,
Et que ma main s'enivre du plaisir
   De palper ton corps électrique,

Je vois ma femme en esprit. Son regard,
   Comme le tien, aimable bête,
Profond et froid, coupe et fend comme un dard,

   Et, des pieds jusques à la tête,
Un air subtil, un dangereux parfum,
   Nagent autour de son corps brun.

THE CAT

Come, my beautiful cat, on my amorous heart; hold back
The claws of your paw, and let me dive
Into your beautiful eyes,
Mingled with metal and agate.

When my fingers caress at leisure
Your head and your back's elasticity,
And when my hand gets drunk with the pleasure
Of feeling your electric body,

I see my wife in spirit.
Her gaze, like yours, amiable beast,
Is deep and cold, cuts and cleaves

Like a dart; and, from her feet
To her head, a subtle air, a dangerous fragrancy,
Are swimming around her brown body.

DUELLUM

Deux guerriers ont couru l'un sur l'autre; leurs armes
Ont éclaboussé l'air de lueurs et de sang.
Ces jeux, ces cliquetis du fer sont les vacarmes
D'une jeunesse en proie à l'amour vagissant.

Les glaives sont brisés! comme notre jeunesse,
Ma chère! Mais les dents, les ongles acérés,
Vengent bientôt l'épée et la dague traîtresse.
—O fureur des coeurs mûrs par l'amour ulcérés!

Dans le ravin hanté des chats-pards et des onces
Nos héros, s'étreignant méchamment, ont roulé,
Et leur peau fleurira l'aridité des ronces.

—Ce gouffre, c'est l'enfer, de nos amis peuplé!
Roulons-y sans remords, amazone inhumaine,
Afin d'éterniser l'ardeur de notre haine!

DUELLUM   (WAR)

Two warriors rushed at one another;
Their weapons splashed the air with sparks and blood.
These games, these clashings of iron are the hubbubs
Of a youth in the throes of newborn love.

The blades are shattered! like our youth, my beloved!
But the teeth, the steely fingernails, avenge very
Soon the sword and the traitorous dagger. —O fury
Of mature hearts ulcerated by love!

In the ravine haunted by mountain cats and snow leopards
Our heroes have rolled, while gripping each other spitefully,
And their skin will adorn with flowers the thorns' aridity.

—That abyss, you see, is hell, populated by our friends!
Let's roll remorselessly there to perpetuate,
Inhuman Amazon, the ardor of our hate!

UN FANTÔME

I. LES TÉNÈBRES

Dans les caveaux d'insondable tristesse
Où le Destin m'a déjà relégué;
Où jamais n'entre un rayon rose et gai;
Où, seul avec la Nuit, maussade hôtesse,

Je suis comme un peintre qu'un Dieu moqueur
Condamne à peindre, hélas! sur les ténèbres;
Où, cuisinier aux appétits funèbres,
Je fais bouillir et je mange mon coeur,

Par instants brille, et s'allonge, et s'étale
Un spectre fait de grâce et de splendeur.
A sa rêveuse allure orientale,

Quand il atteint sa totale grandeur,
Je reconnais ma belle visiteuse:
C'est Elle! noire et pourtant lumineuse.

II. LE PARFUM

Lecteur, as-tu quelquefois respiré
Avec ivresse et lente gourmandise
Ce grain d'encens qui remplit une église,
Ou d'un sachet le musc invétéré?

Charme profond, magique, dont nous grise
Dans le présent le passé restauré!
Ainsi l'amant sur un corps adoré
Du souvenir cueille la fleur exquise.

De ses cheveux élastiques et lourds,
Vivant sachet, encensoir de l'alcôve,
Une senteur montait, sauvage et fauve,

Et des habits, mousseline ou velours,
Tout imprégnés de sa jeunesse pure,
Se dégageait un parfum de fourrure.

III. LE CADRE

Comme un beau cadre ajoute à la peinture,
Bien qu'elle soit d'un pinceau très-vanté,

A PHANTOM

I. THE DARKNESS

In the burial vaults of fathomless sadness
Where Destiny has already secluded me;
Where never a glad or rosy gleam finds entry;
Where, alone with Night, cantankerous hostess,

I am like a painter whom a mocking God
Condemns to paint, alas! upon the darkness;
Where, a cook whose appetites are
Funereal, I bring to a boil and I eat my heart.

At times a specter made of grace and splendor
Glows, and lengthens, and expands its figure.
From its dreaming oriental demeanor,

When it at last attains its total grandeur,
I recognize my beautiful visitor:
It is She! black and yet she's luminous.

II. THE SCENT

Reader, at times have you breathed rapturously
With drunkenness and slow gluttony
That grain of incense that fills a church, or of
A sachet the inveterate musk?

Deep magical spell, with which the past restored
In the present intoxicates us! Thus on a body adored
The lover plucks the
Exquisite flower of memory.

From her elastic and heavy
Hair, a living sachet, the censer of the alcove,
A perfume, savage and musky, rose,

And from her clothes, of muslin or velvet,
Completely imbued with her
Pure youth, there emanated a scent of fur.

III. THE FRAME

In the way that a beautiful frame adds to a picture,
Though it may be by a paint brush granted

Je ne sais quoi d'étrange et d'enchanté
En l'isolant de l'immense nature,

Ainsi bijoux, meubles, métaux, dorure,
S'adaptaient juste à sa rare beauté;
Rien n'offusquait sa parfaite clarté,
Et tout semblait lui servir de bordure.

Même on eût dit parfois qu'elle croyait
Que tout voulait l'aimer; elle noyait
Sa nudité voluptueusement

Dans les baisers du satin et du linge,
Et, lente ou brusque, à chaque mouvement
Montrait la grâce enfantine du singe.

IV. Le Portrait

La Maladie et la Mort font des cendres
De tout le feu qui pour nous flamboya.
De ces grands yeux si fervents et si tendres,
De cette bouche où mon cœur se noya,

De ces baisers puissants comme un dictame,
De ces transports plus vifs que des rayons,
Que reste-t-il? C'est affreux, ô mon âme!
Rien qu'un dessin fort pâle, aux trois crayons,

Qui, comme moi, meurt dans la solitude,
Et que le Temps, injurieux vieillard,
Chaque jour frotte avec son aile rude . . .

Noir assassin de la Vie et de l'Art,
Tu ne tueras jamais dans ma mémoire
Celle qui fut mon plaisir et ma gloire!

Much praise, an indefinable something strange and enchanted
By isolating it from boundless nature,

So jewels, metals, gilded things, furniture,
Adapted themselves precisely to her rare beauty;
Nothing obscured her perfect radiancy,
And everything seemed to serve as a frame for her.

One might even have said sometimes that she believed
That everything wished to love her; she
Would submerge her nudity voluptuously

In the kisses of the satin or the linen,
And, slow or sudden, in every gesture she
Displayed the childlike grace of the simian.

IV. THE PORTRAIT

Disease and Death make ashen dust
Of all the fire that blazed for us.
Of those large eyes so fervent and so fond,
Of those lips in which my heart was drowned,

Of those kisses as powerful as a balm, of those
Transports more fiery than rays of light,
What remains? O my soul, it fills one with fright!
Nothing but a quite pale sketch, in three tones,

Which is dying in solitude, as I am, and
Which Time, injurious old man,
Rubs every day with his rude wing . . .

Assassin dark of Life and of Art,
You shall never kill in my memory
The woman who was my delight and my glory!

RÉVERSIBILITÉ

Ange plein de gaieté, connaissez-vous l'angoisse,
La honte, les remords, les sanglots, les ennuis,
Et les vagues terreurs de ces affreuses nuits
Qui compriment le cœur comme un papier qu'on froisse?
Ange plein de gaieté, connaissez-vous l'angoisse?

Ange plein de bonté, connaissez-vous la haine,
Les poings crispés dans l'ombre et les larmes de fiel,
Quand la Vengeance bat son infernal rappel,
Et de nos facultés se fait le capitaine?
Ange plein de bonté, connaissez-vous la haine?

Ange plein de santé, connaissez-vous les Fièvres,
Qui, le long des grands murs de l'hospice blafard,
Comme des exilés, s'en vont d'un pied traînard,
Cherchant le soleil rare et remuant les lèvres?
Ange plein de santé, connaissez-vous les Fièvres?

Ange plein de beauté, connaissez-vous les rides,
Et la peur de vieillir, et ce hideux tourment
De lire la secrète horreur du dévouement
Dans des yeux où longtemps burent nos yeux avides?
Ange plein de beauté, connaissez-vous les rides?

Ange plein de bonheur, de joie et de lumières,
David mourant aurait demandé la santé
Aux émanations de ton corps enchanté;
Mais de toi je n'implore, ange, que tes prières,
Ange plein de bonheur, de joie et de lumières!

REVERSIBILITY

Angel full of gaiety, do you know agony,
The shame, remorse, the sobs, ennuis,
And vague terrors of those frightful nights that squeeze
The heart like a crumpled leaf?
Angel full of gaiety, do you know agony?

Angel full of kindness, do you know antipathies,
Fists clenched in the dark and the tears of gall
When Vengeance beats its infernal call
To arms and makes itself the captain of our faculties?
Angel full of kindness, do you know antipathies?

Angel full of health, do you know Fevers,
That, along the great walls of the wan
Poorhouse, like exiles, go along with one
Foot dragging, moving their lips and searching for the rare sun?
Angel full of health, do you know Fevers?

Angel full of beauty, do you know wrinkles,
And the fear of aging, and that frightful torture of reading
The secret loathing of devotion in eyes where our greedy
Eyes drank lengthily?
Angel full of beauty, do you know wrinkles?

Angel full of happiness, joy and radiancy,
The dying David would have begged for health from the
Emanations of thy enchanted body;
But, angel, I implore only thy prayers from thee,
Angel full of happiness, joy and radiancy!

HARMONIE DU SOIR

Voici venir les temps où vibrant sur sa tige
Chaque fleur s'évapore ainsi qu'un encensoir;
Les sons et les parfums tournent dans l'air du soir;
Valse mélancolique et langoureux vertige!

Chaque fleur s'évapore ainsi qu'un encensoir;
Le violon frémit comme un cœur qu'on afflige;
Valse mélancolique et langoureux vertige!
Le ciel est triste et beau comme un grand reposoir.

Le violon frémit comme un cœur qu'on afflige,
Un cœur tendre, qui hait le néant vaste et noir!
Le ciel est triste et beau comme un grand reposoir;
Le soleil s'est noyé dans son sang qui se fige.

Un cœur tendre, qui hait le néant vaste et noir,
Du passé lumineux recueille tout vestige!
Le soleil s'est noyé dans son sang qui se fige. . . . .
Ton souvenir en moi luit comme un ostensoir!

EVENING HARMONY

Here come the times when swaying on its stem's crest
Each flower like a censer exhales its fragrancy;
Sounds and scents revolve in the evening's obscurity;
Melancholy waltz and languid dizziness!

Each flower like a censer exhales its fragrancy;
The violin quivers like a heart in distress;
Melancholy waltz and languid dizziness!
The sky like a lofty altar is sad and lovely.

The violin quivers like a heart in distress,
A tender heart, that hates vast black nihility!
The sky like a lofty altar is sad and lovely;
The sun has drowned in its blood that is clotting yet.

A tender heart, that hates vast black nihility,
Is gathering every trace of past luminousness!
The sun has drowned in its blood that is clotting yet. . . . .
Your memory, like a monstrance, shines in me!

L'INVITATION AU VOYAGE

Mon enfant, ma soeur,
Songe à la douceur
D'aller là-bas vivre ensemble!
Aimer à loisir,
Aimer et mourir
Au pays qui te ressemble!
Les soleils mouillés
De ces ciels brouillés
Pour mon esprit ont les charmes
Si mystérieux
De tes traîtres yeux
Brillant à travers leurs larmes.

Là, tout n'est qu'ordre et beauté,
Luxe, calme et volupté.

Des meubles luisants,
Polis par les ans,
Décoreraient notre chambre;
Les plus rares fleurs
Mêlant leurs odeurs
Aux vagues senteurs de l'ambre,
Les riches plafonds,
Les miroirs profonds,
La splendeur orientale,
Tout y parlerait
A l'âme en secret
Sa douce langue natale.

Là, tout n'est qu'ordre et beauté,
Luxe, calme et volupté.

Vois sur ces canaux
Dormir ces vaisseaux
Dont l'humeur est vagabonde;
C'est pour assouvir
Ton moindre désir
Qu'ils viennent du bout du monde.
—Les soleils couchants
Revêtent les champs,
Les canaux, la ville entière,

INVITATION TO THE VOYAGE

My child, my sister, imagine
The sweetness in
Our going to live together there!
To love as time slowly goes by,
To love and to die
In the land that resembles you everywhere!
The wet suns that rise
And set in those murky skies
For my spirit have the charm that inheres
So mysterious
Within your treacherous
Eyes glistening across their tears.

There, all is but order and beauteousness,
Luxury, calm and voluptuousness.

Gleaming furniture
That has been burnished
By the years would adorn our chamber;
The rarest blooms
Blending their perfumes
With the vague fragrancies of amber,
The ceilings, opulent,
The mirrors, deep and intent,
The splendor of the Orient,
There all would speak
To the soul in secrecy
Its native language soft and sweet.

There, all is but order and beauteousness,
Luxury, calm and voluptuousness.

See on those canals
Those sleeping vessels
Whose mood is to sail about aimlessly;
It's to satiate
Your least desire that they
Come from the world's extremity.
—The setting suns
Adorn the open country,
The canals, the entire city's site,

D'hyacinthe et d'or;
Le monde s'endort
Dans une chaude lumière.

Là, tout n'est qu'ordre et beauté,
Luxe, calme et volupté.

With hyacinth and gold;
    The world is going
To sleep in a warmly glowing light.

There, all is but order and beauteousness,
Luxury, calm and voluptuousness.

LA MUSIQUE

La musique souvent me prend comme une mer!
    Vers ma pâle étoile,
Sous un plafond de brume ou dans un vaste éther,
    Je mets à la voile;

La poitrine en avant et les poumons gonflés
    Comme de la toile,
J'escalade le dos des flots amoncelés
    Que la nuit me voile;

Je sens vibrer en moi toutes les passions
    D'un vaisseau qui souffre;
Le bon vent, la tempête et ses convulsions

    Sur l'immense gouffre
Me bercent. D'autres fois, calme plat, grand miroir
    De mon désespoir!

MUSIC

Music often grasps me like a sea!
    In the direction of my pale
Star, under a ceiling of mist or in a vast ether,
    I set sail;

With my chest out front and my lungs swelled fully
    Like a sail, I scale
The back of the heaped-up waves that nighttime veils
    From me;

I feel vibrating in me all the passions of a vessel
    In distress;
Fair wind, the storm and its convulsions cradle me

    On the immense abyss. At other
Times, dead calm, great mirror
    Of my despondency!

LA CLOCHE FÊLÉE

Il est amer et doux, pendant les nuits d'hiver,
D'écouter, près du feu qui palpite et qui fume,
Les souvenirs lointains lentement s'élever
Au bruit des carillons qui chantent dans la brume.

Bienheureuse la cloche au gosier vigoureux
Qui, malgré sa vieillesse, alerte et bien portante,
Jette fidèlement son cri religieux,
Ainsi qu'un vieux soldat qui veille sous la tente!

Moi, mon âme est fêlée, et lorsqu'en ses ennuis
Elle veut de ses chants peupler l'air froid des nuits,
Il arrive souvent que sa voix affaiblie

Semble le râle épais d'un blessé qu'on oublie
Au bord d'un lac de sang, sous un grand tas de morts,
Et qui meurt, sans bouger, dans d'immenses efforts.

THE CRACKED BELL

It is bitter and sweet, during winter nights,
To hear, near the fire that smokes and palpitates,
Distant memories slowly rise
In the clamor of carillons that sing in the haze.

Blessèd is the vigorous-throated bell
That, despite its old age, alert and well,
To its religious cry gives faithful vent,
Like an old soldier on watch beneath the tent!

My own soul is cracked, and when it wishes to throng
In its ennuis nights' cold air with its song,
Its enfeebled voice often seems the dense

Râle of a wounded man forgotten at the side
Of a lake of blood, beneath dead bodies piled high,
Who is dying, without stirring, with efforts immense.

SPLEEN

J'ai plus de souvenirs que si j'avais mille ans.

Un gros meuble à tiroirs encombré de bilans,
De vers, de billets doux, de procès, de romances,
Avec de lourds cheveux roulés dans des quittances,
Cache moins de secrets que mon triste cerveau.
C'est une pyramide, un immense caveau,
Qui contient plus de morts que la fosse commune.
—Je suis un cimetière abhorré de la lune,
Où comme des remords se trainent de longs vers
Qui s'acharnent toujours sur mes morts les plus chers.
Je suis un vieux boudoir plein de roses fanées,
Où gît tout un fouillis de modes surannées,
Où les pastels plaintifs et les pâles Boucher,
Seuls, respirent l'odeur d'un flacon débouché.

Rien n'égale en longueur les boiteuses journées,
Quand sous les lourds flocons des neigeuses années
L'ennui, fruit de la morne incuriosité,
Prend les proportions de l'immortalité.
—Désormais tu n'es plus, ô matière vivante!
Qu'un granit entouré d'une vague épouvante,
Assoupi dans le fond d'un Saharah brumeux;
Un vieux sphinx ignoré du monde insoucieux,
Oublié sur la carte, et dont l'humeur farouche
Ne chante qu'aux rayons du soleil qui se couche.

SPLEEN

I have more memories than were I a thousand years old.

A large chest of drawers encumbered with balance sheets,
With love letters, lawsuits, and heavy hair rolled
Into receipts, with ballads, and lines of poetry,
Hides fewer secrets than my sorrowful brain.
It's a pyramid, a huge burial vault, that contains
More dead than in the potter's field are strewn.
—I am a cemetery abhored by the moon,
Where like remorse long worms crawl along that ceaselessly
Pursue the dead I love most dearly.
I am an old boudoir full of faded roses,
Where a jumble of outmoded styles reposes,
Where the plaintive pastels and the pale Bouchers, alone,
Inhale the odor of a vial left open.

Nothing equals in length the limping days, when beneath
The heavy flakes of the snowy years, ennui,
Fruit of mournful incuriosity,
Takes on the proportions of immortality.
—Henceforth, you are no more, ô living matter!
Than a granite surrounded by a vague terror,
Dozing in the depths of a hazy Sahara;
An old sphinx unknown to the indifferent world, forgotten
On the map, and whose sullen
Humor sings only to the rays of the setting sun.

SPLEEN

Je suis comme le roi d'un pays pluvieux,
Riche, mais impuissant, jeune et pourtant très vieux,
Qui, de ses précepteurs méprisant les courbettes,
S'ennuie avec ses chiens comme avec d'autres bêtes.
Rien ne peut l'égayer, ni gibier, ni faucon,
Ni son peuple mourant en face du balcon.
Du bouffon favori la grotesque ballade
Ne distrait plus le front de ce cruel malade;
Son lit fleurdelisé se transforme en tombeau,
Et les dames d'atour, pour qui tout prince est beau,
Ne savent plus trouver d'impudique toilette
Pour tirer un souris de ce jeune squelette.
Le savant qui lui fait de l'or n'a jamais pu
De son être extirper l'élément corrompu,
Et dans ces bains de sang qui des Romains nous viennent,
Et dont sur leurs vieux jours les puissants se souviennent,
Il n'a su réchauffer ce cadavre hébété
Où coule au lieu de sang l'eau verte du Léthé.

SPLEEN

I am like the king of a rainy country,
Rich, but impotent, young and yet very
Old, who, scorning the bowing and scraping of his teachers,
Is as bored with his dogs as with other dumb creatures.
Nothing can cheer him, neither hunting nor falconry,
Nor his subjects expiring before his balcony.
The ludicrous ballad of his favorite clown
No longer amuses this cruel invalid's brow;
His bed decked with fleurs-de-lis turns into a tomb,
And ladies-in-waiting, for whom every prince is handsome,
No longer know how to find a costume so wanton
As to draw a smile from this young skeleton.
The scholar who makes gold for him could never
Uproot the corrupt component from his nature,
And in those bloodbaths that come to us from the Romans,
And which powerful men remember when they grow old,
He did not know how to warm up that dazed cadaver
Where instead of blood flows Lethe's green water.

SPLEEN

Quand le ciel bas et lourd pèse comme un couvercle
Sur l'esprit gémissant en proie aux longs ennuis,
Et que de l'horizon embrassant tout le cercle
Il nous verse un jour noir plus triste que les nuits;

Quand la terre est changée en un cachot humide,
Où l'Espérance, comme une chauve-souris,
S'en va battant les murs de son aile timide
Et se cognant la tête à des plafonds pourris;

Quand la pluie étalant ses immenses traînées
D'une vaste prison imite les barreaux,
Et qu'un peuple muet d'infâmes araignées
Vient tendre ses filets au fond de nos cerveaux,

Des cloches tout à coup sautent avec furie
Et lancent vers le ciel un affreux hurlement,
Ainsi que des esprits errants et sans patrie
Qui se mettent à geindre opiniâtrement.

—Et de longs corbillards, sans tambours ni musique,
Défilent lentement dans mon âme; l'Espoir,
Vaincu, pleure, et l'Angoisse atroce, despotique,
Sur mon crâne incliné plante son drapeau noir.

SPLEEN

When the low, heavy sky weighs like a lid on the sighing
Spirit a prey to long ennuis,
And when embracing the whole circle of the horizon
It pours us a black day more sorrowful than nights;

When the earth is changed into a humid dungeon,
Where Hope, like a bat, goes plunging
Against the walls with its timorous wings
And hitting its head against the rotted ceilings;

When the rain spreading out its boundless trains
Of a vast prison imitates the bars,
And when a mute multitude of infamous spiders
Comes to stretch its nets in the depths of our brains,

Bells suddenly leap furiously
And hurl a frightful howling towards the sky,
Like spirits wandering without a country
Who begin to moan persistently.

—And long hearses, without drums or music, march slowly
Past in my soul; Hope, vanquished, weeps, and
Anguish, atrocious and despotic, plants
Its black flag on my skull bowed low.

L'HÉAUTONTIMOROUMÉNOS

À J. G. F.

Je te frapperai sans colère
Et sans haine, comme un boucher,
Comme Moïse le rocher!
Et je ferai de ta paupière,

Pour abreuver mon Saharah,
Jaillir les eaux de la souffrance.
Mon désir gonflé d'espérance
Sur tes pleurs salés nagera

Comme un vaisseau qui prend le large,
Et dans mon cœur qu'ils soûleront
Tes chers sanglots retentiront
Comme un tambour qui bat la charge!

Ne suis-je pas un faux accord
Dans la divine symphonie,
Grâce à la vorace Ironie
Qui me secoue et qui me mord?

Elle est dans ma voix, la criarde!
C'est tout mon sang, ce poison noir!
Je suis le sinistre miroir
Où la mégère se regarde!

Je suis la plaie et le couteau!
Je suis le soufflet et la joue!
Je suis les membres et la roue,
Et la victime et le bourreau!

Je suis de mon cœur le vampire,
—Un de ces grands abandonnés
Au rire éternel condamnés,
Et qui ne peuvent plus sourire!

THE SELF-TORTURER

To J.G.F.

I shall strike you without
Ill will, without anger also,
Like a butcher, the way that Moses smote
The rock!* And out

Of your eyelids I shall make
The waters of pain gush forth to slake
My Sahara. My desire inflated with hope
Upon your briny tears will float

Like a ship that's putting out to sea,
And in my heart which they'll intoxicate
Your belovèd sobbings will reverberate
Like the signal to charge that a drum is beating!

Am I not a dissonant chord
In the heavenly symphony,
Thanks to the voracious Irony
That shakes me up and gnaws at me?

She's in my voice, the termagant!
All my blood is this black toxicant!
I am the sinister mirror, the place
In which the shrew looks at her face!

I am the wound and the knife stabbing through!
I am the cheek and the slap that it drew!
I am the rack and the limbs bound thereto,
Both the victim and the torturer, too!

I am the vampire of my own heart,
—One of those great forsaken men
To everlasting laughter condemned,
And who are unable to smile again!

* "And the Lord said unto Moses . . . Behold, I will stand before thee there upon the rock in
Horeb; and thou shalt smite the rock, and there shall come water out of it, that the people may
drink. And Moses did so in the sight of the elders of Israel." (Exodus 17:5–6)

L'HORLOGE

Horloge! dieu sinistre, effrayant, impassible,
Dont le doigt nous menace et nous dit: *"Souviens-toi!*
Les vibrantes Douleurs dans ton coeur plein d'effroi
Se planteront bientôt comme dans une cible;

Le Plaisir vaporeux fuira vers l'horizon
Ainsi qu'une sylphide au fond de la coulisse;
Chaque instant te dévore un morceau du délice
A chaque homme accordé pour toute sa saison.

Trois mille six cents fois par heure, la Seconde
Chuchote: *Souviens-toi!*—Rapide, avec sa voix
D'insecte, Maintenant dit: Je suis Autrefois,
Et j'ai pompé ta vie avec ma trompe immonde!

Remember! *Souviens-toi*! prodigue! *Esto memor*!
(Mon gosier de métal parle toutes les langues.)
Les minutes, mortel folâtre, sont des gangues
Qu'il ne faut pas lâcher sans en extraire l'or!

Souviens-toi que le Temps est un joueur avide
Qui gagne sans tricher, à tout coup! c'est la loi.
Le jour décroît; la nuit augmente; *souviens-toi*!
Le gouffre a toujours soif; la clepsydre se vide.

Tantôt sonnera l'heure où le divin Hasard,
Où l'auguste Vertu, ton épouse encor vierge,
Où le Repentir même (oh! la dernière auberge!),
Où tout te dira: Meurs, vieux lâche! il est trop tard!''

THE CLOCK

Clock! sinister, frightful, impassive god, whose finger
Shakes at us and says to us: *"Remember!*
Vibrant Pains in your fear-filled heart
Will soon plant themselves as in a target;

Vaporous Pleasure towards the horizon will flee
Like a sylphid into the theater's wing; voraciously
Each instant eats from you a morsel of the delight given
To each man for the duration of his season.

Three thousand six hundred times
An hour, the Second whispers: *Remember!*—Fast,
With her insect's voice, Now says: I am the Past,
And with my foul proboscis I've sucked up your life!

Souviens-toi! Remember! prodigal, *Esto
Memor!* (My metal throat speaks all languages.)
The minutes, frolicsome mortal, are gangues
You must not leave without extracting their gold!

Remember that Time is a greedy gambler who wins
Without cheating, at each turn! that's the rule. Day is waning;
Night is rising; *remember!* the abyss
Is always thirsty; the water clock is draining.

Soon the hour will strike when Chance divine,
When august Virtue, your still virgin wife,
When even Repentance (oh! the last inn!) will say
To you: Die, old coward! It is too late!"

LE CYGNE

À Victor Hugo

I

Andromaque, je pense à vous! Ce petit fleuve,
Pauvre et triste miroir où jadis resplendit
L'immense majesté de vos douleurs de veuve,
Ce Simoïs menteur qui par vos pleurs grandit,

A fécondé soudain ma mémoire fertile,
Comme je traversais le nouveau Carrousel.
Le vieux Paris n'est plus (la forme d'une ville
Change plus vite, hélas! que le coeur d'un mortel);

Je ne vois qu'en esprit tout ce camp de baraques,
Ces tas de chapiteaux ébauchés et de fûts,
Les herbes, les gros blocs verdis par l'eau des flaques,
Et, brillant aux carreaux, le bric-à-brac confus.

Là s'étalait jadis une ménagerie;
Là je vis, un matin, à l'heure où sous les cieux
Froids et clairs le Travail s'éveille, où la voirie
Pousse un sombre ouragan dans l'air silencieux,

Un cygne qui s'était évadé de sa cage,
Et, de ses pieds palmés frottant le pavé sec,
Sur le sol raboteux traînait son blanc plumage.
Près d'un ruisseau sans eau la bête ouvrant le bec

Baignait nerveusement ses ailes dans la poudre,
Et disait, le coeur plein de son beau lac natal:
"Eau, quand donc pleuvras-tu? quand tonneras-tu, foudre?"
Je vois ce malheureux, mythe étrange et fatal,

Vers le ciel quelquefois, comme l'homme d'Ovide,
Vers le ciel ironique et cruellement bleu,
Sur son cou convulsif tendant sa tête avide,
Comme s'il adressait des reproches à Dieu!

THE SWAN

To Victor Hugo

I

Andromache, I'm thinking of you. That little river,
Poor and sorrowful mirror where formerly glittered
The immense majesty of your woes of a widow,
That deceitful Simois[1] that by your tears grew bigger,

Has suddenly fecundated my fertile memory,
As I was crossing the new Carrousel.[2]
The old Paris is no more (the form of a city
Changes faster, alas! than the heart of a mortal);

I only see in my mind all this camp of huts,
These heaps of rough-hewn capitals and shafts,
The grasses, the large building blocks grown green from the puddles'
Water, and, sparkling at the windows, the confused bric-a-brac.

Of old a menagerie stretched out there;
There I saw, one morning, at the hour when Work wakes up
Beneath the cold, clear skies, when the roadways thrust
A somber hurricane into the silent air,

A swan that had escaped from its cage,
And, rubbing the dry pavement with its webbed feet,
Was dragging on the rough ground its white plumage.
Near a gutter without water the beast opening its beak

Was nervously bathing its wings in the dust,
And saying, its heart full of its beautiful natal
Lake: "Water, when will you rain? when will you thunder,
Lightning?" I see this wretched creature, myth strange and fatal,

Towards the sky sometimes, like the man of Ovid,[3]
Towards the ironic and cruelly blue sky, on its
Convulsive neck stretching its avid
Head, as if addressing reproaches to God!

[1] After the Trojan War, Hector's widow, Andromache, became the captive of Pyrrhus in Epirus, where she had an artificial river made in order to remind her of the Simois River in Troy. See the *Aeneid*, Book III, line 302, where Andromache is described at the waters of a false Simois (*"falsi Simoentis ad undam"*).
[2] Around Place du Carrousel in Paris, old houses were being demolished and an esplanade was being constructed between the Louvre and the Tuileries.
[3] In Ovid's *Metamorphoses*, man is given a lofty face so that he may look at the sky and the stars (Book I, lines 84–85).

II

Paris change! mais rien dans ma mélancolie
N'a bougé! palais neufs, échafaudages, blocs,
Vieux faubourgs, tout pour moi devient allégorie,
Et mes chers souvenirs sont plus lourds que des rocs.

Aussi devant ce Louvre une image m'opprime:
Je pense à mon grand cygne, avec ses gestes fous,
Comme les exilés, ridicule et sublime,
Et rongé d'un désir sans trêve! et puis à vous,

Andromaque, des bras d'un grand époux tombée,
Vil bétail, sous la main du superbe Pyrrhus,
Auprès d'un tombeau vide en extase courbée;
Veuve d'Hector, hélas! et femme d'Hélénus!

Je pense à la négresse, amaigrie et phthisique,
Piétinant dans la boue, et cherchant, l'oeil hagard,
Les cocotiers absents de la superbe Afrique
Derrière la muraille immense du brouillard;

A quiconque a perdu ce qui ne se retrouve
Jamais, jamais! à ceux qui s'abreuvent de pleurs
Et tettent la Douleur comme une bonne louve!
Aux maigres orphelins séchant comme des fleurs!

Ainsi dans la forêt où mon esprit s'exile
Un vieux Souvenir sonne à plein souffle du cor!
Je pense aux matelots oubliés dans une île,
Aux captifs, aux vaincus! . . . à bien d'autres encor!

II

Paris is changing! but nothing in my melancholy
Has budged! new palaces, scaffoldings, building blocks,
Old suburbs, everything for me becomes allegory,
And my dear memories are heavier than rocks.

And so in front of this Louvre an image oppresses me:
I think of my great swan, with its crazy
Gestures, like exiled people, ridiculous and sublime, and consumed
By a desire unceasingly! and then of you,

Andromache, fallen from the arms of a mighty
Husband, vile cattle, under the hand of the haughty Pyrrhus,
Near an empty tomb you were bent in ecstasy;
Widow of Hector, alas! and wife of Helenus![4]

I think of the Negress, emaciated and consumptive, slogging
Her feet in the mud, and seeking, her eye haggard,
The absent coconut palms of superb Africa
Behind the immense wall of the fog;

Of whoever has lost what is never, never found
Again! of those who with tears quench their thirst
And, as from a good she wolf, from the breast of Suffering, nurse!
Of emaciated orphans drying up like flowers!

Thus in the forest where my spirit exiles
Itself an old Memory sounds the hunting horn with all
Its breath! I think of sailors forgotten on an island,
Of captives, of conquered people! . . . of many others also!

[4] Helenus, Priam's son, was, like Andromache, a slave in Epirus.

LES SEPT VIEILLARDS

À Victor Hugo

Fourmillante cité, cité pleine de rêves,
Où le spectre en plein jour raccroche le passant!
Les mystères partout coulent comme des sèves
Dans les canaux étroits du colosse puissant.

Un matin, cependant que dans la triste rue
Les maisons, dont la brume allongeait la hauteur,
Simulaient les deux quais d'une rivière accrue,
Et que, décor semblable à l'âme de l'acteur,

Un brouillard sale et jaune inondait tout l'espace,
Je suivais, roidissant mes nerfs comme un héros
Et discutant avec mon âme déjà lasse,
Le faubourg secoué par les lourds tombereaux.

Tout à coup, un vieillard dont les guenilles jaunes
Imitaient la couleur de ce ciel pluvieux,
Et dont l'aspect aurait fait pleuvoir les aumônes,
Sans la méchanceté qui luisait dans ses yeux,

M'apparut. On eût dit sa prunelle trempée
Dans le fiel; son regard aiguisait les frimas,
Et sa barbe à longs poils, roide comme une épée,
Se projetait, pareille à celle de Judas.

Il n'était pas voûté, mais cassé, son échine
Faisant avec sa jambe un parfait angle droit,
Si bien que son bâton, parachevant sa mine,
Lui donnait la tournure et le pas maladroit

D'un quadrupède infirme ou d'un juif à trois pattes.
Dans la neige and la boue il allait s'empêtrant,
Comme s'il écrasait des morts sous ses savates,
Hostile à l'univers plutôt qu'indifférent.

Son pareil le suivait: barbe, oeil, dos, bâton, loques,
Nul trait ne distinguait, du même enfer venu,
Ce jumeau centenaire, et ces spectres baroques
Marchaient du même pas vers un but inconnu.

A quel complot infâme étais-je donc en butte,
Ou quel méchant hasard ainsi m'humiliait?

THE SEVEN OLD MEN

To Victor Hugo

Swarming city, city full of reveries,
Where the specter in broad daylight accosts
The passer-by! Everywhere like saps flow mysteries
In the narrow channels of the mighty colossus.

One morning, when the houses, whose height was elongated
By the haze on the sorrowful street, simulated
Both embankments of a swollen
River, and when, a scene like the actor's soul,

A dirty yellow fog flooded all of space,
I observed, while stiffening my nerves like a hero
And arguing with my already tired soul,
The suburbs that the heavy tumbrils jolted.

Suddenly, an old man whose yellow tattered clothes
Imitated the color of those rainy skies,
And whose appearance would have made alms flow,
Were it not for the wickedness that gleamed in his eyes,

Appeared to me. One would have thought his eyeball
Drenched in bile; his gaze the hoar frosts whet,
And his shaggy beard, as rigid as a rapier,
Stood out, like the beard of Judas Iscariot.

He wasn't bent, but broken, his backbone making
A perfect right angle with his leg, so well that his cane,
Completing his appearance, gave
Him the figure and the clumsy gait

Of a crippled quadruped or a three-legged Jew.
Entangling himself in the snow and the fog he went,
As if he crushed the dead beneath his worn-out shoes,
Hostile to the world, rather than indifferent.

His equal followed him: beard, eye, tattered clothes,
Back, cane, no trait distinguished this hundred-year-old
Twin sent from the same hell, and these baroque specters
Walked with the same gait towards an unknown goal.

Of what infamous plot was I the butt, pray tell?
Or what wicked chance humiliated me like this?

Car je comptai sept fois, de minute en minute,
Ce sinistre vieillard qui se multipliait!

Que celui-là qui rit de mon inquiétude,
Et qui n'est pas saisi d'un frisson fraternel,
Songe bien que malgré tant de décrépitude
Ces sept monstres hideux avaient l'air éternel!

Aurais-je, sans mourir, contemplé le huitième,
Sosie inexorable, ironique et fatal,
Dégoûtant Phénix, fils et père de lui-même?
—Mais je tournai le dos au cortège infernal.

Exaspéré comme un ivrogne qui voit double,
Je rentrai, je fermai ma porte, épouvanté,
Malade et morfondu, l'esprit fiévreux et trouble,
Blessé par le mystère et par l'absurdité!

Vainement ma raison voulait prendre la barre;
La tempête en jouant déroutait ses efforts,
Et mon âme dansait, dansait, vieille gabarre
Sans mâts, sur une mer monstrueuse et sans bords!

For I counted seven times, from minute to minute,
That sinister old man who replicated himself!

Let him who laughs at my disquietude,
And who is not seized by a fraternal
Shudder, just think that despite so much decrepitude
These seven hideous monsters seemed eternal!

Would I, without dying, have contemplated the eighth,
Ironic double, fatal, inexorable,
Loathsome Phoenix, son and father of himself?
—But I turned my back on this cortege from hell.

Exasperated like a drunkard seeing double, I
Went home and shut my door; I was terror-struck, shivery
And sick, my mind was feverish and muddled, wounded by
The mystery and by the absurdity!

In vain my reason wished to take the helm;
Its efforts were diverted by the tempest's spree,
And my soul danced, and danced, old barge
Without masts, upon a monstrous, shoreless sea!

RÊVE PARISIEN

À Constantin Guys

I

De ce terrible paysage,
Tel que jamais mortel n'en vit,
Ce matin encore l'image,
Vague et lointaine, me ravit.

Le sommeil est plein de miracles!
Par un caprice singulier
J'avais banni de ces spectacles
Le végétal irrégulier,

Et, peintre fier de mon génie,
Je savourais dans mon tableau
L'enivrante monotonie
Du métal, du marbre et de l'eau.

Babel d'escaliers et d'arcades,
C'était un palais infini,
Plein de bassins et de cascades
Tombant dans l'or mat ou bruni;

Et des cataractes pesantes,
Comme des rideaux de cristal,
Se suspendaient, éblouissantes,
A des murailles de métal.

Non d'arbres, mais de colonnades
Les étangs dormants s'entouraient,
Où de gigantesques naïades,
Comme des femmes, se miraient.

Des nappes d'eau s'épanchaient, bleues,
Entre des quais roses et verts,
Pendant des millions de lieues,
Vers les confins de l'univers;

C'étaient des pierres inouïes
Et des flots magiques; c'étaient
D'immenses glaces éblouies
Par tout ce qu'elles reflétaient!

Insouciants et taciturnes,
Des Ganges, dans le firmament,

PARISIAN DREAM

To Constantin Guys

I

Of this terrible landscape, such
As no mortal ever did see,
This morning still the image,
Far off and vague, seized me.

Sleep is full of miracles!
By a caprice quite singular
I'd expelled from these spectacles
All plant-life, irregular,

And, a painter proud of my genius,
In my picture I relished
The intoxicating sameness
Of water, marble and metal.

A Babel of stairs and arcades,
'Twas a palace of measure untold,
Full of ponds and of cascades
Tumbling into dull or bright gold;

And heavy waterfalls,
Like curtains cut from crystal,
Were suspended there, resplendent,
Upon ramparts made of metal.

The sleeping ponds were surrounded
By colonnades, not trees,
And gigantic naiads, like women,
Admired themselves in these.

Sheets of water, blue, were dispersed
Between embankments pink and green,
For millions and millions of leagues,
Towards the ends of the universe;

There were magical waves and stones
Of wonder unsuspected;
There were boundless ice forms dazzled
By all the things they reflected!

Unconcerned and taciturn,
Ganges Rivers, in the heavens,

Versaient le trésor de leurs urnes
Dans des gouffres de diamant.

Architecte de mes féeries,
Je faisais, à ma volonté,
Sous un tunnel de pierreries
Passer un océan dompté;

Et tout, même la couleur noire,
Semblait fourbi, clair, irisé;
Le liquide enchâssait sa gloire
Dans le rayon cristallisé.

Nul astre d'ailleurs, nuls vestiges
De soleil, même au bas du ciel,
Pour illuminer ces prodiges,
Qui brillaient d'un feu personnel!

Et sur ces mouvantes merveilles
Planait (terrible nouveauté!
Tout pour l'oeil, rien pour les oreilles!)
Un silence d'éternité.

II

En rouvrant mes yeux pleins de flamme
J'ai vu l'horreur de mon taudis,
Et senti, rentrant dans mon âme,
La pointe des soucis maudits;

La pendule aux accents funèbres
Sonnait brutalement midi,
Et le ciel versait des ténèbres
Sur le triste monde engourdi.

Poured the treasure from many an urn
Into abysses of diamonds.

Architect of my fairy scenes,
I made, at my pleasure, beneath
A tunnel of jewels flow
A subjugated ocean;

And all, the color black, even,
Seemed rainbow-like, polished, bright;
The liquid enshrined its glory
In the crystallized beam of light.

No star besides, no signs
Of sun, even in the depths of the sky,
To illuminate these wonders
That shone with a personal fire!

And over these moving marvels
Hovered (terrible novelty!
All sight, no sound!) a silence
Of eternity.

II

I reopened my flame-filled eyes
And saw the horror of my hovel,
And felt, rejoining my soul,
The sting of accursèd troubles;

The clock with funereal tones
Tolled noon brutally, and there swirled
Down darkness from heaven upon
The sorrowful, torpid world.

LE VIN DES AMANTS

Aujourd'hui l'espace est splendide!
Sans mors, sans éperons, sans bride,
Partons à cheval sur le vin
Pour un ciel féerique et divin!

Comme deux anges que torture
Une implacable calenture,
Dans le bleu cristal du matin
Suivons le mirage lointain!

Mollement balancés sur l'aile
Du tourbillon intelligent,
Dans un délire parallèle,

Ma soeur, côte à côte nageant,
Nous fuirons sans repos ni trêves
Vers le paradis de mes rêves!

LOVERS' WINE

Space today is exquisite!
Without spurs, or bridle, or a bit,
Let's go off galloping on wine
For a sky fairylike and divine!

Like two angels in the throes of torture
Of an implacable calenture,
Let's follow into the crystal blue
Of morning the mirage in distant view!

Softly balanced in equilibrium
Upon the intelligent whirlwind, in
A parallel delirium,

My sister as side by side we swim,
We'll flee without rest unceasingly
Towards the paradise of my reveries!

FEMMES DAMNÉES

Comme un bétail pensif sur le sable couchées,
Elles tournent leurs yeux vers l'horizon des mers,
Et leurs pieds se cherchant et leurs mains rapprochées
Ont de douces langueurs et des frissons amers.

Les unes, coeurs épris des longues confidences,
Dans le fond des bosquets où jasent les ruisseaux,
Vont épelant l'amour des craintives enfances
Et creusent le bois vert des jeunes arbrisseaux;

D'autres, comme des soeurs, marchent lentes et graves
A travers les rochers pleins d'apparitions,
Où saint Antoine a vu surgir comme des laves
Les seins nus et pourprés de ses tentations;

Il en est, aux lueurs des résines croulantes,
Qui dans le creux muet des vieux antres païens
T'appellent au secours de leurs fièvres hurlantes,
O Bacchus, endormeur des remords anciens!

Et d'autres, dont la gorge aime les scapulaires,
Qui, recélant un fouet sous leurs longs vêtements,
Mêlent, dans le bois sombre et les nuits solitaires,
L'écume du plaisir aux larmes des tourments.

O vierges, ô démons, ô monstres, ô martyres,
De la réalité grands esprits contempteurs,
Chercheuses d'infini, dévotes et satyres,
Tantôt pleines de cris, tantôt pleines de pleurs,

Vous que dans votre enfer mon âme a poursuivies,
Pauvres soeurs, je vous aime autant que je vous plains,
Pour vos mornes douleurs, vos soifs inassouvies,
Et les urnes d'amour dont vos grands coeurs sont pleins!

CONDEMNED WOMEN

Like pensive cattle lying on the sands,
They turn their eyes towards the seas' horizon, and their feet
Searching for each other's feet and their joined hands
Know bitter thrills and languors sweet.

Some, their hearts in love with lengthy confidences,
In the thickets' depths where brooks are babbling,
Keep spelling out the loves of their timorous childhoods
And dig into the green wood of the young saplings;

Others, slow and solemn, walk like nuns
Across the rocks filled with apparitions, where
Saint Anthony saw surging up like lavas the bare
And crimson breasts of his temptations;

There are those who, in the glints of crumbling resins,
Within the silent pit of old pagan caverns
Appeal to you for relief from their howling fevers,
O Bacchus, who puts our ancient remorse to sleep!

And others, whose bosoms love the scapulars,
Who, concealing a birch rod under their long garments,
Mix, in the somber woods and the lonely nights,
The sweat of pleasure with the tears of torments.

O virgins, ô demons, ô monsters, ô martyrs, great spirits
Who despise reality,
Seekers after infinity,
Devout and satyrs, now full of cries, now full of tears,

You whom my soul has pursued into
Your hell, poor sisters, I love you as much as I pity you,
For your unquenched thirsts, your mournful
Woes, and the urns of love with which your great hearts are full!

LE VOYAGE

À Maxime Du Camp

I

Pour l'enfant, amoureux de cartes et d'estampes,
L'univers est égal à son vaste appétit.
Ah! que le monde est grand à la clarté des lampes!
Aux yeux du souvenir que le monde est petit!

Un matin nous partons, le cerveau plein de flamme,
Le coeur gros de rancune et de désirs amers,
Et nous allons, suivant le rhythme de la lame,
Berçant notre infini sur le fini des mers:

Les uns, joyeux de fuir une patrie infâme;
D'autres, l'horreur de leurs berceaux, et quelques-uns,
Astrologues noyés dans les yeux d'une femme,
La Circé tyrannique aux dangereux parfums.

Pour n'être pas changés en bêtes, ils s'enivrent
D'espace et de lumière et de cieux embrasés;
La glace qui les mord, les soleils qui les cuivrent,
Effacent lentement la marque des baisers.

Mais les vrais voyageurs sont ceux-là seuls qui partent
Pour partir; coeurs légers, semblables aux ballons,
De leur fatalité jamais ils ne s'écartent,
Et, sans savoir pourquoi, disent toujours: Allons!

Ceux-là dont les désirs ont la forme des nues,
Et qui rêvent, ainsi qu'un conscrit le canon,
De vastes voluptés, changeantes, inconnues,
Et dont l'esprit humain n'a jamais su le nom!

II

Nous imitons, horreur! la toupie et la boule
Dans leur valse et leurs bonds; même dans nos sommeils
La Curiosité nous tourmente et nous roule,
Comme un Ange cruel qui fouette des soleils.

Singulière fortune où le but se déplace,
Et, n'étant nulle part, peut être n'importe où!
Où l'Homme, dont jamais l'espérance n'est lasse,
Pour trouver le repos court toujours comme un fou!

THE VOYAGE

To Maxime Du Camp

I

For the child, whom maps and prints enthrall,
The universe is equal to his vast appetite.
Ah! how large the world is in the lamps' bright light!
In the eyes of memory how the world is small!

One morning we depart, our brains full of flame,
Our hearts swollen with rancor and bitter desires, and we
Go, following the rhythm of the wave,
Rocking our infinity on the finitude of the seas:

Some, glad to flee an infamous country;
Others, the horror of their cradles, and some,
Astrologers drowned in the eyes of a woman,
With her dangerous scents, the tyrannical Circe.

So as not to be changed into beasts, they become intoxicated
On space and light and fiery skies;
The ice that gnaws them, the suns that bronze them, erase
The mark of kisses by and by.

But the true travelers are those alone
Who leave in order to leave; hearts buoyant, like balloons,
From their fate they never stray, and, without knowing
Why, always say: Let's go!

Those whose longings have the shape of clouds,
And who dream, as a conscript does of the cannon,
Of vast voluptuous pleasures, unknown, changing,
Of which the human mind has never known the name!

II

We imitate, horror! in their waltz and their leaps
The spinning top and the ball; even in our sleeps
Curiosity torments and tosses us,
Like a cruel Angel who whips suns.

Singular fortune where the target goes
From place to place, and being nowhere, can
Be any place! Where, with his hope never weary, Man
Always runs like a madman in order to find repose!

Notre âme est un trois-mâts cherchant son Icarie;
Une voix retentit sur le pont: "Ouvre l'oeil!"
Une voix de la hune, ardente et folle, crie:
"Amour . . . gloire . . . bonheur!" Enfer! c'est un écueil!

Chaque îlot signalé par l'homme de vigie
Est un Eldorado promis par le Destin;
L'Imagination qui dresse son orgie
Ne trouve qu'un récif aux clartés du matin.

O le pauvre amoureux des pays chimériques!
Faut-il le mettre aux fers, le jeter à la mer,
Ce matelot ivrogne, inventeur d'Amériques
Dont le mirage rend le gouffre plus amer?

Tel le vieux vagabond, piétinant dans la boue,
Rêve, le nez en l'air, de brillants paradis;
Son oeil ensorcelé découvre une Capoue
Partout où la chandelle illumine un taudis.

III

Étonnants voyageurs! quelles nobles histoires
Nous lisons dans vos yeux profonds comme les mers!
Montrez-nous les écrins de vos riches mémoires,
Ces bijoux merveilleux, faits d'astres et d'éthers.

Nous voulons voyager sans vapeur et sans voile!
Faites, pour égayer l'ennui de nos prisons,
Passer sur nos esprits, tendus comme une toile,
Vos souvenirs avec leurs cadres d'horizons.

Dites, qu'avez-vous vu?

IV

                    "Nous avons vu des astres
Et des flots; nous avons vu des sables aussi;
Et, malgré bien des chocs et d'imprévus désastres,
Nous nous sommes souvent ennuyés, comme ici.

La gloire du soleil sur la mer violette,
La gloire des cités dans le soleil couchant,

Our soul is a three-masted ship that seeks
Its Icaria; a voice rings on deck: "Open up your eyes!"
Aloft a voice, ardent and crazy, cries
Out: "Love . . . glory . . . happiness!" Hell, it's a reef!

Each islet signalized by the lookout man
Is an Eldorado promised by Destiny;
The Imagination which prepares its orgy
Finds only a reef in the morning's clarities.

O the poor lover of chimerical countries!
Must he be put in fetters, thrown into the sea,
This drunken sailor, inventor of Americas
Whose mirage makes the abyss more bitter?

Just as the old vagabond, stamping in the mud,
Dreams of radiant paradises, his nose in the air;
So his bewitched eye discovers a Capua everywhere
A candle illuminates a hovel.

III

Astonishing travelers! what noble stories
We read in your eyes profound as the seas!
Show us the jewel boxes of your rich memories,
Those marvelous gems, made of stars and of ethers.

We wish to travel without steam or sail! To enliven
The ennui of our prisons, send across,
On our spirits, stretched taut
Like a canvas, your recollections framed by horizons.

Tell us, what have you seen?

IV

                              "We have seen
Stars and waves; we have seen sands furthermore;
And, in spite of many shocks and unforeseen
Disasters, as here, we were often bored.

The glory of the sun on the violet sea,
The glory of cities in the setting sun,

Allumaient dans nos coeurs une ardeur inquiète
De plonger dans un ciel au reflet alléchant.

Les plus riches cités, les plus grands paysages,
Jamais ne contenaient l'attrait mystérieux
De ceux que le hasard fait avec les nuages.
Et toujours le désir nous rendait soucieux!

—La jouissance ajoute au désir de la force.
Désir, vieil arbre à qui le plaisir sert d'engrais,
Cependant que grossit et durcit ton écorce,
Tes branches veulent voir le soleil de plus près!

Grandiras-tu toujours, grand arbre plus vivace
Que le cyprès?—Pourtant nous avons, avec soin,
Cueilli quelques croquis pour votre album vorace,
Frères qui trouvez beau tout ce qui vient de loin!

Nous avons salué des idoles à trompe;
Des trônes constellés de joyaux lumineux;
Des palais ouvragés dont la féerique pompe
Serait pour vos banquiers un rêve ruineux;

Des costumes qui sont pour les yeux une ivresse;
Des femmes dont les dents et les ongles sont teints,
Et des jongleurs savants que le serpent caresse.»

V

Et puis, et puis encore?

VI

"O cerveaux enfantins!

Pour ne pas oublier la chose capitale,
Nous avons vu partout, et sans l'avoir cherché,
Du haut jusques en bas de l'échelle fatale,
Le spectacle ennuyeux de l'immortel péché:

La femme, esclave vile, orgueilleuse et stupide,
Sans rire s'adorant et s'aimant sans dégoût;
L'homme, tyran goulu, paillard, dur et cupide,
Esclave de l'esclave et ruisseau dans l'égout;

Kindled in our hearts a restless ardency
To dive into a sky with an alluring reflection.

The richest cities, the greatest landscapes, never
Contained the attractive mystery
That chance makes with the clouds. And every
Moment desire filled us with anxiety!

—Enjoyment adds strength to desire. Desire, old tree
For which pleasure serves as a fertilizer,
While your bark enlarges and becomes harder,
Your branches want to see the sun more closely!

Will you always grow, great tree longer-lived than the cypress?
—Still we have gathered some sketches, carefully,
For your voracious album, brothers who admire
Whatever comes from distant countries!

We've hailed idols with elephants' trunks; thrones constellated
With luminous jewels; decorated
Palaces whose fairylike pomp would be
For your bankers a ruinous reverie;

Costumes that for eyes are a drunkenness;
Women whose teeth and nails are dyed,
And skillful jugglers whom serpents caress."

V

And then what else did you find?

VI

                              "O childish minds!

Not to forget the most important thing, without having
Looked for it, we saw wherever we've been,
From the top to the bottom of the fatal ladder,
The tedious spectacle of immortal sin:

Woman, base, arrogant and stupid slave, loving
Herself without laughing and adoring herself without disgust;
Man, gluttonous tyrant, greedy, hard and lewd,
Slave of the slave and gutter into the sewer;

Le bourreau qui jouit, le martyr qui sanglote;
La fête qu'assaisonne et parfume le sang;
Le poison du pouvoir énervant le despote,
Et le peuple amoureux du fouet abrutissant;

Plusieurs religions semblables à la nôtre,
Toutes escaladant le ciel; la Sainteté,
Comme en un lit de plume un délicat se vautre,
Dans les clous et le crin cherchant la volupté;

L'Humanité bavarde, ivre de son génie,
Et, folle maintenant comme elle était jadis,
Criant à Dieu, dans sa furibonde agonie:
«O mon semblable, ô mon maître, je te maudis!»

Et les moins sots, hardis amants de la Démence,
Fuyant le grand troupeau parqué par le Destin,
Et se réfugiant dans l'opium immense!
—Tel est du globe entier l'éternel bulletin.»

VII

Amer savoir, celui qu'on tire du voyage!
Le monde, monotone et petit, aujourd'hui,
Hier, demain, toujours, nous fait voir notre image:
Une oasis d'horreur dans un désert d'ennui!

Faut-il partir? rester? Si tu peux rester, reste;
Pars, s'il le faut. L'un court, et l'autre se tapit
Pour tromper l'ennemi vigilant et funeste,
Le Temps! Il est, hélas! des coureurs sans répit,

Comme le Juif errant et comme les apôtres,
A qui rien ne suffit, ni wagon ni vaisseau,
Pour fuir ce rétiaire infâme; il en est d'autres
Qui savent le tuer sans quitter leur berceau.

Lorsque enfin il mettra le pied sur notre échine,
Nous pourrons espérer et crier: En avant!
De même qu'autrefois nous partions pour la Chine,
Les yeux fixés au large et les cheveux au vent,

Nous nous embarquerons sur la mer des Ténèbres
Avec le coeur joyeux d'un jeune passager.

The martyr who sobs, the torturer who enjoys;
The festival seasoned and scented with blood; the poison
Of power enervating the despot, and the masses
In love with the brutalizing lash;

Several religions similar to ours, all scaling
The sky; and like a fastidious person wallowing
In a featherbed, Holiness
In nails and horsehair seeking voluptuousness;

Intoxicated with its genius, prating Humanity,
As crazy now as it was formerly,
Crying out to God, in its furious death agony:
"O my likeness, ô my master, I curse thee!"

And the least foolish, bold lovers of Insanity,
Shunning the large flock penned up by Destiny,
And taking refuge in immeasurable opium!
—Such is of the globe the eternal bulletin."

VII

Bitter knowledge, that one gathers from the voyage!
The world, monotonous and small, today,
Yesterday, tomorrow, always, makes us see
Our image: An oasis of horror in a desert of ennui!

Should one leave? or stay? Stay, if you can stay; leave,
If you must. One man runs, another crouches to deceive
The vigilant and fatal enemy, Time!
There are, alas! some runners who have no reprieve,

Like the wandering Jew and like the apostles, for whom nothing
Suffices, neither coach nor ship, to flee this infamous
Retiarius; there are others who are able
To kill him without leaving their cradles.

When he puts his foot on our spine at last,
We'll be able to hope and to cry out: Forward! As in the past
We set out for China, our eyes fixed on the open sea
And our hair in the wind, so we

Will embark upon the sea of Darkness with the cheerful
Heart of a young passenger. Do you hear

Entendez-vous ces voix, charmantes et funèbres,
Qui chantent: "Par ici! vous qui voulez manger

Le Lotus parfumé! c'est ici qu'on vendange
Les fruits miraculeux dont votre coeur a faim;
Venez vous enivrer de la douceur étrange
De cette après-midi qui n'a jamais de fin!"

A l'accent familier nous devinons le spectre;
Nos Pylades là-bas tendent leurs bras vers nous.
"Pour rafraîchir ton coeur nage vers ton Électre!"
Dit celle dont jadis nous baisions les genoux.

VIII

O Mort, vieux capitaine, il est temps! levons l'ancre!
Ce pays nous ennuie, ô Mort! Appareillons!
Si le ciel et la mer sont noirs comme de l'encre,
Nos coeurs que tu connais sont remplis de rayons!

Verse-nous ton poison pour qu'il nous réconforte!
Nous voulons, tant ce feu nous brûle le cerveau,
Plonger au fond du gouffre, Enfer ou Ciel, qu'importe?
Au fond de l'Inconnu pour trouver du *nouveau!*

Those voices, charming and funereal,
That sing: "This way! you who wish to eat

The Lotus perfumed!
It's here that one vintages the miraculous fruits
For which your heart hungers; come and become intoxicated on
The strange sweetness of this never-ending afternoon!"

At the familiar tone we divine the specter;
Our Pylades over there stretch their arms towards us. "To refresh
Your heart swim towards your Electra!" says she
Whose knees we used to kiss formerly.

VIII

O Death, old captain, it's time! weigh anchor!
This country wearies us, ô Death! Let's get under way!
If the sky and the sea are black as ink, our hearts
Which you know are filled with gleaming rays!

Pour us your poison so that it may comfort us!
We wish, this fire burns our brains so much, to plunge
Into the depths of the abyss, Hell or Heaven, what matter? Into
The depths of the Unknown to find something *new*!

LE LÉTHÉ

Viens sur mon coeur, âme cruelle et sourde,
Tigre adoré, monstre aux airs indolents;
Je veux longtemps plonger mes doigts tremblants
Dans l'épaisseur de ta crinière lourde;

Dans tes jupons remplis de ton parfum
Ensevelir ma tête endolorie,
Et respirer, comme une fleur flétrie,
Le doux relent de mon amour défunt.

Je veux dormir! dormir plutôt que vivre!
Dans un sommeil aussi doux que la mort,
J'étalerai mes baisers sans remord
Sur ton beau corps poli comme le cuivre.

Pour engloutir mes sanglots apaisés
Rien ne me vaut l'abîme de ta couche;
L'oubli puissant habite sur ta bouche,
Et le Léthé coule dans tes baisers.

A mon destin, désormais mon délice,
J'obéirai comme un prédestiné;
Martyr docile, innocent condamné,
Dont la ferveur attise le supplice,

Je sucerai, pour noyer ma rancoeur,
Le népenthès et la bonne ciguë
Aux bouts charmants de cette gorge aiguë,
Qui n'a jamais emprisonné de coeur.

LETHE

Come on my heart, soul deaf and inhumane,
Adored tiger, monster with indolent airs; I wish to
Plunge my trembling fingers a long while into
The thickness of your heavy mane;

In your petticoats filled with your scent to shroud
My aching head,
And to inhale, like a withered flower,
The sweet mustiness of my love now dead.

I wish to sleep! to sleep rather than to live! In a sleep
As sweet as death,
On your beautiful body burnished like copper I'll spread
My kisses remorselessly.

To engulf my quieted sobs nothing equals for me
Your bed's abyss;
Potent oblivion inhabits your mouth and Lethe
Flows in your kisses.

My destiny, henceforth my delight, I'll obey
Like one predestined;
A docile martyr, an innocent condemned,
Whose fervor fans his torture's flames,

I'll suck in, to drown my rancor, nepenthes
And good hemlock,
At the charming tips of that sharp
Bosom that has never imprisoned a heart.

LES BIJOUX

La très-chère était nue, et, connaissant mon coeur,
Elle n'avait gardé que ses bijoux sonores,
Dont le riche attirail lui donnait l'air vainqueur
Qu'ont dans leurs jours heureux les esclaves des Mores.

Quand il jette en dansant son bruit vif et moqueur,
Ce monde rayonnant de métal et de pierre
Me ravit en extase, et j'aime à la fureur
Les choses où le son se mêle à la lumière.

Elle était donc couchée et se laissait aimer,
Et du haut du divan elle souriait d'aise
A mon amour profond et doux comme la mer,
Qui vers elle montait comme vers sa falaise.

Les yeux fixés sur moi, comme un tigre dompté,
D'un air vague et rêveur elle essayait des poses,
Et la candeur unie à la lubricité
Donnait un charme neuf à ses métamorphoses;

Et son bras et sa jambe, et sa cuisse et ses reins,
Polis comme de l'huile, onduleux comme un cygne,
Passaient devant mes yeux clairvoyants et sereins;
Et son ventre et ses seins, ces grappes de ma vigne,

S'avançaient, plus câlins que les Anges du mal,
Pour troubler le repos où mon âme était mise,
Et pour la déranger du rocher de cristal
Où, calme et solitaire, elle s'était assise.

Je croyais voir unis par un nouveau dessin
Les hanches de l'Antiope au buste d'un imberbe,
Tant sa taille faisait ressortir son bassin.
Sur ce teint fauve et brun le fard était superbe!

—Et la lampe s'étant résignée à mourir,
Comme le foyer seul illuminait la chambre,
Chaque fois qu'il poussait un flamboyant soupir,
Il inondait de sang cette peau couleur d'ambre!

THE JEWELS

My dearly beloved was nude, and, knowing my heart,
She had kept on only her sonorous jewelry,
Whose rich adornments gave her the victorious air
Of Moorish slaves on their days that are happy.

When it hurls in dancing its alive and mocking jingle,
This radiant world of metal and stone grips me
With ecstasy, and I love passionately
The things in which sound and light commingle.

So she was lying down and let herself be loved,
And with pleasure she smiled from the divan above
Upon my love as deep and gentle as the sea,
That towards her, as towards its cliff, rose up.

With her eyes fixed on me, like a tiger made tame,
In a vague and dreamy way she tried out poses,
And her candor combined with her lubricity
Gave a novel charm to her metamorphoses;

And her arm and her leg, and her loins and her thighs,
As smooth as oil, as sinuous as a swan,
Moved past before my serene and clearsighted eyes;
And her belly and her breasts, those clusters of my vine,

Advanced, more wheedling than the Angels of evil,
To trouble the resting place where my soul had gone,
And to dislodge it from the crystalline rock whereon
It had seated itself, solitary and calm.

I thought I saw the hips of Antiope*
Joined with a boy's bust in a new design,
Her waist set off her pelvis to such a degree.
On that fawnlike and dusky complexion the rouge was sublime!

—And while the lamp was resigning itself to die,
As the hearth alone illuminated the chamber,
Each time that it uttered a flaming sigh,
It deluged with blood that skin the color of amber!

* Antiope was a nymph loved by Zeus, who approached her in the shape of a satyr when she
was asleep. She gave birth to twins, Amphion and Zethus. There are paintings of Antiope by
Watteau and Ingres.

RECUEILLEMENT

Sois sage, ô ma Douleur, et tiens-toi plus tranquille.
Tu réclamais le Soir; il descend; le voici:
Une atmosphère obscure enveloppe la ville,
Aux uns portant la paix, aux autres le souci.

Pendant que des mortels la multitude vile,
Sous le fouet du Plaisir, ce bourreau sans merci,
Va cueillir des remords dans la fête servile,
Ma Douleur, donne-moi la main; viens par ici,

Loin d'eux. Vois se pencher les défuntes Années,
Sur les balcons du ciel, en robes surannées;
Surgir du fond des eaux le Regret souriant;

Le Soleil moribond s'endormir sous une arche,
Et, comme un long linceul traînant à l'Orient,
Entends, ma chère, entends la douce Nuit qui marche.

MEDITATION

Be good, ô my Grief, and behave more quietly.
You clamored for Evening; it's descending; it's here:
The town is enveloped in an obscure atmosphere,
To some bringing peace, to others anxiety.

While the vile multitude of mortals, under
The whip of Pleasure, that pitiless tormentor,
Will cull remorse in the servile holiday,
My Grief, give me your hand; come this way,

Far from them. See the dead Years in old-fashioned dresses
Bending over the balconies of heaven;
Smiling Regret rising from the waters deep;

The dying Sun falling asleep beneath an arch, and,
Like a long shroud trailing in the East,
Hear, my dear, hear the gentle Night advance.

Rimbaud (by Coussins)

RIMBAUD

SENSATION

Par les soirs bleus d'été, j'irai dans les sentiers,
Picoté par les blés, fouler l'herbe menue:
Rêveur, j'en sentirai la fraîcheur à mes pieds.
Je laisserai le vent baigner ma tête nue.

Je ne parlerai pas, je ne penserai rien:
Mais l'amour infini me montera dans l'âme,
Et j'irai loin, bien loin, comme un bohémien,
Par la Nature,—heureux comme avec une femme.

Mars 1870

FEELING

On blue summer evenings, I'll go on the paths,
Where the corn stalks prickle, to trample the slender grass:
A dreamer, I'll feel its coolness where I tread.
And I'll let the wind bathe my bare head.

I'll not speak, I'll not think anything at all:
But infinite love will rise in my soul,
And I'll go far, quite far, like a bohemian,
Through Nature,—as happy as if with a woman.

March 1870

VÉNUS ANADYOMÈNE

Comme d'un cercueil vert en fer blanc, une tête
De femme à cheveux bruns fortement pommadés
D'une vieille baignoire émerge, lente et bête,
Avec des déficits assez mal ravaudés;

Puis le col gras et gris, les larges omoplates
Qui saillent; le dos court qui rentre et qui ressort;
Puis les rondeurs des reins semblent prendre l'essor;
La graisse sous la peau paraît en feuilles plates;

L'échine est un peu rouge, et le tout sent un goût
Horrible étrangement; on remarque surtout
Des singularités qu'il faut voir à la loupe . . .

Les reins portent deux mots gravés: *Clara Venus*;
—Et tout ce corps remue et tend sa large croupe
Belle hideusement d'un ulcère à l'anus.

VENUS ANADYOMENE

As from a green tin coffin, a woman's head
With its brown hair pomaded exceedingly,
Emerges from an old bathtub stupidly
And slow, with quite poorly mended deficiencies;

Then the fat, gray neck, the broad, projecting shoulder
Blades; the short back which juts out and retreats;
Then the rounded lines of the loins appear to take flight;
The fat beneath the skin seems like flat sheets;

The spine is somewhat red, and all smells strangely
Horrible; one notes especially
Some oddities you should use a lens to see . . .

The loins bear two engraved words: *Clara Venus*;
—And this whole body moves and bends its broad rump hideously
Beautiful with an ulcer on the anus.

LES EFFARÉS

Noirs dans la neige et dans la brume,
Au grand soupirail qui s'allume,
   Leurs culs en rond

À genoux, cinq petits,—misère!—
Regardent le boulanger faire
   Le lourd pain blond . . .

Ils voient le fort bras blanc qui tourne
La pâte grise, et qui l'enfourne
   Dans un trou clair.

Ils écoutent le bon pain cuire.
Le boulanger au gras sourire
   Chante un vieil air.

Ils sont blottis, pas un ne bouge,
Au souffle du soupirail rouge,
   Chaud comme un sein.

Et quand, pendant que minuit sonne,
Façonné, pétillant et jaune,
   On sort le pain,

Quand, sous les poutres enfumées,
Chantent les croûtes parfumées,
   Et les grillons,

Quand ce trou chaud souffle la vie
Ils ont leur âme si ravie
   Sous leurs haillons,

Ils se ressentent si bien vivre,
Les pauvres petits pleins de givre!
   —Qu'ils sont là, tous,

Collant leurs petits museaux roses
Au grillage, chantant des choses,
   Entre les trous,

Mais bien bas,—comme une prière . . .
Repliés vers cette lumière
   Du ciel rouvert,

THE BEWILDERED ONES

Black in the snow and in the haze,
At the large vent that begins to blaze,
   Their backsides rounded,

Kneeling, five children,—misery!—
Watch as the baker makes the heavy
   Light-colored bread . . .

They see the strong white arm that molds
The greyish dough
   And puts it in the oven in a bright hole.

They listen to the good bread bake. Meanwhile
The baker with his broad smile
   Sings a tune that's old.

They are huddled, not even one of them
Is stirring, at the breath of the red vent,
   As warm

As a breast. And when, as midnight tolls,
The bread is brought out, crackling, yellow
   And formed,

When, under the beams that smoke has blackened,
Sing the crusts scented sweetly, and
   The crickets also,

When this warm hole breathes life
The children's souls are so delighted
   Under their tattered clothes,

They feel so wholly alive at this time,
The poor little children full of rime!
   —That there they are now, all

Of them pasting
Their little pink muzzles on the metal grating,
   While singing things between the holes,

But very softly,—like
A prayer . . . Bent downward towards that light
   Of the sky reopened,

—Si fort, qu'ils crèvent leur culotte,
—Et que leur lange blanc tremblote
  Au vent d'hiver . . .

20 Septembre 1870

—So hard, that they split their trousers open,
—And their white swaddling clothes flutter in
  The winter wind . . .

September 20, 1870

LE DORMEUR DU VAL

C'est un trou de verdure où chante une rivière
Accrochant follement aux herbes des haillons
D'argent; où le soleil, de la montagne fière,
Luit: c'est un petit val qui mousse de rayons.

Un soldat jeune, bouche ouverte, tête nue,
Et la nuque baignant dans le frais cresson bleu,
Dort; il est étendu dans l'herbe, sous la nue,
Pâle dans son lit vert où la lumière pleut.

Les pieds dans les glaïeuls, il dort. Souriant comme
Sourirait un enfant malade, il fait un somme:
Nature, berce-le chaudement: il a froid.

Les parfums ne font pas frissonner sa narine;
Il dort dans le soleil, la main sur sa poitrine
Tranquille. Il a deux trous rouges au côté droit.

Octobre 1870

THE SLEEPER OF THE VALLEY

It's a gap of greenness where a singing river
Madly hooks upon the grasses silver
Shreds; where the sun, from the lofty mountain's height,
Shines down: it's a valley that froths with rays of light.

A young soldier, open-mouthed, bare-headed, is sleeping,
With the nape of his neck bathing in the fresh blue cress;
Beneath the clouds, he is stretched out on the grass,
He is pale in his green bed where the light is seeping.

With his feet in the sword grasses, he is sleeping. While
He takes a nap, he smiles as a sick child would smile:
Nature, rock him warmly: he is cold.

Sweet smells do not make his nostrils quiver; still
He lies sleeping in the sun, with his hand on his tranquil
Breast. In his right side he has two red holes.

October 1870

MA BOHÈME

(*Fantaisie*)

Je m'en allais, les poings dans mes poches crevées;
Mon paletot aussi devenait idéal;
J'allais sous le ciel, Muse! et j'étais ton féal;
Oh! là! là! que d'amours splendides j'ai rêvées!

Mon unique culotte avait un large trou.
—Petit-Poucet rêveur, j'égrenais dans ma course
Des rimes. Mon auberge était à la Grande-Ourse.
—Mes étoiles au ciel avaient un doux frou-frou

Et je les écoutais, assis au bord des routes,
Ces bons soirs de septembre où je sentais des gouttes
De rosée à mon front, comme un vin de vigueur;

Où, rimant au milieu des ombres fantastiques,
Comme des lyres, je tirais les élastiques
De mes souliers blessés, un pied près de mon coeur!

MY BOHEMIAN LIFE

(*Fantasy*)

Off I went, my fists in my pockets with split open seams;
My overcoat was also becoming ideal; under the sky
I went, Muse! and your trusty friend was I;
Oh! la! la! how many splendid loves I dreamed!

My unique trousers had a large hole.
—A dreaming Tom Thumb, I told rhymes
On my way. My inn was at the Great Bear's sign.
—My stars had a sweet rustling in the sky

And I listened to them, as I sat by the roads on those fine
September nights, when I
Felt dewdrops on my forehead, like a vigorous wine;

When, amid fantastic shadows I versified,
And plucked, like lyres, the laces of my
Wounded shoes, one foot at my heart's side.

LES CORBEAUX

Seigneur, quand froide est la prairie,
Quand dans les hameaux abattus,
Les longs angelus se sont tus . . .
Sur la nature défleurie
Faites s'abattre des grands cieux
Les chers corbeaux délicieux.

Armée étrange aux cris sévères,
Les vents froids attaquent vos nids!
Vous, le long des fleuves jaunis,
Sur les routes aux vieux calvaires,
Sur les fossés et sur les trous
Dispersez-vous, ralliez-vous!

Par milliers, sur les champs de France,
Où dorment des morts d'avant-hier,
Tournoyez, n'est-ce pas, l'hiver,
Pour que chaque passant repense!
Sois donc le crieur du devoir,
Ô notre funèbre oiseau noir!

Mais, saints du ciel, en haut du chêne,
Mât perdu dans le soir charmé,
Laissez les fauvettes de mai
Pour ceux qu'au fond du bois enchaîne,
Dans l'herbe d'où l'on ne peut fuir,
La défaite sans avenir.

THE CROWS

Lord, when the meadowland is chilled,
When in the demolished hamlets' gloom,
The lengthy angelus bells are stilled . . .
Upon nature that has lost its bloom
Make swoop down from the vast skies those
Belovèd and delicious crows.

Strange army with your cries severe,
Your nests are attacked by winds which freeze!
You, along the yellowed rivers here,
Upon the roads of old calvaries,
Upon the ditches and upon
The holes, disperse, and rally, go on!

By the thousands, over French fields, where men
Who died the day before yesterday sleep,
In the winter, won't you, round and round sweep,
So each passer-by may think again!
The crier of duty therefore be,
O our bird black and funerary!

But, saints of the sky, atop the oak tree,
A mast lost in the charmed evening, refrain
From touching the May warblers for those who
In the depths of the woods are enchained,
In the grass from which one cannot flee,
By defeat without prospects for the future.*

* One of the meanings of "avenir" is "prospects." For a fuller discussion of this, see Enid
Rhodes Peschel, "Rimbaud's 'Les Corbeaux': A Hymn of Hopelessness—and of Hope" in
French Review, Vol. LII, No. 3 (Feb. 1979), 418–22.

LES ASSIS

Noirs de loupes, grêlés, les yeux cerclés de bagues
Vertes, leurs doigts boulus crispés à leurs fémurs,
Le sinciput plaqué de hargnosités vagues
Comme les floraisons lépreuses des vieux murs;

Ils ont greffé dans des amours épileptiques
Leur fantasque ossature aux grands squelettes noirs
De leurs chaises; leurs pieds aux barreaux rachitiques
S'entrelacent pour les matins et pour les soirs!

Ces vieillards ont toujours fait tresse avec leurs sièges,
Sentant les soleils vifs percaliser leur peau,
Ou, les yeux à la vitre où se fanent les neiges,
Tremblant du tremblement douloureux du crapaud.

Et les Sièges leur ont des bontés: culottée
De brun, la paille cède aux angles de leurs reins;
L'âme des vieux soleils s'allume emmaillotée
Dans ces tresses d'épis où fermentaient les grains.

Et les Assis, genoux aux dents, verts pianistes,
Les dix doigts sous leur siège aux rumeurs de tambour,
S'écoutent clapoter des barcarolles tristes,
Et leurs caboches vont dans des roulis d'amour.

—Oh! ne les faites pas lever! C'est le naufrage . . .
Ils surgissent, grondant comme des chats giflés,
Ouvrant lentement leurs omoplates, ô rage!
Tout leur pantalon bouffe à leur reins boursouflés.

Et vous les écoutez, cognant leurs têtes chauves
Aux murs sombres, plaquant et plaquant leurs pieds tors,
Et leurs boutons d'habit sont des prunelles fauves
Qui vous accrochent l'oeil du fond des corridors!

Puis ils ont une main invisible qui tue:
Au retour, leur regard filtre ce venin noir
Qui charge l'oeil souffrant de la chienne battue,
Et vous suez pris dans un atroce entonnoir.

Rassis, les poings noyés dans des manchettes sales,
Ils songent à ceux-qui les ont fait lever

THE SEATED ONES

Black with wens, pock-marked, their eyes encircled with green
Rings, their knotty[1] fingers clenched on their femurs,
Their sinciputs caked with vague gallings[2]
Like the leprous efflorescences of old walls;

They have grafted in epileptic loves their fantastic frames
To the large black skeletons of their chairs; their feet
On the rachitic crossbars interlace
For mornings and for evenings!

These old men have always braided themselves into
Their seats, while feeling fiery suns percalize their skins,
Or with their eyes on the windows where snows
Fade away, they tremble with the pained tremor of the toad.

And the Seats are good to them:
Breeched in brown, the straw surrenders to the angles
Of their loins; the souls of old suns kindle
Wrapped up in these braided ears of corn where the grains fermented.

And with their knees to their teeth, the Seated Ones, green
Pianists, whose ten fingers make the din of drums below
Their seats, hear themselves plashing sad barcaroles,
And in rollings of love their pates careen.

—Oh! don't make them get up! That's disaster surely . . .
Like tomcats struck, they rise in snarling outrage,
Spreading out slowly their shoulder blades, ô rage!
At their bloated loins their trousers swell angrily.

And you hear them, bumping their bald heads on the dark walls,
While stamping and stamping their crooked feet on the floors,
And the buttons on their clothes are fulvous eyeballs
That hook your eye from the depths of the corridors!

And then they have an invisible hand that kills:
When they return, their gaze filters that black venom that fills
The beaten bitch's suffering
Eye, and you sweat caught in an atrocious funnel.

Reseated, with their fists in their dirty cuffs immersed,
They think about those who made them rise and, from dawn till evening,

[1] *Boulu*, a neologism, may suggest *boule* (ball) and *boulures* (excrescences that begin to grow on the bottom of plants).
[2] *Hargnosités* is a noun invented by Rimbaud from the adjective *hargneux*, which denotes irritation and bad humor.

187

Et, de l'aurore au soir, des grappes d'amygdales
Sous leurs mentons chétifs s'agitent à crever.

Quand l'austère sommeil a baissé leurs visières,
Ils rêvent sur leur bras de sièges fécondés,
De vrais petits amours de chaises en lisière
Par lesquelles de fiers bureaux seront bordés;

Des fleurs d'encre crachant des pollens en virgule
Les bercent, le long des calices accroupis
Tels qu'au fil des glaïeuls le vol des libellules
—Et leur membre s'agace à des barbes d'épis.

Bunches of tonsils beneath
Their puny chins agitate enough to burst.

When stern sleep has lowered their eye-shades, they dream
Upon their arms of fecundated
Seats, of real little loves of chairs in leading
Strings that around proud desks will be located;

Ink flowers spitting out comma-shaped pollens rock them, along
The calyxes where they've crouched like dragonflies in flight
Through the sword grasses—and their members are excited
By the beards of the ears of corn.

TÊTE DE FAUNE

Dans la feuillée, écrin vert taché d'or,
Dans la feuillée incertaine et fleurie
De fleurs splendides où le baiser dort,
Vif et crevant l'exquise broderie,

Un faune effaré montre ses deux yeux
Et mord les fleurs rouges de ses dents blanches.
Brunie et sanglante ainsi qu'un vin vieux,
Sa lèvre éclate en rires sous les branches.

Et quand il a fui—tel qu'un écureuil—
Son rire tremble encore à chaque feuille,
Et l'on voit épeuré par un bouvreuil
Le Baiser d'or du Bois, qui se receuille.

FAUN'S HEAD

In the bower, green jewel box flecked with gold,
In the wavering bower flowery
With splendid flowers where the kiss is sleeping,
Alive and splitting the exquisite embroidery,

A frightened faun shows his two eyes and
Bites the red blossoms with his white
Teeth. Burnished and blood-colored like an old wine,
His lip bursts out in laughs beneath the branches.

And when he has fled—the way a squirrel flees—
His laugh still trembles on each leaf,
And by a bullfinch frightened one sees
The golden Kiss of the Woods, musing silently.

ORAISON DU SOIR

Je vis assis, tel qu'un ange aux mains d'un barbier,
Empoignant une chope à fortes cannelures,
L'hypogastre et le col cambrés, une Gambier
Aux dents, sous l'air gonflé d'impalpables voilures.

Tels que les excréments chauds d'un vieux colombier,
Mille Rêves en moi font de douces brûlures:
Puis par instants mon coeur triste est comme un aubier
Qu'ensanglante l'or jeune et sombre des coulures.

Puis, quand j'ai ravalé mes rêves avec soin,
Je me tourne, ayant bu trente ou quarante chopes,
Et me recueille, pour lâcher l'âcre besoin:

Doux comme le Seigneur du cèdre et des hysopes,
Je pisse vers les cieux bruns, très haut et très loin,
Avec l'assentiment des grands héliotropes.

EVENING PRAYER

I lived seated, like an angel in a barber's hands,
Grasping a beer mug with grooved details,
In my teeth a pipe with curved hypogastrium and
Neck, beneath the air swelled with impalpable sails.

Like the warm excrements of an old dovecote,
A thousand Dreams burn gently in me: then at moments
My sorrowful heart is like a sapwood blood-
Stained by the young and somber gold of its flowings.

Then, when I've swallowed my dreams again carefully,
I turn around having drunk thirty or forty mugs of beer,
And collect myself, to release the bitter need:

Gentle like the Lord of hyssops and of cedar,
I piss toward the brown skies, to high and distant scopes,
With the assent of the large heliotropes.

LE COEUR VOLÉ

Mon triste coeur bave à la poupe,
Mon coeur couvert de caporal:
Ils y lancent des jets de soupe,
Mon. triste coeur bave à la poupe:
Sous les quolibets de la troupe
Qui pousse un rire général,
Mon triste coeur bave à la poupe,
Mon coeur couvert de caporal!

Ithyphalliques et pioupiesques
Leurs quolibets l'ont dépravé!
Au gouvernail on voit des fresques
Ithyphalliques et pioupiesques.
O flots abracadabrantesques,
Prenez mon coeur, qu'il soit lavé!
Ithyphalliques et pioupiesques
Leurs quolibets l'ont dépravé!

Quand ils auront tari leurs chiques,
Comment agir, ô coeur volé?
Ce seront des hoquets bachiques
Quand ils auront tari leurs chiques:
J'aurai des sursauts stomachiques,
Moi, si mon coeur est ravalé:
Quand ils auront tari leurs chiques
Comment agir, ô coeur volé?

Mai 1871

THE PLUNDERED HEART

My sad heart's slobbering at the poop,
My heart overlaid with caporal:
They're hurling on it streams of soup,
My sad heart's slobbering at the poop:
Under the tauntings of the troop
Bursting out in a laugh that's general,
My sad heart's slobbering at the poop,
My heart overlaid with caporal!

Ithyphallic and barracks-lewd
Their taunting words have made it depraved!
At the helm are frescoes to be viewed
Ithyphallic and barracks-lewd.
O abracadabrical waves here strewed,
Come take my heart, let it be bathed!
Ithyphallic and barracks-lewd
Their taunting words have made it depraved!

When they've dried up the quids they're chewing,
How to act, ô plundered heart?
There will be Bacchic hiccuping
When they've dried up the quids they're chewing:
I'll feel my stomach sputtering,
I will, if they belittle my heart:
When they've dried up the quids they're chewing
How to act, ô plundered heart?

May 1871

VOYELLES

A noir, E blanc, I rouge, U vert, O bleu: voyelles,
Je dirai quelque jour vos naissances latentes:
A, noir corset velu des mouches éclatantes
Qui bombinent autour des puanteurs cruelles,

Golfes d'ombre; E, candeurs des vapeurs et des tentes,
Lances des glaciers fiers, rois blancs, frissons d'ombelles;
I, pourpres, sang craché, rire des lèvres belles
Dans la colère ou les ivresses pénitentes;

U, cycles, vibrements divins des mers virides,
Paix des pâtis semés d'animaux, paix des rides
Que l'alchimie imprime aux grands fronts studieux;

O, suprême Clairon plein des strideurs étranges,
Silences traversés des Mondes et des Anges:
—O l'Oméga, rayon violet de Ses Yeux!

"L'ÉTOILE A PLEURÉ ROSE . . ."

L'étoile a pleuré rose au coeur de tes oreilles,
L'infini roulé blanc de ta nuque à tes reins;
La mer a perlé rousse à tes mammes vermeilles
Et l'Homme saigné noir à ton flanc souverain.

VOWELS

A black, E white, I red, U green, O blue: vowels,
Some day your latent births I shall relate:
A, black hairy corset of dazzling flies that bombinate
Around cruel and foul

Smells, gulfs of shadow; E, whitenesses of tents and vapors,
White kings, shivers of umbels, lances of proud glaciers;
I, purples, spat blood, laughter of beautiful lips
In anger or penitent intoxications;

U, cycles, divine vibrations of viridian seas,
Peace of pastures sown with animals, peace
Of wrinkles that alchemy prints on large studious foreheads;

O, supreme Clarion full of strange strident cries,
Silences traversed of Worlds and of Angels:
—O the Omega, violet ray of His Eyes!

"THE STAR WEPT PINK . . ."

The star wept pink in the core of your ears,
The infinite rolled white from your nape to your back;
The sea formed russet beads at your vermilion mammae
And Man at your sovereign side bled black.

LES CHERCHEUSES DE POUX

Quand le front de l'enfant, plein de rouges tourmentes,
Implore l'essaim blanc des rêves indistincts,
Il vient près de son lit deux grandes soeurs charmantes
Avec de frêles doigts aux ongles argentins.

Elles assoient l'enfant devant une croisée
Grande ouverte où l'air bleu baigne un fouillis de fleurs,
Et dans ses lourds cheveux où tombe la rosée
Promènent leurs doigts fins, terribles et charmeurs.

Il écoute chanter leurs haleines craintives
Qui fleurent de longs miels végétaux et rosés,
Et qu'interrompt parfois un sifflement, salives
Reprises sur la lèvre ou désirs de baisers.

Il entend leurs cils noirs battant sous les silences
Parfumés; et leurs doigts électriques et doux
Font crépiter parmi ses grises indolences
Sous leurs ongles royaux la mort des petits poux.

Voilà que monte en lui le vin de la Paresse,
Soupir d'harmonica qui pourrait délirer;
L'enfant se sent, selon la lenteur des caresses,
Sourdre et mourir sans cesse un désir de pleurer.

THE WOMEN WHO SEEK FOR LICE

When the boy's forehead, full of red tempests,
Implores the white swarm of dreams with hazy details,
There come close to his bed two large charming sisters
With fragile fingers and silvery fingernails.

They seat the child at a casement opened wide at which
A jumble of flowers is bathing in blue air,
And where the dew falls in his heavy hair
Run their slender fingers, terrible and bewitching.

He listens to their fearful breaths sing that smell
Of long honeys pink and vegetal,
And these at times are interrupted by hisses,
Salivas sucked back on lips or desires for kisses.

He hears their black eyelashes beating in the scented silences;
And their fingers, electric and gentle,
Make crackle under their majestic nails the deaths
Of the small lice amid his gray indolences.

Now there rises in him the wine of Laziness, harmonica's sigh
That could be delirious; the child feels, according to
The slowness of their caresses, welling and dying
Unceasingly a desire to cry.

LE BATEAU IVRE

Comme je descendais des Fleuves impassibles,
Je ne me sentis plus guidé par les haleurs:
Des Peaux-Rouges criards les avaient pris pour cibles
Les ayant cloués nus aux poteaux de couleurs.

J'étais insoucieux de tous les équipages,
Porteur de blés flamands ou de cotons anglais.
Quand avec mes haleurs ont fini ces tapages
Les Fleuves m'ont laissé descendre où je voulais.

Dans les clapotements furieux des marées,
Moi, l'autre hiver, plus sourd que les cerveaux d'enfants,
Je courus! Et les Péninsules démarrées
N'ont pas subi tohu-bohus plus triomphants.

La tempête a béni mes éveils maritimes.
Plus léger qu'un bouchon j'ai dansé sur les flots
Qu'on appelle rouleurs éternels de victimes,
Dix nuits, sans regretter l'oeil niais des falots!

Plus douce qu'aux enfants la chair des pommes sûres,
L'eau verte pénétra ma coque de sapin
Et des taches de vins bleus et des vomissures
Me lava, dispersant gouvernail et grappin.

Et dès lors, je me suis baigné dans le Poème
De la Mer, infusé d'astres, et lactescent,
Dévorant les azurs verts; où, flottaison blême
Et ravie, un noyé pensif parfois descend;

Où, teignant tout à coup les bleuités, délires
Et rhythmes lents sous les rutilements du jour,
Plus fortes que l'alcool, plus vastes que nos lyres,
Fermentent les rousseurs amères de l'amour!

Je sais les cieux crevant en éclairs, et les trombes
Et les ressacs et les courants: je sais le soir,
L'Aube exaltée ainsi qu'un peuple de colombes,
Et j'ai vu quelquefois ce que l'homme a cru voir!

J'ai vu le soleil bas, taché d'horreurs mystiques,
Illuminant de longs figements violets,

THE DRUNKEN BOAT

As I was sailing down impassive Rivers,
I no longer felt steered by the haulers of boats:
Some screaming Redskins had taken these men for targets
By nailing their naked bodies to colored posts.

I was heedless of all ships' crews, a carrier
Of English cottons or Flemish grains.
When with my haulers these noises expired
The Rivers let me sail down where I desired.

In the tides' furious lappings, I, the other
Winter, deafer than children's brains,
I ran! And Peninsulas unmoored
Have not endured any more triumphant disorders.

The tempest blessed my maritime awakings.
Lighter than a cork I danced on the waves
That are called endless rollers of victims, for ten nights,
Without missing the silly glow of the lanterns' lights!

Sweeter than the flesh of sour apples
To children, green water penetrated my hull of pine
And washed from me the stains left by blue wines
And vomit, while scattering my rudder and grappling.

And since then, I have bathed in the Poem
Of the Sea, infused with stars, and lactescent,
Devouring the green azures; where, a pale flotsam in ecstasy,
A pensive drowned man sinks occasionally;

Where, suddenly staining the bluenesses, slow deliriums
And rhythms beneath the red glimmers of
The day, stronger than alcohol, vaster than our lyres,
There ferment the bitter rednesses of love!

I know skies bursting into lightnings, and waterspouts
And undertows and currents: I know evening, Dawn
Exalted like a flock of doves,
And I have seen sometimes what man believed he saw!

I have seen the sunken sun, stained with mystical horrors,
Illuminating long violet curdlings, like actors in plays

Pareils à des acteurs de drames très-antiques
Les flots roulant au loin leurs frissons de volets!

J'ai rêvé la nuit verte aux neiges éblouies,
Baiser montant aux yeux des mers avec lenteurs,
La circulation des sèves inouïes,
Et l'éveil jaune et bleu des phosphores chanteurs!

J'ai suivi, des mois pleins, pareille aux vacheries
Hystériques, la houle à l'assaut des récifs,
Sans songer que les pieds lumineux des Maries
Pussent forcer le mufle aux Océans poussifs!

J'ai heurté, savez-vous, d'incroyables Florides
Mêlant aux fleurs des yeux de panthères à peaux
D'hommes! Des arcs-en-ciel tendus comme des brides
Sous l'horizon des mers, à de glauques troupeaux!

J'ai vu fermenter les marais énormes, nasses
Où pourrit dans les joncs tout un Léviathan!
Des écroulements d'eaux au milieu des bonaces,
Et les lointains vers les gouffres cataractant!

Glaciers, soleils d'argent, flots nacreux, cieux de braises!
Échouages hideux au fond des golfes bruns
Où les serpents géants dévorés des punaises
Choient, des arbres tordus, avec de noirs parfums!

J'aurais voulu montrer aux enfants ces dorades
Du flot bleu, ces poissons d'or, ces poissons chantants.
—Des écumes de fleurs ont bercé mes dérades
Et d'ineffables vents m'ont ailé par instants.

Parfois, martyr lassé des pôles et des zones,
La mer dont le sanglot faisait mon roulis doux
Montait vers moi ses fleurs d'ombre aux ventouses jaunes
Et je restais, ainsi qu'une femme à genoux . . .

Presque île, ballottant sur mes bords les querelles
Et les fientes d'oiseaux clabaudeurs aux yeux blonds.
Et je voguais, lorsqu'à travers mes liens frêles
Des noyés descendaient dormir, à reculons!

Or moi, bateau perdu sous les cheveux des anses,
Jeté par l'ouragan dans l'éther sans oiseau,

Of very-ancient days,
The waves rolling far away their shivers of window shutters!

I have dreamed of green night with dazzled snows,
A kiss slowly rising to the oceans' eyes, the flowing
Of wonderful saps, and the awakening
In blue and yellow of phosphorus that sing!

I have followed the swell assailing the reefs
Like hysterical cowsheds, for whole
Months, without dreaming that the luminous feet
Of the Marys could force a muzzle on the wheezing Oceans!

I have hurtled against incredible Floridas, you know,
That mix panthers' eyes in men's skins with flowers! Rainbows
Stretched like bridles beneath the horizon
Of the seas, to glaucous droves!

I have seen huge fens fermenting, traps within
The rushes where a whole Leviathan
Lies rotting! Downfalls of waters amid calm seas,
And distances cataracting towards vortices!

Glaciers, silver suns, skies of embers, pearly waves!
Hideous runnings aground on the bed of brown bays
Where gigantic snakes that voracious bugs attack
Fall down, from twisted trees, with odors black!

I'd have liked to show children those dorados
Of the blue wave, those fish of gold, those fish that sing.
—Foams of flowers rocked my sea-driven wanderings
And at moments ineffable winds endowed me with wings.

Sometimes, a martyr tired of poles and of zones,
When the sea whose sobbing made me roll with ease
Raised towards me her flowers of shade with yellow sucking
Cups, I'd remain, like a woman on her knees . . .

A peninsula, tossing about on my sides the quarrels
And droppings of fair-eyed, brawling birds. And as
I sailed along, through my frail bonds there would sweep
By me drowned men sinking backwards into sleep!

Now I, a boat lost under the hair of the coves,
And hurled by the hurricane into the birdless ether,

Moi dont les Monitors et les voiliers des Hanses
N'auraient pas repêché la carcasse ivre d'eau;

Libre, fumant, monté de brumes violettes,
Moi qui trouais le ciel rougeoyant comme un mur
Qui porte, confiture exquise aux bons poètes,
Des lichens de soleil et des morves d'azur,

Qui courais, taché de lunules électriques,
Planche folle, escorté des hippocampes noirs,
Quand les juillets faisaient crouler à coups de triques
Les cieux ultramarins aux ardents entonnoirs;

Moi qui tremblais, sentant geindre à cinquante lieues
Le rut des Béhémots et les Maelstroms épais,
Fileur éternel des immobilités bleues,
Je regrette l'Europe aux anciens parapets!

J'ai vu des archipels sidéraux! et des îles
Dont les cieux délirants sont ouverts au vogueur:
—Est-ce en ces nuits sans fond que tu dors et t'exiles,
Million d'oiseaux d'or, ô future Vigueur?—

Mais, vrai, j'ai trop pleuré! Les Aubes sont navrantes.
Toute lune est atroce et tout soleil amer:
L'âcre amour m'a gonflé de torpeurs enivrantes.
Ô que ma quille éclate! Ô que j'aille à la mer!

Si je désire une eau d'Europe, c'est la flache
Noire et froide où vers le crépuscule embaumé
Un enfant accroupi plein de tristesses, lâche
Un bateau frêle comme un papillon de mai.

Je ne puis plus, baigné de vos langueurs, ô lames,
Enlever leur sillage aux porteurs de cotons,
Ni traverser l'orgueil des drapeaux et des flammes,
Ni nager sous les yeux horribles des pontons.

I whose carcass drunk with water the Monitors
And Hanse ships would not have fished up from the ocean;

Free, and smoking, mounted by violet hazes,
I who bored through the reddening heavens as through
A wall that brings, exquisite jam for good poets,
Lichens of sun and mucus of sky blue,

Who ran, spotted with electric lunulae,
A crazy plank, escorted by black sea horses, when the Julys
With their bludgeon blows made the lapis lazuli skies
With ardent funnels shake unsteadily;

I who quaked, feeling fifty leagues away moans of rutting
Behemoths and dense Maelstroms, an eternal spinner
Of the blue immobilities, I have regrets:
I miss Europe with its ancient parapets!

I saw astral archipelagoes! and islands
Whose delirious skies are open to the sea traveler:
—Is it in those bottomless nights that you sleep and exile
Yourself, million birds of gold, ô future Vigor?—

But, really, I've wept too much! The Dawns are distressing.
Each moon is atrocious and each sun depressing:
With intoxicating torpors bitter love swelled me.
O let my keel burst! O let me go into the sea!

If there is a water in Europe that I desire,
It's the black, cold puddle where in the embalmed air of twilight
A crouching child filled with sadnesses, releases
A boat as frail as a Maytime butterfly.

I can no longer, bathed in your languors, make trips,
O waves, in the wake of cotton-bearing ships,
Or sail across the pride of flags and pennants,
Or pull past the horrible eyes of prison ships.

LA RIVIÈRE DE CASSIS

La Rivière de Cassis roule ignorée
  En des vaux étranges:
La voix de cent corbeaux l'accompagne, vraie
  Et bonne voix d'anges:
Avec les grands mouvements des sapinaies
  Quand plusieurs vents plongent.

Tout roule avec des mystères révoltants
  De campagnes d'anciens temps;
De donjons visités, de parcs importants:
  C'est en ces bords qu'on entend
Les passions mortes des chevaliers errants:
  Mais que salubre est le vent!

Que le piéton regarde à ces clairevoies:
  Il ira plus courageux.
Soldats des forêts que le Seigneur envoie,
  Chers corbeaux délicieux!
Faites fuire d'ici le paysan matois
  Qui trinque d'un moignon vieux.

Mai 1872

THE BLACK CURRANT RIVER

The Black Currant River rolls along unknown
  In valleys narrow and strange:
The sounds of a hundred crows escort it, good sounds
  And genuine of angels:
With the great movements which through the fir groves range
  When several winds swoop down.

All rolls with the revolting mysteries
  Of campaigns of ancient times;
Of important parks, of visited castles' keeps:
  It's on these shores that you listen
To dead passions of knights-
  Errant: But how salubrious is the wind!

Let him who walks look at these clerestories:
  He'll go more courageously.
Soldiers of the forests whom the Lord sends, dear
  Delicious crows! Make the crafty
Peasant who clinks glasses with his old stump flee
  Away from here.

May 1872

COMÉDIE DE LA SOIF

1. LES PARENTS

    Nous sommes tes Grands-Parents,
      Les Grands!
    Couverts des froides sueurs
    De la lune et des verdures.
    Nos vins secs avaient du coeur!
    Au soleil sans imposture
    Que faut-il à l'homme? boire.

MOI.—Mourir aux fleuves barbares.

    Nous sommes tes Grands-Parents
      Des champs.
    L'eau est au fond des osiers:
    Vois le courant du fossé
    Autour du château mouillé.
    Descendons en nos celliers;
    Après, le cidre et le lait.

MOI.—Aller où boivent les vaches.

    Nois sommes tes Grands-Parents;
      Tiens, prends
    Les liqueurs dans nos armoires;
    Le Thé, le Café, si rares,
    Frémissent dans les bouilloires.
    —Vois les images, les fleurs.
    Nous rentrons du cimetière.

MOI.—Ah! tarir toutes les urnes!

2. L'ESPRIT

    Éternelles Ondines,
      Divisez l'eau fine.
    Vénus, soeur de l'azur,
      Émeus le flot pur.

    Juifs errants de Norwège,
      Dites-moi la neige.
    Anciens exilés chers,
      Dites-moi la mer.

MOI.—Non, plus ces boissons pures,
      Ces fleurs d'eau pour verres;

COMEDY OF THIRST

1. THE PARENTS

> We are your Grandparents,
>   The Ones of Eminence!
> Covered with the cold
> Sweats of the moon and verdures.
> Our dry wines had soul!
> In the sun without imposture
> What does man need? to imbibe.

I:—In the barbarous rivers to die.

> We are your Grandparents
>   Of the country lands.
> Beneath the willows there is water:
> See the stream of the moat around
> The moist castle. Let's go down
> Into our cellars;
> After, milk and cider.

I:—To go where the cows are drinking.

> We are your Grandparents;
>   Take hence,
> Liqueurs from our cupboards; Tea
> And Coffee, very
> Rare, simmer in the kettles.—See
> The images, the flowers. We
> Are returning from the cemetery.

I:—Ah! to dry up all the urns!

2. THE SPIRIT

> Eternal Undines,
>   Divide the fine water. Stir
> The pure wave, Venus, sister
>   Of the azure.

> Wandering Jews of Norway tell me
>   About the snow.
> Exiles belovèd and old,
>   Tell me about the sea.

I:—No, no more
    Of these pure drinks, these water-

Légendes ni figures
  Ne me désaltèrent;

Chansonnier, ta filleule
  C'est ma soif si folle
Hydre intime sans gueules
  Qui mine et désole.

3. LES AMIS

Viens, les Vins vont aux plages,
Et les flots par millions!
Vois le Bitter sauvage
Rouler du haut des monts!

Gagnons, pèlerins sages,
L'Absinthe aux verts piliers . . .

MOI.—Plus ces paysages.
  Qu'est-ce l'ivresse, Amis?

J'aime autant, mieux, même,
Pourrir dans l'étang,
Sous l'affreuse crème,
Près des bois flottants.

4. LE PAUVRE SONGE

Peut-être un Soir m'attend
Où je boirai tranquille
En quelque vieille Ville,
Et mourrai plus content:
Puisque je suis patient!

Si mon mal se résigne,
Si j'ai jamais quelque or,
Choisirai-je le Nord
Ou le Pays des Vignes? . . .
—Ah! songer est indigne

Puisque c'est pure perte!
Et si je redeviens
Le voyageur ancien,

Flowers for glasses; my thirst was not quenched by either
   Legends or figures;

Song-writer, your girl godchild
   There's my thirst so wild
Hydra mouthless and intimate
   That consumes and makes desolate.

3. THE FRIENDS

Come on, Wines go to the beaches, and billows
By the millions!
See the savage Bitter
Rolling from the hilltops!

Let's take, wise pilgrims,
Green-pillared absinthe . . .

I:—To these landscapes put an end.
   What's drunkenness, Friends?

I love just as much, more even,
To grow rotten in the pond,
Beneath the frightful cream,
Near the timbers drifting on.

4. THE POOR MAN DREAMS

Perhaps an Evening's in store for me
When I'll drink peacefully
In some old City,
And I'll die more content:
Because I am patient!

If my misfortune resigns
Itself, if I have some gold some time,
Is it the North that I
Will choose or the Land of the Vines? . . .
—Ah! to dream is worthless

Since it's to no purpose!
And if I become once more
The traveler I was before,

Jamais l'auberge verte
Ne peut bien m'être ouverte.

5. CONCLUSION

Les pigeons qui tremblent dans la prairie,
Le gibier, qui court et qui voit la nuit,
Les bêtes des eaux, la bête asservie,
Les derniers papillons! . . . ont soif aussi.

Mais fondre où fond ce nuage sans guide,
—Oh! favorisé de ce qui est frais!
Expirer en ces violettes humides
Dont les aurores chargent ces forêts?

Mai 1872

Never can the green inn be
Really opened to me.

CONCLUSION

The pigeons that flutter in the meadow,
The game, that runs and that sees
The night, the water beasts, the conquered beast,
The last butterflies! . . . are thirsty also.

But to dissolve where this unguided
Cloud dissolves,—Oh! favored by what is fresh!
To die in these humid violets
Whose auroras fill these forests?

May 1872

FÊTES DE LA PATIENCE

BANNIÈRES DE MAI

Aux branches claires des tilleuls
Meurt un maladif hallali.
Mais des chansons spirituelles
Voltigent parmi les groseilles.
Que notre sang rie en nos veines,
Voici s'enchevêtrer les vignes.
Le ciel est joli comme un ange.
L'azur et l'onde communient.
Je sors. Si un rayon me blesse
Je succomberai sur la mousse.

Qu'on patiente et qu'on s'ennuie
C'est trop simple. Fi de mes peines.
Je veux que l'été dramatique
Me lie à son char de fortune.
Que par toi beaucoup, ô Nature,
—Ah moins seul et moins nul!—je meure.
Au lieu que les Bergers, c'est drôle,
Meurent à peu près par le monde.

Je veux bien que les saisons m'usent.
À toi, Nature, je me rends;
Et ma faim et toute ma soif.
Et, s'il te plaît, nourris, abreuve.
Rien de rien ne m'illusionne;
C'est rire aux parents, qu'au soleil,
Mais moi je ne veux rire à rien;
Et libre soit cette infortune.

Mai 1872

FESTIVALS OF PATIENCE

1. MAY BANNERS
2. SONG OF THE HIGHEST TOWER
3. ETERNITY
4. GOLDEN AGE

MAY BANNERS

In the lindens' bright
Boughs a sickly mort is dying.
But spiritual songs among
The currant bushes are hovering.
Let our blood laugh in our veins,
Here vines become entangled.
The sky is lovely like an angel.
The azure and the wave
Commune. I'm going out. If a ray of light wounds
Me I'll succumb on the moss.

That one should be patient and feel ennui,
That's too simple. Fie on my griefs.
I want dramatic summer to bind
Me to its chariot of fortune.
That through you very much, ô Nature,
—Ah less alone and less nothing!—I may die.
Whereas Shepherds, it's droll,
Die more or less by means of the world.

I'm willing to be worn out by the seasons.
To you, Nature, I surrender;
Both my hunger and all my thirst.
And, please, nourish, give water.
Nothing at all gives me delusions;
It's to laugh at parents, to laugh at the sun,
But I don't want to laugh at anything myself;
And may this misfortune be unconfined.

May 1872

CHANSON DE LA PLUS HAUTE TOUR

Oisive jeunesse
À tout asservie,
Par délicatesse
J'ai perdu ma vie.
Ah! Que le temps vienne
Où les coeurs s'éprennent.

Je me suis dit: laisse,
Et qu'on ne te voie:
Et sans la promesse
De plus hautes joies.
Que rien ne t'arrête
Auguste retraite.

J'ai tant fait patience
Qu'à jamais j'oublie;
Craintes et souffrances
Aux cieux sont parties.
Et la soif malsaine
Obscurcit mes veines.

Ainsi la Prairie
À l'oubli livrée,
Grandie, et fleurie
D'encens et d'ivraies
Au bourdon farouche
De cent sales mouches.

Ah! Mille veuvages
De la si pauvre âme
Qui n'a que l'image
De la Notre-Dame!
Est-ce qu'on prie
La Vierge Marie?

Oisive jeunesse
À tout asservie
Par délicatesse
J'ai perdu ma vie.
Ah! Que le temps vienne
Où les coeurs s'éprennent!

Mai 1872

SONG OF THE HIGHEST TOWER

Idle young days
To everything enslaved,
Through delicacy I
Have lost my life.
Ah! let the time come
When hearts with love are overcome.

I told myself: leave be,
And do not let them see
You: and without the promise
Of higher joys.
Let nothing make you cease
Majestic retreat.

I have endured so patiently
That I have lost all memory
Forever; fears and pains
To the skies are departed.
And the dangerous thirst darkens
My veins.

Thus the Meadow given
Over to oblivion,
Grown taller, and flowering with
Frankincense and rye
Grass amid the fierce bourdon of
A hundred filthy flies.

Ah! Thousand widowhoods of the so
Poor soul
That has the image only
Of Our Lady!
Does one beseech
The Virgin Mary?

Idle young days
To everything enslaved
Through delicacy I
Have lost my life.
Ah! Let the time come
When hearts with love are overcome!

May 1872

L'ÉTERNITÉ

Elle est retrouvée.
Quoi?—L'Éternité.
C'est la mer allée
Avec le soleil.

Âme sentinelle,
Murmurons l'aveu
De la nuit si nulle
Et du jour en feu.

Des humains suffrages,
Des communs élans
Là tu te dégages
Et voles selon.

Puisque de vous seules,
Braises de satin,
Le Devoir s'exhale
Sans qu'on dise: enfin.

Là pas d'espérance,
Nul orietur.
Science avec patience,
Le supplice est sûr.

Elle est retrouvée.
Quoi?—L'Éternité.
C'est la mer allée
Avec le soleil.

Mai 1872

ETERNITY

It is found and won
Again. What?—Eternity.
It is the sea
Gone off with the sun.

Sentinel soul,
Let us softly suspire
The avowal of the night so null
And the day on fire.

From human approvals,
From common drives
You break loose and fly
According to.

Because from you only,
Embers of satin, Duty
Is exhaled and no
One says: finally.

Not any hope there,
No *orietur.**
Knowledge with patience,
The torment is sure.

It is found and won
Again. What?—Eternity.
It is the sea
Gone off with the sun.

May 1872

---

* From the Latin *orior, oriri, ortus sum*, meaning "to rise." Rimbaud is probably referring to religion here.

ÂGE D'OR

Quelqu'une des voix
Toujours angélique
—Il s'agit de moi,—
Vertement s'explique:

Ces mille questions
Qui se ramifient
N'amènent, au fond,
Qu'ivresse et folie;

Reconnais ce tour
Si gai, si facile:
Ce n'est qu'onde, flore,
Et c'est ta famille!

Puis elle chante. Ô
Si gai, si facile,
Et visible à l'oeil nu . . .
—Je chante avec elle,—

Reconnais ce tour
Si gai, si facile,
Ce n'est qu'onde, flore,
Et c'est ta famille! . . . etc.

Et puis une voix
—Est-elle angélique!—
Il s'agit de moi,
Vertement s'explique;

Et chante à l'instant
En soeur des haleines:
D'un ton Allemand,
Mais ardente et pleine:

Le monde est vicieux;
Si cela t'étonne!
Vis et laisse au feu
L'obscure infortune.

Ô joli château!
Que ta vie est claire!
De quel Âge es-tu,

GOLDEN AGE

One of the voices
Always angelically,
—It is about me,—
Explains itself sharply:

These thousand questions
That ramify
Lead only, finally,
To drunkenness and folly;

Recognize this circuit so gay,
So easy:
It's only flora, wave,
And it's your family.

And then it sings. O so gay,
So easy, and visible
To the naked eye . . .
—I sing with it,—

Recognize this circuit so gay,
So easy,
It's only flora, wave,
And it's your family! . . . etc. . .

And then a voice—
—Is it angelic!—
It is about me,
Explains itself sharply:

And sings immediately
As a sister to the winds:
With a German intonation,
But fully and ardently:

The world is vicious;
If that astonishes
You! Live and to fire leave
Gloomy adversity.

O pretty castle! How bright
Is your life!
From what Age are

Nature princière
De notre grand frère! etc . . .

Je chante aussi, moi:
Multiples soeurs! voix
Pas du tout publiques!
Environnez-moi
De gloire pudique . . . etc. . .

Juin 1872

You, princely nature
Of our big brother! etc . . .

And I, I sing also:
Many
Sisters! Voices not public at all!
Encircle me
With humble glory . . . etc. . .

June 1872

Entends comme brame
près des acacias
en avril la rame
viride du pois!

Dans sa vapeur nette,
vers Phoebé! tu vois
s'agiter la tête
de saints d'autrefois . . .

Loin des claires meules
des caps, des beaux toits,
ces chers Anciens veulent
ce philtre sournois . . .

Or ni fériale
ni astrale! n'est
la brume qu'exhale
ce nocturne effet.

Néanmoins ils restent,
—Sicile, Allemagne,
dans ce brouillard triste
et blêmi, justement!

Hear how in April near
the acacia trees
the viridian stick is belling
of the peas!

In its clean haze,
towards Phoebe! you see
saints' heads of bygone days
moving restlessly.

Far from the bright haystacks
of the capes, from the beautiful
roofs, these belovèd Ancients
want this artful philter . . .

Gold neither astral nor ferial!
is but the mist
exhaled by this
nocturnal effect.

However, they remain,
—Sicily, Germany,
in this sorrowful haze
grown pallid, justly!

HONTE

Tant que la lame n'aura
Pas coupé cette cervelle,
Ce paquet blanc, vert et gras,
À vapeur jamais nouvelle,

(Ah! Lui, devrait couper son
Nez, sa lèvre, ses oreilles,
Son ventre! et faire abandon
De ses jambes! ô merveille!)

Mais, non; vrai, je crois que tant
Que pour sa tête la lame,
Que les cailloux pour son flanc,
Que pour ses boyaux la flamme,

N'auront pas agi, l'enfant
Gêneur, la si sotte bête,
Ne doit cesser un instant
De ruser et d'être traître,

Comme un chat des Monts-Rocheux,
D'empuantir toutes sphères!
Qu'à sa mort pourtant, ô mon Dieu!
S'élève quelque prière!

SHAME

As long as the blade has not cut through
This brain, this greasy
Package white and green,
Its vapor never new,

(Ah! He, should cut his nose, his lip,
His ears, his abdomen!
His legs he should surrender then!
O the miracle of it!)

Why, no; really, I think that as long
As for his head the blade,
That pebbles for his side, that for
His bowels flame,

Have not had their effect, the pesterous
Child, the so silly beast,
Should not for an instant cease
From using ruses and from being treacherous,

Like a cat from the mountains of Roche,*
From polluting spheres everywhere!
At his death however, ô
My God! let there arise some prayer!

* Rimbaud came from Roche (in the Attigny district, in the Ardennes). In a letter to Verlaine, Ernest Delahaye calls Rimbaud "le monstre hypothétiquement rocheux" which implies "the monster who is perhaps in Roche right now" (December 31, 1881). The word *rocheux* "was therefore part of the jargon used by Rimbaud and his friends," write Marc Ascione and Jean-Pierre-Chambon, "Les 'Zolismes' de Rimbaud," *Europe*, 51° année, Nos. 529–530 (mai-juin 1973), 130–31, n. 6.

MÉMOIRE

I

L'eau claire; comme le sel des larmes d'enfance,
L'assaut au soleil des blancheurs des corps de femmes;
la soie, en foule et de lys pur, des oriflammes
sous les murs dont quelque pucelle eut la défense;

l'ébat des anges;—Non . . . le courant d'or en marche,
meut ses bras, noirs, et lourds, et frais surtout, d'herbe. Elle
sombre, ayant le Ciel bleu pour ciel-de-lit, appelle
pour rideaux l'ombre de la colline et de l'arche.

II

Eh! l'humide carreau tend ses bouillons limpides!
L'eau meuble d'or pâle et sans fond les couches prêtes.
Les robes vertes et déteintes des fillettes
font les saules, d'où sautent les oiseaux sans brides.

Plus pure qu'un louis, jaune et chaude paupière
le souci d'eau—ta foi conjugale, ô l'Épouse!—
au midi prompt, de son terne miroir, jalouse
au ciel gris de chaleur la Sphère rose et chère.

III

Madame se tient trop debout dans la prairie
prochaine où neigent les fils du travail; l'ombrelle
aux doigts; foulant l'ombelle; trop fière pour elle;
des enfants lisant dans la verdure fleurie

leur livre de maroquin rouge! Hélas, Lui, comme
mille anges blancs qui se séparent sur la route,
s'éloigne par delà la montagne! Elle, toute
froide, et noire, court! après le départ de l'homme!

IV

Regret des bras épais et jeunes d'herbe pure!
Or des lunes d'avril au coeur du saint lit! Joie

MEMORY

I

Clear water; like the salt of children's tears, the
assault on the sun of the whitenesses of women's bodies;
the silk, in crowds and of pure lily, of the oriflammes
beneath the walls defended by some virgin maid;

the frolic of angels;—No . . . the gold tide on the march,
moves its arms, black, and heavy, and blooming above all, with grass. She
sinks, having the blue Sky for her canopy,
calls as curtains the shade of the hill and the arch.

II

Ah! the humid floor spreads out its clear bubbles!
The water furnishes with pale, bottomless gold the ready beds.
The little girls' green and faded dresses
form willows, from which unbridled birds leap up.

Purer than a louis, warm and yellow eye
the marsh marigold—your conjugal faith, ô Wife!—
at prompt noon, from its lusterless mirror, envies
in the sky gray with heat the Sphere belovèd and rosy.

III

In the nearby meadow Madame stands too stiffly
where the sons of toil snow down; her parasol in
her fingers; crushing the umbel; too haughty for her;
children reading in the flowery verdure

their book bound with red Morocco leather! Alas, He,
like a thousand white angels who part on the path,
goes away beyond the mountain! She,
quite black, and chilly, runs! after the departure of the man!

IV

Yearning for the arms of pure grass, young and stout!
Gold of April moons in the heart of the holy bed! Joy

des chantiers riverains à l'abandon, en proie
aux soirs d'août qui faisaient germer ces pourritures!

Qu'elle pleure à présent sous les remparts! l'haleine
des peupliers d'en haut est pour la seule brise.
Puis, c'est la nappe, sans reflets, sans source, grise:
un vieux, dragueur, dans sa barque, immobile peine.

V

Jouet de cet oeil d'eau morne, je n'y puis prendre,
ô canot immobile! oh! bras trop courts! ni l'une
ni l'autre fleur: ni la jaune qui m'importune,
là; ni la bleue, amie à l'eau couleur de cendre.

Ah! la poudre des saules qu'une aile secoue!
Les roses des roseaux dès longtemps dévorées!
Mon canot, toujours fixe; et sa chaîne tirée
Au fond de cet oeil d'eau sans bords,—à quelle boue?

Of riverside sites in utter neglect, a prey
To August evenings that made these putrescences sprout!

Let her weep now beneath the ramparts! the poplars' breath
from above counts as the sole breeze. Then, it's the sheet,
without reflections, springless, gray:
an old man, a dredger, in his motionless boat, toils away.

V

The plaything of this eye of mournful water,
I cannot grasp in it, ô motionless dinghy!
oh! too short arms! either flower: not the yellow one that troubles me,
there; or the blue one, friend of the ashen water.

Ah! the dust of the willows shaken by a wing!
The roses of the reeds devoured a long time
ago! My dinghy, always still; and its cable stretched
to the bottom of this shoreless eye of water,—to what slime?

O saisons, ô châteaux,
Quelle âme est sans défauts?

O saisons, ô châteaux,

J'ai fait la magique étude
Du Bonheur, que nul n'élude.

O vive lui, chaque fois
Que chante son coq gaulois.

Mais! je n'aurai plus d'envie,
Il s'est chargé de ma vie.

Ce Charme! il prit âme et corps,
Et dispersa tous efforts.

Que comprendre à ma parole?
Il fait qu'elle fuie et vole!

O saisons, ô châteaux!

[Et, si le malheur m'entraîne,
Sa disgrâce m'est certaine.

Il faut que son dédain, las!
Me livre au plus prompt trépas!

—O Saisons, ô Châteaux!]

O seasons, ô châteaux,
Is there any flawless soul?

O seasons, ô châteaux,

The magic study I have pursued
Of Happiness, which no one eludes.

Long live he, O,
Each time his Gallic cock does crow!

Why! I shall have no more desire,
He has taken charge of my life entire.

This Charm! soul and body he captivated,
And all efforts dissipated.

What to understand of what I say?
My word he makes fly and soar away!

O seasons, ô châteaux!

[And, if I'm swept off by misery,
His disfavor is certain to me.

His disdain, alas! necessarily
To the quickest death would deliver me!

—O Seasons, ô Châteaux!]

Verlaine

VERLAINE

NEVERMORE

Souvenir, souvenir, que me veux-tu? L'automne
Faisait voler la grive à travers l'air atone,
Et le soleil dardait un rayon monotone
Sur le bois jaunissant où la bise détone.

Nous étions seul à seule et marchions en rêvant,
Elle et moi, les cheveux et la pensée au vent.
Soudain, tournant vers moi son regard émouvant:
"Quel fut ton plus beau jour?" fit sa voix d'or vivant,

Sa voix douce et sonore, au frais timbre angélique.
Un sourire discret lui donna la réplique,
Et je baisai sa main blanche, dévotement.

—Ah! les premières fleurs, qu'elles sont parfumées!
Et qu'il bruit avec un murmure charmant
Le premier *oui* qui sort de lèvres bien-aimées!

AUTUMN SONG

The sobs long drawn
Of the autumn
Violins
Cause a wound in
My heart of a monotonous
Languorousness.

Quite choking
And pallid, when
The hour is tolling,
I remember
The days gone by
And I cry;

And I go off in
The evil wind
That carries me ahead
To this area
And that, like the
Leaf that is dead.

L'HEURE DU BERGER

La lune est rouge au brumeux horizon;
Dans un brouillard qui danse la prairie
S'endort fumeuse, et la grenouille crie
Par les joncs verts où circule un frisson;

Les fleurs des eaux referment leurs corolles;
Des peupliers profilent aux lointains,
Droits et serrés, leurs spectres incertains;
Vers les buissons errent les lucioles;

Les chats-huants s'éveillent, et sans bruit
Rament l'air noir avec leurs ailes lourdes,
Et le zénith s'emplit de lueurs sourdes.
Blanche, Vénus émerge, et c'est la Nuit.

THE TIME FOR LOVERS

The moon upon the hazy horizon is red;
In a dancing mist the smoky meadow
Falls asleep, and the frog cries out
Through green rushes where a shiver moves about;

Water flowers close their corollas again. Far away,
Poplars profile, straight and pressed together,
Their uncertain specters;
Towards the bushes the fireflies stray;

The tawny owls wake up, and silently
Row the black air with their heavy wings,
And the zenith fills with muted lights.
White, Venus emerges, and it is Night.

CLAIR DE LUNE

Votre âme est un paysage choisi
Que vont charmant masques et bergamasques
Jouant du luth et dansant et quasi
Tristes sous leurs déguisements fantasques.

Tout en chantant sur le mode mineur
L'amour vainqueur et la vie opportune,
Ils n'ont pas l'air de croire à leur bonheur
Et leur chanson se mêle au clair de lune,

Au calme clair de lune triste et beau,
Qui fait rêver les oiseaux dans les arbres
Et sangloter d'extase les jets d'eau,
Les grands jets d'eau sveltes parmi les marbres.

MOONLIGHT

Your soul is a selected landscape that maskers
And bergamasche* go about beguiling
Playing the lute and dancing and quasi
Sad beneath their fantastical disguises.

While singing in the minor mood
Triumphant love and life that is opportune,
They do not seem to believe in their good fortune
And their song mingles with the moonlight,

With the calm moonlight sad and beautiful,
That makes the birds dream in the trees
And the fountains weep with ecstasy,
The great svelte fountains amid the marble statues.

* Derived from Bergamo, the Italian city, bergamasca (the plural is bergamasche) means a fast
dance similar to the tarantella, or the music for this dance.

LE FAUNE

Un vieux faune de terre cuite
Rit au centre des boulingrins,
Présageant sans doute une suite
Mauvaise à ces instants sereins

Qui m'ont conduit et t'ont conduite,
—Mélancoliques pèlerins,—
Jusqu'à cette heure dont la fuite
Tournoie au son des tambourins.

THE FAUN

An old terra-cotta faun laughs out
In the heart of the bowling green,
Portending an evil sequel no doubt
To these instants that are serene

That have led me and have led you,
Madame,—melancholy pilgrims,—
Unto this hour whose flight whirls to
The sound of the tambourins.*

* *Le tambourin* (English, tambourin) is a long, narrow drum from Provence.

MANDOLINE

Les donneurs de sérénades
Et les belles écouteuses
Échangent des propos fades
Sous les ramures chanteuses.

C'est Tircis et c'est Aminte,
Et c'est l'éternel Clitandre,
Et c'est Damis qui pour mainte
Cruelle fait maint vers tendre.

Leurs courtes vestes de soie,
Leurs longues robes à queues,
Leur élégance, leur joie
Et leurs molles ombres bleues

Tourbillonnent dans l'extase
D'une lune rose et grise,
Et la mandoline jase
Parmi les frissons de brise.

MANDOLIN

The serenaders and
The beautiful listeners bandy
About some vapid remarks
Beneath the singing branches.

It's Tircis and it's Aminta,
And it's the eternal Clitandre,
And it's Damis* who for many an unkind
Girl writes many a tender line.

Their short and silken jackets,
Their floor-length gowns with trains,
Their elegance, their gladness
And their soft and blue shadows

Swirl in the ecstasies
Of a moon that is pink and gray,
And the mandolin chatters away
Amid the shivers of the breeze.

* Traditional names in pastorals and Italian comedy.

EN SOURDINE

Calmes dans le demi-jour
Que les branches hautes font,
Pénétrons bien notre amour
De ce silence profond.

Fondons nos âmes, nos coeurs
Et nos sens extasiés,
Parmi les vagues langueurs
Des pins et des arbousiers.

Ferme tes yeux à demi,
Croise tes bras sur ton sein,
Et de ton coeur endormi
Chasse à jamais tout dessein.

Laissons-nous persuader
Au souffle berceur et doux
Qui vient à tes pieds rider
Les ondes de gazon roux.

Et quand, solennel, le soir
Des chênes noirs tombera,
Voix de notre désespoir,
Le rossignol chantera.

WITH MUTED STRINGS

Calm in the twilight that
The high branches make above,
With this profound silence let's
Completely imbue our love.

Let's blend our souls, our hearts
And our senses in ecstasies,
Among the vague languors of
The pines and the strawberry trees.

Now close your eyes halfway,
Cross your arms upon your breast,
And all schemes from your heart at rest
Forever chase away.

Let's let ourselves be persuaded
In the breath cradling and sweet
That comes rippling at your feet
The waves of russet grass.

And when the solemn evening
Falls from the black oaks,
Voice of our hopelessness,
The nightingale will sing.

COLLOQUE SENTIMENTAL

Dans le vieux parc solitaire et glacé,
Deux formes ont tout à l'heure passé.

Leurs yeux sont morts et leurs lèvres sont molles,
Et l'on entend à peine leurs paroles.

Dans le vieux parc solitaire et glacé,
Deux spectres ont évoqué le passé.

—Te souvient-il de notre extase ancienne?
—Pourquoi voulez-vous donc qu'il m'en souvienne?

—Ton coeur bat-il toujours à mon seul nom?
Toujours vois-tu mon âme en rêve?—Non.

—Ah! les beaux jours de bonheur indicible
Où nous joignions nos bouches!—C'est possible.

—Qu'il était bleu, le ciel, et grand, l'espoir!
—L'espoir a fui, vaincu, vers le ciel noir.

Tels ils marchaient dans les avoines folles,
Et la nuit seule entendit leurs paroles.

SENTIMENTAL COLLOQUY

In the deserted old park now frozen fast,
Two forms only moments ago just passed.

Their lips barely move and their eyes are dead,
And one scarcely hears the words they said.

In the deserted old park now frozen fast,
Two specters conjured up the past.

—Do you remember our old ecstasy?
—*Why* do you want it to be remembered by me?

—Does your heart still hearing my name throb so?
Does my soul still appear in your reveries?—No.

—Ah! the beautiful days of inexpressible
Bliss when we joined our lips.—It's possible.

—How blue was the sky, and hope, full-grown!
—Hope, vanquished, towards the black sky has flown.

In the wild oats thus their steps they led,
And night alone heard the words they said.

Avant que tu ne t'en ailles,
Pâle étoile du matin,
   —Mille cailles
Chantent, chantent dans le thym.—

Tourne devers le poète,
Dont les yeux sont pleins d'amour,
   —L'alouette
Monte au ciel avec le jour.—

Tourne ton regard que noie
L'aurore dans son azur;
   —Quelle joie
Parmi les champs de blé mûr!—

Puis fais luire ma pensée
Là-bas,—bien loin, oh! bien loin!
   —La rosée
Gaîment brille sur le foin.—

Dans le doux rêve où s'agite
Ma mie endormie encor . . .
   —Vite, vite,
Car voici le soleil d'or.—

Before you depart,
Pale morning star,
   —A thousand quails in
The thyme are singing, singing.—

Turn towards the poet, whose eyes
Are filled with love,
   —The lark soars above
With day into the skies.—

Turn your gaze that dawn
Drowns in its azure;
   —What joyous pleasure
Amid the ripe fields of corn!—

Then make my thought gleam there,—quite far,
Oh! quite far away!
   —The dewdrops are
Gaily glittering on the hay!—

In the sweet reverie
Where my still sleeping love moves restlessly . . .
   —Quick, quick, for here comes
The golden sun.—

La lune blanche
Luit dans les bois;
De chaque branche
Part une voix
Sous la ramée . . .

Ô bien-aimée.

L'étang reflète,
Profond miroir,
La silhouette
Du saule noir
Où le vent pleure . . .

Rêvons, c'est l'heure.

Un vaste et tendre
Apaisement
Semble descendre
Du firmament
Que l'astre irise . . .

C'est l'heure exquise.

The moon shines white
In the forest tonight;
From every bough
A voice calls out
Beneath the arbor . . .

O my darling.

The pool reflects,
A mirror deep,
The silhouette
Of the black willow
Where the wind weeps . . .

It's the hour, let's dream.

A calm vast and tender
Seems to descend
From the firmament
Made iridescent
By the star . . .

It's the exquisite hour.

Il pleut doucement sur la ville.
(ARTHUR RIMBAUD)

Il pleure dans mon coeur
Comme il pleut sur la ville;
Quelle est cette langueur
Qui pénètre mon coeur?

Ô bruit doux de la pluie
Par terre et sur les toits!
Pour un coeur qui s'ennuie
Ô le chant de la pluie!

Il pleure sans raison
Dans ce coeur qui s'écoeure.
Quoi! nulle trahison? . . .
Ce deuil est sans raison.

C'est bien la pire peine
De ne savoir pourquoi
Sans amour et sans haine
Mon coeur a tant de peine!

It's raining gently on the town.
(ARTHUR RIMBAUD)

In my heart there is weeping
Like rain sweeping on the town;
What is this languor seeping
Through all of my heart's being?

O gentle noise of the rain
On the ground and on the roofs!
For a heart knowing boredom's pain
O the singing of the rain!

There is weeping without a reason
In this heart losing heart.
What! no betrayal or treason? . . .
This mourning's without a reason.

And really the worst pain
Is not to understand why
Without love or hate to explain
My heart feels so much pain!

Son joyeux, importun, d'un clavecin sonore.
(PÉTRUS BOREL)

Le piano que baise une main frêle
Luit dans le soir rose et gris vaguement,
Tandis qu'avec un très léger bruit d'aile
Un air bien vieux, bien faible et bien charmant
Rôde discret, épeuré quasiment,
Par le boudoir longtemps parfumé d'Elle.

Qu'est-ce que c'est que ce berceau soudain
Qui lentement dorlote mon pauvre être?
Que voudrais-tu de moi, doux Chant badin?
Qu'as-tu voulu, fin refrain incertain
Qui vas tantôt mourir vers la fenêtre
Ouverte un peu sur le petit jardin?

Joyful sound, importunate, of a resonant harpsichord.
(PÉTRUS BOREL)

The piano that a frail hand kisses gleams
In the vaguely gray and rosy evening,
While with a very faint noise of a wing
A quite old air, quite feeble and quite charming
Prowls discreetly, frightened nearly,
Through the boudoir perfumed a long while by Her.

What is this sudden cradle that slowly
Coddles my wretched being?
What would you wish for from me, sweet playful
Song? What did you wish for, subtle uncertain refrain
That towards the slightly opened window will die
Above the little garden by and by?

Dans l'interminable
Ennui de la plaine
La neige incertaine
Luit comme du sable.

Le ciel est de cuivre
Sans lueur aucune.
On croirait voir vivre
Et mourir la lune.

Comme des nuées
Flottent gris les chênes
Des forêts prochaines
Parmi les buées.

Le ciel est de cuivre
Sans lueur aucune.
On croirait voir vivre
Et mourir la lune.

Corneille poussive
Et vous, les loups maigres,
Par ces bises aigres
Quoi donc vous arrive?

Dans l'interminable
Ennui de la plaine
La neige incertaine
Luit comme du sable.

In the endless ennui
Of the meadowland
Snow falling unsteadily
Glistens like sand.

Copper-hued is the sky
Without any gleam.
You'd think you were seeing
The moon live and die.

Like clouds oaks in
The near forest swim
Gray amid the stream
Of the windowpane's steam.

Copper-hued is the sky
Without any gleam.
You'd think you were seeing
The moon live and die.

Wheezy crow and you,
The skinny wolves, in
These raw north winds
Just what happens to you?

In the endless ennui
Of the meadowland
Snow falling unsteadily
Glistens like sand.

BRUXELLES

Chevaux de Bois

Par saint-Gille,
Viens-nous-en,
Mon agile
Alezan!
(V. HUGO)

Tournez, tournez, bons chevaux de bois,
Tournez cent tours, tournez mille tours,
Tournez souvent et tournez toujours,
Tournez, tournez au son des hautbois.

Le gros soldat, la plus grosse bonne
Sont sur vos dos comme dans leur chambre,
Car en ce jour au bois de la Cambre
Les maîtres sont tous deux en personne.

Tournez, tournez, chevaux de leur coeur,
Tandis qu'autour de tous vos tournois
Clignote l'oeil du filou sournois,
Tournez au son du piston vainqueur.

C'est ravissant comme ça vous soûle
D'aller ainsi dans ce cirque bête:
Bien dans le ventre et mal dans la tête,
Du mal en masse et du bien en foule.

Tournez, tournez sans qu'il soit besoin
D'user jamais de nuls éperons
Pour commander à vos galops ronds,
Tournez, tournez, sans espoir de foin.

Et dépêchez, chevaux de leur âme:
Déjà voici que la nuit qui tombe
Va réunir pigeon et colombe
Loin de la foire et loin de madame.

Tournez, tournez! le ciel en velours
D'astres en or se vêt lentement.
Voici partir l'amante et l'amant.
Tournez au son joyeux des tambours!

Champ de foire de Saint-Gilles, août 72

BRUSSELS
Merry-Go-Round

By Saint Gilles,
Come with us, do,
My agile horse
Of chestnut hue!
(V. Hugo)

Go round, go round, good merry-go-round,
Go round a hundred turns, go round a thousand
Turns, go round often and forever go round,
Go round, go round to the oboes' sound.

The stout soldier, the even stouter maidservant
Are on your back as in their chamber,
For on this day in the woods of Cambre*
Both of the masters are there in person.

Go round, go round, horses of their hearts,
While around all of your tournaments
The eye of the shifty pickpocket winks,
Go round to the sound of the conquering piston.

It's entrancing how drunk it makes you to go
Like this in this silly carrousel:
Well-being in the belly and in the head, aching, so
Much aching and heaps of feeling well.

Go round, go round, without a need
To use any spurs on any day
To command all of your gallopings round,
Go round, go round, without hope for hay.

And hurry, horses of their souls:
Already here comes the evening twilight
That will reunite the pigeon and
The dove far from the fair and far from madame.

Go round, go round! the sky in velvet slowly comes
To array itself with golden stars.
Now the lover and his mistress depart.
Go round to the joyful sound of the drums!

The fairground of Saint-Gilles, August [18]72

---

* The woods of Cambre is an elegant public promenade south of Brussels.

GREEN

Voici des fruits, des fleurs, des feuilles et des branches
Et puis voici mon coeur qui ne bat que pour vous.
Ne le déchirez pas avec vos deux mains blanches
Et qu'à vos yeux si beaux l'humble présent soit doux.

J'arrive tout couvert encore de rosée
Que le vent du matin vient glacer à mon front.
Souffrez que ma fatigue à vos pieds reposée
Rêve des chers instants qui la délasseront.

Sur votre jeune sein laissez rouler ma tête
Toute sonore encor de vos derniers baisers;
Laissez-la s'apaiser de la bonne tempête,
Et que je dorme un peu puisque vous reposez.

GREEN

Here are some fruits, some flowers, some branches and
Some leaves and then here is my heart that only beats
For you. Do not tear it with your two white hands
And in your so beautiful eyes may the humble present be sweet.

I arrive quite covered yet with dew that the morning
Wind has frozen on my forehead. Let
My weariness laid down at your feet to rest
Dream of the dear moments that will refresh it.

Let my head roll back and forth on your young breast,
My head quite resonant still with your last kisses;
Let it calm down from the good tempest,
And let me sleep a little since you are resting.

STREETS

Dansons la gigue!

J'aimais surtout ses jolis yeux,
Plus clairs que l'étoile des cieux,
J'aimais ses yeux malicieux.

Dansons la gigue!

Elle avait des façons vraiment
De désoler un pauvre amant,
Que c'en était vraiment charmant!

Dansons la gigue!

Mais je trouve encore meilleur
Le baiser de sa bouche en fleur
Depuis qu'elle est morte à mon coeur.

Dansons la gigue!

Je me souviens, je me souviens
Des heures et des entretiens,
Et c'est le meilleur de mes biens.

Dansons la gigue!

Soho.

STREETS

I

Let's dance the jig!

I loved above all her pretty eyes,
Even brighter than the star in the skies,
I loved her mischievous eyes.

Let's dance the jig!

She had some ways, you'd better believe,
Of making a poor lover grieve,
That really it was charming indeed!

Let's dance the jig!

But even better I find
The kiss of her lips in bloom since the time
When to my heart she died.

Let's dance the jig!

I remember, I remember
The hours and the talking sessions,
And that's the best of my possessions.

Let's dance the jig!

Soho.

Mon Dieu m'a dit: Mon fils, il faut m'aimer. Tu vois
Mon flanc percé, mon coeur qui rayonne et qui saigne,
Et mes pieds offensés que Madeleine baigne
De larmes, et mes bras douloureux sous le poids

De tes péchés, et mes mains! Et tu vois la croix,
Tu vois les clous, le fiel, l'éponge, et tout t'enseigne
À n'aimer, en ce monde amer où la chair règne,
Que ma Chair et mon Sang, ma parole et ma voix.

Ne t'ai-je pas aimé jusqu'à la mort moi-même,
Ô mon frère en mon Père, ô mon fils en l'Esprit,
Et n'ai-je pas souffert, comme c'était écrit?

N'ai-je pas sangloté ton angoisse suprême
Et n'ai-je pas sué la sueur de tes nuits,
Lamentable ami qui me cherches où je suis?

My God said to me: My son, you must love me. You see
My side pierced open, my heart that radiates and bleeds,
And my injured feet that Magdalene bathes
With tears, and my arms aching under the weight

Of your sins, and my hands! And you see the nails,
You see the cross, the gall, the sponge, and all teaches
You, in this bitter world where the flesh prevails,
To love only my Flesh and my Blood, my voice and my speech.

Haven't I myself loved you unto
Death, ô my brother in my Father, ô my son
In the Spirit, and haven't I suffered, as it was destined?

Haven't I sobbed your utmost anguish and haven't
I sweated the sweat of your nighttimes, pitiable friend
Who seeks for me where I am?

L'espoir luit comme un brin de paille dans l'étable.
Que crains-tu de la guêpe ivre de son vol fou?
Vois, le soleil toujours poudroie à quelque trou.
Que ne t'endormais-tu, le coude sur la table?

Pauvre âme pâle, au moins cette eau du puits glacé,
Bois-la. Puis dors après. Allons, tu vois, je reste,
Et je dorloterai les rêves de ta sieste,
Et tu chantonneras comme un enfant bercé.

Midi sonne. De grâce, éloignez-vous, madame.
Il dort. C'est étonnant comme les pas de femme
Résonnent au cerveau des pauvres malheureux.

Midi sonne. J'ai fait arroser dans la chambre.
Va, dors! L'espoir luit comme un caillou dans un creux.
Ah, quand refleuriront les roses de septembre!

Hope shines like a blade of straw in the cattle stable.
What do you fear from the wasp drunk with its mad flight?
See, at some hole the sun always rises in motes of light.
Why wouldn't you sleep, with your elbow on the table?

Poor pale soul, at least this water from the icy
Well, drink it. And then sleep. Come on, you see,
I'm staying, and I'll coddle your siesta's dreams,
And you will hum like a child who is rocked to sleep.

Noon tolls. Have pity, go away, madame. He's asleep.
It's astonishing how a woman's footsteps keep
On echoing in the brains of poor wretched men.

Noon tolls. I've had the room watered down. Go on, sleep!
Hope shines like a pebble in a pit. Ah, when
Will the roses of September flower again?

Un grand sommeil noir
Tombe sur ma vie:
Dormez, tout espoir,
Dormez, toute envie!

Je ne vois plus rien,
Je perds la mémoire
Du mal et du bien . . .
Ô la triste histoire!

Je suis un berceau
Qu'une main balance
Au creux d'un caveau:
Silence, silence!

A great dark drowsiness
Is falling upon my days:
Stay sleeping, every hope,
Stay sleeping, all envious ways!

Not a thing any more do I see,
I am losing the memory
Of good and iniquity . . .
O the sorrowful history!

I am a cradle that
A hand is rocking in
The pit of a burial vault:
Be silent, be silent!

Le ciel est, par-dessus le toit,
    Si bleu, si calme!
Un arbre, par-dessus le toit,
    Berce sa palme.

La cloche, dans le ciel qu'on voit,
    Doucement tinte.
Un oiseau sur l'arbre qu'on voit
    Chante sa plainte.

Mon Dieu, mon Dieu, la vie est là,
    Simple et tranquille.
Cette paisible rumeur-là
    Vient de la ville.

—Qu'as-tu fait, ô toi que voilà
    Pleurant sans cesse,
Dis, qu'as-tu fait, toi que voilà,
    De ta jeunesse?

The sky is, above the roof,
   So blue, so calm!
A tree, above the roof,
   Is rocking its palm.

The bell, in the sky that one sees,
   Is softly ringing.
A bird in the tree that one sees
   Is plaintively singing.

Dear me, dear me, life exists there,
   Simply, tranquilly.
That peaceful murmur there
   Comes from the city.

—What have you done, ô you there
   Shedding ceaseless tears,
Tell, what have you done, you there,
   With your youthful years?

Le son du cor s'afflige vers les bois
D'une douleur on veut croire orpheline
Qui vient mourir au bas de la colline
Parmi la bise errant en courts abois.

L'âme du loup pleure dans cette voix
Qui monte avec le soleil qui décline
D'une agonie on veut croire câline
Et qui ravit et qui navre à la fois.

Pour faire mieux cette plainte assoupie,
La neige tombe à long traits de charpie
À travers le couchant sanguinolent,

Et l'air a l'air d'être un soupir d'automne,
Tant il fait doux par ce soir monotone
Où se dorlote un paysage lent.

The hunting horn grieves towards the forest with
A suffering one wants to think orphaned that dies
At the bottom of the hill amid
The north wind roving in short baying cries.

The wolf's soul is weeping in this voice that rises
With the sun that wanes in a death agony
One wants to think caressing that both delights
And distresses simultaneously.

To make this lamentation heavier with sleep,
The snow is falling in long streaks
Of lint across the sanguinolent western sky,

And the air has the air of being an autumn sigh,
For such sweetness on this monotonous evening dwells
In which a sluggish landscape coddles itself.

KALÉIDOSCOPE

À Germain Nouveau

Dans une rue, au coeur d'une ville de rêve,
Ce sera comme quand on a déjà vécu:
Un instant à la fois très vague et très aigu . . .
Ô ce soleil parmi la brume qui se lève!

Ô ce cri sur la mer, cette voix dans les bois!
Ce sera comme quand on ignore des causes:
Un lent réveil après bien des métempsychoses:
Les choses seront plus les mêmes qu'autrefois

Dans cette rue, au coeur de la ville magique
Où des orgues moudront des gigues dans les soirs,
Où les cafés auront des chats sur les dressoirs,
Et que traverseront des bandes de musique.

Ce sera si fatal qu'on en croira mourir:
Des larmes ruisselant douces le long des joues,
Des rires sanglotés dans le fracas des roues,
Des invocations à la mort de venir,

Des mots anciens comme un bouquet de fleurs fanées!
Les bruits aigres des bals publics arriveront,
Et des veuves avec du cuivre après leur front,
Paysannes, fendront la foule des traînées

Qui flânent là, causant avec d'affreux moutards
Et des vieux sans sourcils que la dartre enfarine,
Cependant qu'à deux pas, dans des senteurs d'urine,
Quelque fête publique enverra des pétards.

Ce sera comme quand on rêve et qu'on s'éveille!
Et que l'on se rendort et que l'on rêve encor
De la même féerie et du même décor,
L'été, dans l'herbe, au bruit moiré d'un vol d'abeille.

KALEIDOSCOPE

For Germain Nouveau

On a street, in the heart of a dream city,
It will be like when one lived previously:
One moment at once very sharp and very vague . . .
O that sun amid the rising haze!

O that voice in the woods, that cry over the sea!
It will be like when one doesn't know causes:
A slow awakening after many metempsychoses:
Things will be even more the same than formerly

On that street, in the heart of the magic city
Where organs will grind out jigs in the evenings,
Where cafés will have cats on their sideboards,
And where bands of musicians will travel across.

It will be so fatal that you think you'll die
Of it: tears streaming, sweet, along cheeks,
Laughs sobbed in the fracas of the wheels,
Invocations to death to arrive,

Ancient words like a bouquet of faded flowers!
Shrill noises of public dances will occur,
And widows wearing copper helmets,* like peasants,
Will elbow through the crowd of streetwalkers

Who stroll there, talking with frightful kids and old men
Without eyebrows whom scurf flours, while two steps from them,
Amid the scents of urine, firecrackers will be
Sent off in some public festivity.

It will be like when one dreams and one wakes from sleep!
And one falls asleep again and one dreams once more
Of the same enchantment and the same décor,
In the summer's grass, to the moiré noise of the flight of a bee.

---

* Verlaine himself elucidated the meaning of these words. In *Two Weeks in Holland* (1893),
he wrote about Amsterdam: "It's there that I see, or rather see again, women with helmets; I
had already come across some, twenty years ago, in Brussels, whence that very old line of mine:
'Et des femmes avec du cuivre après leur front' " (Verlaine, *Oeuvres complètes*, Vol. II [Paris:
Le Club du Meilleur Livre, 1960], p. 897).

ART POÉTIQUE

À Charles Morice

De la musique avant toute chose,
Et pour cela préfère l'Impair
Plus vague et plus soluble dans l'air,
Sans rien en lui qui pèse ou qui pose.

Il faut aussi que tu n'ailles point
Choisir tes mots sans quelque méprise:
Rien de plus cher que la chanson grise
Où l'Indécis au Précis se joint.

C'est des beaux yeux derrière des voiles,
C'est le grand jour tremblant de midi,
C'est, par un ciel d'automne attiédi,
Le bleu fouillis des claires étoiles.

Car nous voulons la Nuance encor,
Pas la Couleur, rien que la nuance!
Oh! la nuance seule fiance
Le rêve au rêve et la flûte au cor!

Fuis du plus loin la Pointe assassine,
L'Esprit cruel et le Rire impur,
Qui font pleurer les yeux de l'Azur,
Et tout cet ail de basse cuisine!

Prends l'éloquence et tords-lui son cou!
Tu feras bien, en train d'énergie,
De rendre un peu la Rime assagie.
Si l'on n'y veille, elle ira jusqu'où?

Ô qui dira les torts de la Rime?
Quel enfant sourd ou quel nègre fou
Nous a forgé ce bijou d'un sou
Qui sonne creux et faux sous la lime?

De la musique encore et toujours!
Que ton vers soit la chose envolée

ART OF POETRY

To Charles Morice

Music before anything else, and for such composing
Prefer the Uneven-Syllabled Line
Vaguer and more soluble in air, with nothing
In it ponderous or posing.

You also must not make your choice
Of words without taking something wrong:
Nothing more belovèd than the gray song
Where the Indecisive to the Precise is joined.

It's beautiful eyes behind veils,
It's the full noon's trembling light,
It's the blue jumble of bright
Stars in a tepid autumn sky!

For Nuance is still what we wish for,
Not Color, nothing but nuances!
Oh! only the nuance affiances
The dream to the dream and the flute to the horn!

Flee as far as you can from the murderous Quip,
The impure Laugh and cruel Wit,
Which make the eyes of the Azure weep,
And all that garlic of common cuisine!

Take eloquence and wring its neck!
You will do well, while in an energetic
Mood, to make Rhyme a little wiser. If you
Don't watch over it, where will it go to?*

O who will tell the offenses of Rhyme? What child
Who is deaf or what Negro fool
Forged for us this jewel worth a sou
That sounds hollow and false beneath the file?

Music again and all the time!
Let your line be the thing that has taken wing

---

* With his rhyme on "cou /. . . . ./ qu'où" (suggesting the cuckoo, "coucou"), Verlaine
illustrates the awkwardness that results when the poet does not watch over his rhyme.

Qu'on sent qui fuit d'une âme en allée
Vers d'autres cieux à d'autres amours.

Que ton vers soit la bonne aventure
Éparse au vent crispé du matin
Qui va fleurant la menthe et le thym . . .
Et tout le reste est littérature.

That one feels fleeing from a soul going
Towards other loves and other skies.

Let your line be the prophecy of future
Good luck dispersed in the shriveling morning wind
Which always smells of thyme and of mint . . .
And all the rest is literature.

ALLÉGORIE

À Jules Valadon

Despotique, pesant, incolore, l'Été,
Comme un roi fainéant présidant un supplice,
S'étire par l'ardeur blanche du ciel complice
Et bâille. L'homme dort loin du travail quitté.

L'alouette au matin, lasse, n'a pas chanté,
Pas un nuage, pas un souffle, rien qui plisse
Ou ride cet azur implacablement lisse
Où le silence bout dans l'immobilité.

L'âpre engourdissement a gagné les cigales
Et sur leur lit étroit de pierres inégales
Les ruisseaux à moitié taris ne sautent plus.

Une rotation incessante de moires
Lumineuses étend ses flux et ses reflux . . .
Des guêpes, çà et là, volent, jaunes et noires.

ALLEGORY

To Jules Valadon

Despotic, heavy, colorless, the Summer,
Like an idle king presiding over a torture,
Stretches through the white ardor of the accomplice sky
And yawns. Man sleeps far from his toil laid aside.

The lark, weary, in the morning did not sing,
Not a cloud, not a breath, not a thing
That ripples or wrinkles this implacably
Smooth azure where silence boils in immobility.

Bitter torpor has overtaken the cicadas and over
Their narrow bed of uneven stones
The half dried up brooks do not leap any more.

An incessant rotation of luminous moires
Extends its flowings and its flowings back . . .
Wasps, here and there, are flying, yellow and black.

CRIMEN AMORIS

À Villiers de l'Isle-Adam

DANS un palais, soie et or, dans Ecbatane,
De beaux démons, des Satans adolescents,
Au son d'une musique mahométane,
Font litière aux Sept Péchés de leurs cinq sens.

C'est la fête aux Sept Péchés: ô qu'elle est belle!
Tous les Désirs rayonnaient en feux brutaux;
Les Appétits, pages prompts que l'on harcèle,
Promenaient des vins roses dans des cristaux.

Des danses sur des rhythmes d'épithalames
Bien doucement se pâmaient en longs sanglots
Et de beaux choeurs de voix d'hommes et de femmes
Se déroulaient, palpitaient comme des flots,

Et la bonté qui s'en allait de ces choses
Était puissante et charmante tellement
Que la campagne autour se fleurit de roses
Et que la nuit paraissait en diamant.

Or le plus beau d'entre tous ces mauvais anges
Avait seize ans sous sa couronne de fleurs.
Les bras croisés sur les colliers et les franges,
Il rêve, l'oeil plein de flammes et de pleurs.

En vain la fête autour se faisait plus folle,
En vain les Satans, ses frères et ses soeurs,
Pour l'arracher au souci qui le désole
L'encourageaient d'appels de bras caresseurs:

Il résistait à toutes câlineries,
Et le chagrin mettait un papillon noir
À son cher front tout brûlant d'orfèvreries.
Ô l'immortel et terrible désespoir!

Il leur disait: « Ô vous, laissez-moi tranquille! »
Puis, les ayant baisés tous bien tendrement,
Il s'évada d'avec eux d'un geste agile,
Leur laissant aux mains des pans de vêtement.

Le voyez-vous sur la tour la plus céleste
Du haut palais avec une torche au poing?

CRIMEN AMORIS   (THE CRIME OF LOVE)

To Villiers de l'Isle-Adam

In a palace, silk and gold, in Ecbatana,*
Beautiful demons, adolescent Satans,
To a music of the Mohammedans,
Bear aloft with their five senses the Seven Sins.

It's the festival of the Seven Sins: ô how beautiful
It is! All desires beamed in brutal fires;
The Appetites, prompt pages one harasses,
Bore rosé wines around in crystal glasses.

Dances to the rhythms of epithalamiums
Were swooning in long sobs quite tenderly
And beautiful choirs of men's and women's voices
Were rolling in, palpitating like waves of the sea,

And the Goodness that issued from these things was so potent
And so charming that the countryside
Around adorned itself with roses
And night appeared in diamond.

Now the handsomest of all those evil angels
Beneath his crown of flowers was sixteen years
Of age. With his arms crossed on the collars and the fringes,
He dreams, his eye filled with flames and with tears.

In vain the festival all around became wilder,
In vain the Satans, his brothers and his sisters,
To tear him away from the worries distressing
Him, encouraged him with appeals from arms that were caressing:

He resisted all cajoleries,
And chagrin placed a black butterfly on
His belovèd forehead quite burning with jewelry.
O the immortal and terrible despondency!

He said to them: "O you, leave me alone!"
Then, having kissed them all very tenderly,
He escaped from them by moving agilely,
Leaving in their hands some bits of clothing.

Do you see him on the most celestial tower of
The lofty palace with a torch in his fist? He is shaking

*Ecbatana (Persia) is the ancient name of Hamadan.

Il la brandit comme un héros fait d'un ceste:
D'en bas on croit que c'est une aube qui point.

Qu'est-ce qu'il dit de sa voix profonde et tendre
Qui se marie au claquement clair du feu
Et que la lune est extatique d'entendre?
«Oh! je serai celui-là qui créera Dieu!

» Nous avons tous trop souffert, anges et hommes,
» De ce conflit entre le Pire et le Mieux.
» Humilions, misérables que nous sommes,
» Tous nos élans dans le plus simple des voeux.

» Ô vous tous, ô nous tous, ô les pécheurs tristes,
» Ô les gais Saints, pourquoi ce schisme têtu?
» Que n'avons-nous fait, en habiles artistes,
» De nos travaux la seule et même vertu!

» Assez et trop de ces luttes trop égales!
» Il va falloir qu'enfin se rejoignent les
» Sept Péchés aux Trois Vertus Théologales!
» Assez et trop de ces combats durs et laids!

» Et pour réponse à Jésus qui crut bien faire
» En maintenant l'équilibre de ce duel,
» Par moi l'enfer dont c'est ici le repaire
» Se sacrifie à l'Amour universel! »

La torche tombe de sa main éployée,
Et l'incendie alors hurla s'élevant,
Querelle énorme d'aigles rouges noyée
Au remous noir de la fumée et du vent.

L'or fond et coule à flots et la marbre éclate;
C'est un brasier tout splendeur et tout ardeur;
La soie en courts frissons comme de l'ouate
Vole à flocons tout ardeur et tout splendeur.

Et les Satans mourants chantaient dans les flammes,
Ayant compris, comme ils s'étaient résignés!
Et de beaux choeurs de voix d'hommes et de femmes
Montaient parmi l'ouragan des bruits ignés.

Et lui, les bras croisés d'une sorte fière,
Les yeux au ciel où le feu monte en léchant,

It with a flourish as a hero does a cestus:
From below one thinks that it's a dawn that's breaking.

What is it that he's saying with his deep
And tender voice that marries the bright cracking of
The fire and that the moon hears rapturously?
"Oh! I will be the one who will create God!

"We have all suffered too much, angels and men,
"From this conflict between the Worst and the Best. Let us now,
"Wretched creatures that we are, humble all
"Our enthusiasms in the simplest of vows.

"Why this stubborn schism, ô all of you,
"O all of us, ô sorrowful sinners, ô cheerful
"Saints? Why haven't we made, as skillful
"Artists, from our labors the same and single virtue!

"Enough and too much of these too equal struggles!
"At last the Seven Sins will have to reunite
"With the Three Theological Virtues! Enough
"And too much of these hard and ugly fights!

"And to answer Jesus who believed that he did well
"By maintaining the equilibrium of
"This duel, through me now hell
"Whose lair is here sacrifices itself to universal Love!"

The torch tumbles from his outspread hand,
And then the fire, while mounting, dinned,
An enormous wrangling of red eagles drowned
In the black eddy of the smoke and of the wind.

The gold melts and flows in waves and the marble
Flashes; it's a brazier all splendor and all ardor;
Like wadding, the silk in fleeting shudders
Flies in tufts, all ardent and all splendor.

And the dying Satans were singing in the flames,
Having understood, since they had resigned themselves!
And beautiful choirs of men's and women's voices
Were rising amid the storm of the igneous noises.

And he, with his arms crossed in a haughty air,
With his eyes on the sky where the licking fire climbs along,

Il dit tout bas une espèce de prière,
Qui va mourir dans l'allégresse du chant.

Il dit tout bas une espèce de prière,
Les yeux au ciel où le feu monte en léchant . . .
Quand retentit un affreux coup de tonnerre,
Et c'est la fin de l'allégresse et du chant.

On n'avait pas agréé le sacrifice:
Quelqu'un de fort et de juste assurément
Sans peine avait su démêler la malice
Et l'artifice en un orgueil qui se ment.

Et du palais aux cent tours aucun vestige,
Rien ne resta dans ce désastre inouï,
Afin que par le plus effrayant prodige
Ceci ne fût qu'un vain rêve évanoui . . .

Et c'est la nuit, la nuit bleue aux mille étoiles;
Une campagne évangélique s'étend,
Sévère et douce, et, vagues comme des voiles,
Les branches d'arbre ont l'air d'ailes s'agitant.

De froids ruisseaux courent sur un lit de pierre;
Les doux hiboux nagent vaguement dans l'air
Tout embaumé de mystère et de prière;
Parfois un flot qui saute lance un éclair.

La forme molle au loin monte des collines
Comme un amour encore mal défini,
Et le brouillard qui s'essore des ravines
Semble un effort vers quelque but réuni.

Et tout cela comme un coeur et comme une âme,
Et comme un verbe, et d'un amour virginal,
Adore, s'ouvre en une extase et réclame
Le Dieu clément qui nous gardera du mal.

He recites in a whisper a kind of prayer,
That will die in the gaiety of the song.

He recites in a whisper a kind of prayer,
With his eyes on the sky where the licking fire climbs along . . .
When a frightful clap of thunder reverberates there,
And that is the end of the gaiety and the song.

Someone had not accepted the sacrifice:
Someone powerful and just assuredly
Had known how to discern the malice easily
And the artifice in a pride that disguises itself.

And of the hundred-towered palace no trace to be seen,
Not a thing remained in this unparalleled calamity,
So that for the most terrifying prodigy
This was but a vain and vanished dream . . .

And it is night, blue night with a thousand stars;
An evangelical plain stretches out,
Severe and peaceful, and, vague like veils,
The tree branches look like wings waving about.

Over a bed of stone cold brooks are gliding;
The gentle owls float vaguely in the air
Quite embalmed with mystery and with prayer;
At times a wave that leaps hurls a flash of lightning.

The soft shape in the distance mounts from the hills
Like a love defined unclearly still,
And the mists that from the ravines ascend
Seem an effort towards some reconciled end.

And all that like a heart and like a soul,
And like a word, and with a virginal love,
Adores, expands in an ecstasy and beseeches
The merciful God who will keep us from evil.

Mallarmé (photograph by Félix Nadar)

MALLARMÉ

SALUT

Rien, cette écume, vierge vers
A ne désigner que la coupe;
Telle loin se noie une troupe
De sirènes mainte à l'envers.

Nous naviguons, ô mes divers
Amis, moi déjà sur la poupe
Vous l'avant fastueux qui coupe
Le flot de foudres et d'hivers;

Une ivresse belle m'engage
Sans craindre même son tangage
De porter debout ce salut

Solitude, récif, étoile
A n'importe ce qui valut
Le blanc souci de notre toile.

SALUTATION*

Nothing, this foam, virgin verse
To designate the cup only;
Thus a troop of sirens drowns in the distance
Many a one inversely.

We are sailing, ô my friends diverse,
On the stern already am I
You the sumptuous bow that traverses
Through the wave of winters and of lightnings;

A beautiful intoxication
Urges me without even fearing
Its pitching to bear standing up this salutation

Solitude, rocky reef, star
To whatever was worth
The white care of our sail cloth.

---

* Mallarmé was asked in January 1893 to give a toast at a banquet of young writers. "Salut" is that toast—his greeting which, as its Latin etymology suggests (*salus, salutis*), is also concerned with the poet's "salvation." Throughout, Mallarmé mingles images of a sea voyage with figures of versification, intoxication and salvation. See, for example, his puns on forms of the word "verse."

APPARITION

La lune s'attristait. Des séraphins en pleurs
Rêvant, l'archet aux doigts, dans le calme des fleurs
Vaporeuses, tiraient de mourantes violes
De blancs sanglots glissant sur l'azur des corolles.
—C'était le jour béni de ton premier baiser.
Ma songerie aimant à me martyriser
S'enivrait savamment du parfum de tristesse
Que même sans regret et sans déboire laisse
La cueillaison d'un Rêve au coeur qui l'a cueilli.
J'errais donc, l'oeil rivé sur le pavé vieilli
Quand avec du soleil aux cheveux, dans la rue
Et dans le soir, tu m'es en riant apparue
Et j'ai cru voir la fée au chapeau de clarté
Qui jadis sur mes beaux sommeils d'enfant gâté
Passait, laissant toujours de ses mains mal fermées
Neiger de blancs bouquets d'étoiles parfumées.

APPARITION

The moon grew sorrowful. Seraphim dreaming in tears,
With fiddle bows in their fingers,
In the calm of vaporous flowers, drew from dying violas
White sobs gliding over the azure of the corollas.
—It was the blessèd day of your first kiss. My dreaming
Fond of martyrizing me
Became drunk with the scent of sadness knowingly
That even without regret or aftertaste the culling of a Dream
Leaves in the heart that has culled it. And so
I was roaming, with my eye fixed on the agèd road
When with sunlight in your hair, on the street
And in the evening, laughing you appeared to me
And I thought I saw the fairy wearing the hat of light who in former
Times would pass over my beautiful slumbers
Of a spoiled child, always letting from her hands left ajar
Snow white bouquets of scented stars.

LE PITRE CHÂTIÉ

Yeux, lacs avec ma simple ivresse de renaître
Autre que l'histrion qui du geste évoquais
Comme plume la suie ignoble des quinquets,
J'ai troué dans le mur de toile une fenêtre.

De ma jambe et des bras limpide nageur traître,
A bonds multipliés, reniant le mauvais
Hamlet! c'est comme si dans l'onde j'innovais
Mille sépulcres pour y vierge disparaître.

Hilaire or de cymbale à des poings irrité,
Tout à coup le soleil frappe la nudité
Qui pure s'exhala de ma fraîcheur de nacre,

Rance nuit de la peau quand sur moi vous passiez,
Ne sachant pas, ingrat! que c'était tout mon sacre,
Ce fard noyé dans l'eau perfide des glaciers.

THE CHASTENED CLOWN

Eyes, lakes with my simple intoxication to be
Reborn other than the actor who with a gesture evoked
Like feather the ignoble soot of the filthy
Oil lamps, I have bored in the canvas wall a window.

A limpid, traitorous swimmer, with multiplied bounds
Of my leg and arms, forswearing
The bad Hamlet! it's as though I innovated a thousand
Sepulchers in the wave to vanish virgin there.

Hilarious gold of a cymbal irritated
By fists, all at once the sun strikes the nudity
That pure was exhaled from my freshness of nacre,

Rancid night of the skin when you passed over me,
Not knowing, ingrate! that that was all my consecration,
That paint drowned in the perfidious water of the glaciers.

BRISE MARINE

La chair est triste, hélas! et j'ai lu tous les livres.
Fuir! là-bas fuir! Je sens que des oiseaux sont ivres
D'être parmi l'écume inconnue et les cieux!
Rien, ni les vieux jardins reflétés par les yeux
Ne retiendra ce coeur qui dans la mer se trempe
O nuits! ni la clarté déserte de ma lampe
Sur le vide papier que la blancheur défend
Et ni la jeune femme allaitant son enfant.
Je partirai! Steamer balançant ta mâture,
Lève l'ancre pour une exotique nature!

Un Ennui, désolé par les cruels espoirs,
Croit encore à l'adieu suprême des mouchoirs!
Et, peut-être, les mâts, invitant les orages
Sont-ils de ceux qu'un vent penche sur les naufrages
Perdus, sans mâts, sans mâts, ni fertiles îlots . . .
Mais, ô mon coeur, entends le chant des matelots!

SEA BREEZE

The flesh is sad, alas! and I have read all the books. To flee!
Over there to flee! I feel birds are drunk with being
Amid the unknown foam and the skies!
Nothing, not the old gardens reflected in eyes
Will hold back this heart that steeps itself in the sea, O nights!
Not my lamp's deserted brightness
On the blank paper defended/forbidden by its whiteness
And not the young wife nursing her child at her breast.
I will depart! Steamer swaying your masts and spars,
Weigh anchor for an exotic nature!

An Ennui, tormented by cruel hopes, still believes
In the supreme farewell of handkerchiefs!
And, perhaps, the masts, inviting tempests
Are the kind which a wind bends over lost shipwrecks,
Without masts, without masts, or fertile islets . . .
But, ô my heart, to the sailors' singing, listen!

DON DU POÈME

Je t'apporte l'enfant d'une nuit d'Idumée!
Noire, à l'aile saignante et pâle, déplumée,
Par le verre brûlé d'aromates et d'or,
Par les carreaux glacés, hélas! mornes encor,
L'aurore se jeta sur la lampe angélique.
Palmes! et quand elle a montré cette relique
A ce père essayant un sourire ennemi,
La solitude bleue et stérile a frémi.
O la berceuse, avec ta fille et l'innocence
De vos pieds froids, accueille une horrible naissance:
Et ta voix rappelant viole et clavecin,
Avec le doigt fané presseras-tu le sein
Par qui coule en blancheur sibylline la femme
Pour les lèvres que l'air du vierge azure affame?

GIFT OF THE POEM

I bring you the child of a night of Idumaea!
Black, and plucked, with a pallid, bleeding
Wing, through the glass burnt with aromatics and with gold,
Through the panes still mournful, alas! and frozen cold,
Dawn threw herself upon the angelic
Lamp. Palm branches! and when she showed this relic
To this father attempting
A hostile smile, the blue and sterile solitude trembled.
With your daughter and the innocence of your chilled feet
And hers, O cradler, a horrible birth now greet:
And your voice recalling viol and harpsichord, will you press
With your faded finger the breast
Through which flows in sibylline whiteness the woman for
The lips starving for the air of the virgin azure?

L'APRÈS-MIDI D'UN FAUNE

Églogue

LE FAUNE

Ces nymphes, je les veux perpétuer.
                                        Si clair,
Leur incarnat léger, qu'il voltige dans l'air
Assoupi de sommeils touffus.

                                Aimai-je un rêve?
Mon doute, amas de nuit ancienne, s'achève
En maint rameau subtil, qui, demeuré les vrais
Bois mêmes, prouve, hélas! que bien seul je m'offrais
Pour triomphe la faute idéale de roses.
Réfléchissons . . .

                        ou si les femmes dont tu gloses
Figurent un souhait de tes sens fabuleux!
Faune, l'illusion s'échappe des yeux bleus
Et froids, comme une source en pleurs de la plus chaste:
Mais, l'autre tout soupirs, dis-tu qu'elle contraste
Comme brise du jour chaude dans ta toison?
Que non! par l'immobile et lasse pâmoison
Suffoquant de chaleurs le matin frais s'il lutte,
Ne murmure point d'eau que ne verse ma flûte
Au bosquet arrosé d'accords; et le seul vent
Hors des deux tuyaux prompt à s'exhaler avant
Qu'il disperse le son dans une pluie aride,
C'est, à l'horizon pas remué d'une ride,
Le visible et serein souffle artificiel
De l'inspiration, qui regagne le ciel.

O bords siciliens d'un calme marécage
Qu'à l'envi de soleils ma vanité saccage,
Tacite sous les fleurs d'étincelles, CONTEZ
« *Que je coupais ici les creux roseaux domptés*
» *Par le talent; quand, sur l'or glauque de lointaines*
» *Verdures dédiant leur vigne à des fontaines,*
» *Ondoie une blancheur animale au repos:*
» *Et qu'au prélude lent où naissent les pipeaux*

A FAUN'S AFTERNOON

Eclogue

THE FAUN

These nymphs, these I want to perpetuate.
                              So clear,
Their light flesh color, that it hovers in the air
Made drowsy with tufted sleeps.

                    Did I love a dream?
My doubt, a heap of ancient night, completes
Itself in many a subtle branch, which, having stayed
The real woods, proves, alas! that all alone I gave
Myself as a triumph the ideal lack of roses.
Let us reflect . . .

                    or if the women your thought glozes
Figure a wish of your fabulous senses! There flies
Away illusion from the cold, blue eyes
Or the more chaste nymph, like a weeping spring, Faun:
But, the other all sighs, do you think she forms
A contrast like the day's warm breeze in your fleece?
Surely not! through the immobile, weary swoon suffocating with
    heats
The cool morning if it struggles, no water
Murmurs that is not poured forth
By my flute on the thicket sprinkled with harmonies;
And the only wind outside of the two reeds
Prompt to be exhaled before in an arid rain it spreads
Forth sound, is, on the horizon where no wrinkle moves by,
The visible and serene artificial breath
Of inspiration, which regains the sky.

O shores of a quiet marsh in Sicily
That vying with suns my vanity
Ransacks, tacit beneath the flowers of sparkles, TELL
"That here I was cutting the hollow reeds that talent quelled;
When, on the glaucous gold of far off verdures dedicating
Their vines to fountains, there undulates
An animal whiteness at repose:
And that at the slow prelude where those

» Ce vol de cygnes, non! de naïades se sauve
» Ou plonge . . . »

        Inerte, tout brûle dans l'heure fauve
Sans marquer par quel art ensemble détala
Trop d'hymen souhaité de qui cherche le *la*:
Alors m'éveillerai-je à la ferveur première,
Droit et seul, sous un flot antique de lumière,
Lys! et l'un de vous tous pour l'ingénuité.

Autre que ce doux rien par leur lèvre ébruité,
Le baiser, qui tout bas des perfides assure,
Mon sein, vierge de preuve, atteste une morsure
Mystérieuse, due à quelque auguste dent;
Mais, bast! arcane tel élut pour confident
Le jonc vaste et jumeau dont sous l'azur on joue:
Qui, détournant à soi le trouble de la joue,
Rêve, dans un solo long, que nous amusions
La beauté d'alentour par des confusions
Fausses entre elle-même et notre chant crédule;
Et de faire aussi haut que l'amour se module
Évanouir du songe ordinaire de dos
Ou de flanc pur suivis avec mes regards clos,
Une sonore, vaine et monotone ligne.

Tâche donc, instrument des fuites, ô maligne
Syrinx, de refleurir aux lacs où tu m'attends!
Moi, de ma rumeur fier, je vais parler longtemps
Des déesses; et par d'idolâtres peintures,
A leur ombre enlever encore des ceintures:
Ainsi, quand des raisins j'ai sucé la clarté,
Pour bannir un regret par ma feinte écarté,
Rieur, j'élève au ciel d'été la grappe vide
Et, soufflant dans ses peaux lumineuses, avide
D'ivresse, jusqu'au soir je regarde au travers.

O nymphes, regonflons des SOUVENIRS divers.
« Mon oeil, trouant les joncs, dardait chaque encolure
» Immortelle, qui noie en l'onde sa brûlure
» Avec un cri de rage au ciel de la forêt;
» Et le splendide bain de cheveux disparaît
» Dans les clartés et les frissons, ô pierreries!

Reed pipes are born this flock of swans, no! of naïads flees
Or plunges . . ."

                      Inert, all burns in the tawny
Hour without marking by what art at the same time ran away
Too much marriage desired by him who seeks the note *A*:
Then will I awaken to the pristine fervor, upright
And alone, beneath an ancient wave of light,
A lily! and one of all you lilies for ingenuousness.

Different from that sweet nothing made known by their lips, the kiss,
Which in a whisper assures me of the perfidious girls, my breast,
Of proof virgin, a mysterious bite attests,
Owed to some august tooth; but, I shan't
Say more! such a secret chose for its confidant
The vast twin rush on which one plays beneath the blueness:
Which rush, turning to itself the cheek's distress,
Dreams, in a lengthy solo, that we were amusing
The surrounding beauty by false confusions
Between itself and our credulous song; and of making
Just as high as love modulates
Itself vanish from the ordinary dream of a back
Or pure flank that my closed glances track,
A sonorous, vain and monotonous line.

Go try, instrument of flights, ô malign
Syrinx, to flower again on the lakes where you wait for me!
I, proud of my clamor, will speak lengthily
Of the goddesses; and through idolatrous paintings,
In their shadow I'll carry their girdles away
Again: Just as, when from the grapes I've sucked the clearness,
To banish a regret brushed aside by my artifice,
Laughing, I raise to the summer sky the empty
Bunch and, blowing into its luminous skins, greedy
For intoxication, till evening I look through them.

O nymphs, let's inflate diverse MEMORIES again.
"My eye, piercing holes in the rushes, speared each immortal nape,
That drowns in the wave its burning with a cry of rage
To the forest's sky; and the splendid bath of hair
Disappears in lights and shivers, ô gems! I run up there;

» J'accours; quand, à mes pieds, s'entrejoignent (meurtries
» De la langueur goûtée à ce mal d'être deux)
» Des dormeuses parmi leurs seuls bras hasardeux;
» Je les ravis, sans les désenlacer, et vole
»A ce massif, haï par l'ombrage frivole,
» De roses tarissant tout parfum au soleil,
» Où notre ébat au jour consumé soit pareil. »
Je t'adore, courroux des vierges, ô délice
Farouche du sacré fardeau nu qui se glisse
Pour fuir ma lèvre en feu buvant, comme un éclair
Tressaille! la frayeur secrète de la chair:
Des pieds de l'inhumaine au coeur de la timide
Que délaisse à la fois une innocence, humide
De larmes folles ou de moins tristes vapeurs.
« Mon crime, c'est d'avoir, gai de vaincre ces peurs
»Traîtresses, divisé la touffe échevelée
»De baisers que les dieux gardaient si bien mêlée:
» Car, à peine j'allais cacher un rire ardent
» Sous les replis heureux d'une seule (gardant
» Par un doigt simple, afin que sa candeur de plume
»Se teignît à l'émoi de sa soeur qui s'allume,
»La petite, naïve et ne rougissant pas:)
»Que de mes bras, défaits par de vagues trépas,
» Cette proie, à jamais ingrate se délivre
»Sans pitié du sanglot dont j'étais encore ivre. »

Tant pis! vers le bonheur d'autres m'entraîneront
Par leur tresse nouée aux cornes de mon front:
Tu sais, ma passion, que, pourpre et déjà mûre,
Chaque grenade éclate et d'abeilles murmure;
Et notre sang, épris de qui le va saisir,
Coule pour tout l'essaim éternel du désir.
A l'heure où ce bois d'or et de cendres se teinte
Une fête s'exalte en la feuillée éteinte:
Etna! c'est parmi toi visité de Vénus
Sur ta lave posant ses talons ingénus,
Quand tonne un somme triste ou s'épuise la flamme.
Je tiens la reine!

                O sûr châtiment . . .

                                Non, mais l'âme

When at my feet, interjoin (bruised by the languor tasted
From that pain of being two) the sleeping nymphs amid
Just their hazardous arms; I carry them away,
Without disentangling them, and fly to that clump, hated
By the frivolous shade, of roses drying up all perfume
In the sun, where our frolic may be like the day consumed."
I adore you, wrath of virgins, ô fierce delight of the sacred
Naked burden that slips away
To flee from my lip on fire drinking, like a flash
Of lightning trembling! the secret terror of the flesh:
From the feet of the inhuman nymph to the heart
Of the timid one from whom at the same time an innocence departs,
Humid with mad tears or with vapors less sorrowful.
"My crime, it is to have divided, gleeful
To conquer those treacherous fears, the dishevelled
Tuft of kisses that the gods kept so well mingled:
For, an ardent laugh I was scarcely going to hide
Beneath the happy creases of one nymph (keeping by
Just a simple finger, so that her whiteness of feather
Might color at the emotion of her sister
Becoming inflamed, the small nymph, naïve and not blushing:)
When from my arms, undone by vague deaths, goes rushing
That forever ungrateful prey, which frees itself without pity
For the sob that was still intoxicating me."

Never mind! towards happiness others will carry me
By their tresses tied to the horns of my forehead:
You know, my passion, that, purple and ripe already,
Each pomegranate bursts and murmurs with bees;
And our blood, in love with what is going to seize
It, flows for all the eternal swarm of desire. At the hour
When this wood is tinged with gold and ashes a festivity
Is exalted in the extinguished bower:
Etna! it's amid you visited by Venus
Placing upon your lava her ingenuous
Heels, when thunders a sorrowful nap or the flame exhausts its glow.
I hold the queen!

O certain punishment . . .

No,

De paroles vacante et ce corps alourdi
Tard succombent au fier silence de midi:
Sans plus il faut dormir en l'oubli du blasphème,
Sur le sable altéré gisant et comme j'aime
Ouvrir ma bouche à l'astre efficace des vins!

Couple, adieu; je vais voir l'ombre que tu devins.

But the soul empty of words and this heavy body
Succumb to noon's proud silence tardily:
Without more ado one must sleep in oblivion of
The blasphemy on the thirsty sand lying down and how I love
To open my mouth to the star that makes wines effectively!*

Adieu, couple; I'll visit the shade that you came to be.

* The French "efficace" (effective and/or efficacious) derives from the Latin *efficio, efficere, effeci, effectum*, meaning to do, to produce, to effect, to make.

LA CHEVELURE . . .

La chevelure vol d'une flamme à l'extrême
Occident de désirs pour la tout déployer
Se pose (je dirais mourir un diadème)
Vers le front couronné son ancien foyer

Mais sans or soupirer que cette vive nue
L'ignition du feu toujours intérieur
Originellement la seule continue
Dans le joyau de l'oeil véridique ou rieur

Une nudité de héros tendre diffame
Celle qui ne mouvant astre ni feux au doigt
Rien qu'à simplifier avec gloire la femme
Accomplit par son chef fulgurante l'exploit

De semer de rubis le doute qu'elle écorche
Ainsi qu'une joyeuse et tutélaire torche.

THE HAIR . . .

The hair flight of a flame at the far West
Of desires to unfurl it all comes to rest
(I should say to die a diadem)
Toward the crowned forehead its ancient fireside

But without gold sighing that this cloud alive
The ignition of the always inner
Fire originally the sole one may continue in
The jewel of the truthful or laughing eye

A nudity of a tender hero defames her
Who moving no star nor fires on her finger
Only to simplify with glory the woman achieves
By her head as she fulgurates the remarkable deed

Of sowing with ruby the doubt that she grazes or
Peels off just like a joyous and tutelary torch.

SAINTE

A la fenêtre recelant
Le santal vieux qui se dédore
De sa viole étincelant
Jadis avec flûte ou mandore,

Est la Sainte pâle, étalant
Le livre vieux qui se déplie
Du Magnificat ruisselant
Jadis selon vêpre et complie:

A ce vitrage d'ostensoir
Que frôle une harpe par l'Ange
Formée avec son vol du soir
Pour la délicate phalange

Du doigt que, sans le vieux santal
Ni le vieux livre, elle balance
Sur le plumage instrumental,
Musicienne du silence.

SAINT*

At the window containing/concealing
The old santal whose gilt is peeling
From her viol glittering in
The past with flute or mandolin,**

Is the pallid Saint, exposing
For view the old book that is unfolding
Some of the Magnificat streaming in
The past according to vespers and compline:

At this monstrance of stained glass
That a harp is brushing lightly past
Created by the Angel thanks
To his evening flight toward the delicate phalanx

Of her finger that, with neither
The old book nor the old santal,
She balances on the instrumental
Plumage, she the musician of silence.

* Mallarmé's first title for this poem was "Saint Cecelia Playing on a Cherub's Wing." Saint Cecelia, a martyr, is the patron saint of music.
** *Une mandore* is a large mandolin that was used until the 18th century.

PROSE

pour des Esseintes

Hyperbole! de ma mémoire
Triomphalement ne sais-tu
Te lever, aujourd'hui grimoire
Dans un livre de fer vêtu:

Car j'installe, par la science,
L'hymne des coeurs spirituels
En l'oeuvre de ma patience,
Atlas, herbiers et rituels.

Nous promenions notre visage
(Nous fûmes deux, je le maintiens)
Sur maints charmes de paysage,
O soeur, y comparant les tiens.

L'ère d'autorité se trouble
Lorsque, sans nul motif, on dit
De ce midi que notre double
Inconscience approfondit

Que, sol des cent iris, son site,
Ils savent s'il a bien été,
Ne porte pas de nom que cite
L'or de la trompette d'Été.

Oui, dans une île que l'air charge
De vue et non de visions
Toute fleur s'étalait plus large
Sans que nous en devisions.

Telles, immenses, que chacune
Ordinairement se para

PROSE

*for des Esseintes**

Hyperbole! from my memory
Can't you arise triumphantly,
A gramarye today
In a book in iron arrayed:

For I install, through science,
The hymn of hearts that are spiritual
In the work of my patience,
Atlases, herbals and rituals.

We were letting our gaze explore
(We were two, this I maintain)
The many charms of the landscape,
O sister, comparing theirs with yours.

The age of authority is troubled
When, with no motive, one relates
About this noon that our double
Unconsciousness investigates

That, soil of the hundred irises,
They know if it really did exist,
No name is borne by this site
That the gold of Summer's trumpet cites.

Yes, on an island that the air fills
With view and not with visions
Each flower stretched out more amply without
Our chatting about it.

Such flowers, immense,
That each one adorned itself usually

* Des Esseintes is the protagonist of Joris-Karl Huysmans's novel *A rebours* (*Against the Grain*), which helped introduce Mallarmé to the public in 1884. Des Esseintes is a symbolist or decadent aesthete who likes to read Mallarmé. The word "Prose" may have its liturgical meaning—a hymn sung in the Eucharistic service, originating from a practice of setting words to the jubilatio of the alleluia. Mallarmé's poem would then be a sort of hymn to celebrate the transubstantiation of the poet's word into the Word. Or "Prose" may be ironic, for the poem is anything but an example of commonplace or dull expression, the ordinary form of spoken or written language. This "prose" is meant only for initiated readers: for des Esseintes and for others who enjoy the art of Mallarmé, the religious experience of his poetry.

D'un lucide contour, lacune,
Qui des jardins la sépara.

Gloire du long désir, Idées
Tout en moi s'exaltait de voir
La famille des iridées
Surgir à ce nouveau devoir,

Mais cette soeur sensée et tendre
Ne porta son regard plus loin
Que sourire et, comme à l'entendre
J'occupe mon antique soin.

Oh! sache l'Esprit de litige,
A cette heure où nous nous taisons,
Que de lis multiples la tige
Grandissait trop pour nos raisons

Et non comme pleure la rive,
Quand son jeu monotone ment
A vouloir que l'ampleur arrive
Parmi mon jeune étonnement

D'ouïr tout le ciel et la carte
Sans fin attestés sur mes pas,
Par le flot même qui s'écarte,
Que ce pays n'exista pas.

L'enfant abdique son extase
Et docte déjà par chemins
Elle dit le mot: Anastase!
Né pour d'éternels parchemins,

Avant qu'un sépulcre ne rie
Sous aucun climat, son aïeul,
De porter ce nom: Pulchérie!
Caché par le trop grand glaïeul.

With a lucid contour, lacuna
That separated it from the gardens.

Glory of long desire, Ideas
All in me became exalted to see
The family of irideas**
Rise to this new duty,

But that sensible, tender sister did not bear
Her gaze farther than a smile
And, as if to understand her
I occupy my ancient care.

Oh! Spirit of litigation know,
At this hour when we are silent,
That the stalk of multiple lilies was growing
Too much for our reasons

And not as the river bank laments,
When its monotonous game tells lies
In wishing that amplitude may arrive
Amid my young astonishment

At hearing all the map and the sky
Attested endlessly in my footsteps, by
The very wave which is
Withdrawing, that this land did not exist.

The child abdicates her ecstasy
And learnèd already by pathways worn
She says the word: Anastase!***
For eternal parchments born,

Before a sepulcher can laugh beneath
Any climate, its ancestor,
At bearing this name: Pulchérie!****
By the too large gladiolus concealed.

** Mallarmé invented the word "iridées," which combines elements of iridescence and ideas, to describe a type of ideal flower.
*** Anastase derives from the Greek *Anastasios*, meaning "Of the resurrection."
**** Pulchérie derives from the Latin *pulcher*, meaning "beautiful."

ÉVENTAIL

de Madame Mallarmé

Avec comme pour langage
Rien qu'un battement aux cieux
Le futur vers se dégage
Du logis très précieux

Aile tout bas la courrière
Cet éventail si c'est lui
Le même par qui derrière
Toi quelque miroir a lui

Limpide (où va redescendre
Pourchassée en chaque grain
Un peu d'invisible cendre
Seule à me rendre chagrin)

Toujours tel il apparaisse
Entre tes mains sans paresse.

FAN

of Madame Mallarmé

With as for language nothing but
A flutter
To the skies the future verse frees itself
From the very precious dwelling

With its wing very low
The messenger this fan if it is
The same by means of which
Behind you some mirror shone

Limpid (where will
Come down again pursued in each gust of wind
A bit of invisible
Ash alone to make me chagrined)

Thus may it appear for times limitless
Between your hands without idleness.

AUTRE ÉVENTAIL

de Mademoiselle Mallarmé

O rêveuse, pour que je plonge
Au pur délice sans chemin,
Sache, par un subtil mensonge,
Garder mon aile dans ta main.

Une fraîcheur de crépuscule
Te vient à chaque battement
Dont le coup prisonnier recule
L'horizon délicatement.

Vertige! voici que frissonne
L'espace comme un grand baiser
Qui, fou de naître pour personne,
Ne peut jaillir ni s'apaiser.

Sens-tu le paradis farouche
Ainsi qu'un rire enseveli
Se couler du coin de ta bouche
Au fond de l'unanime pli!

Le sceptre des rivages roses
Stagnants sur les soirs d'or, ce l'est,
Ce blanc vol fermé que tu poses
Contre le feu d'un bracelet.

ANOTHER FAN

of Mademoiselle Mallarmé

O dreamer, in order that I may dive
Into pure delight by no path spanned,
Know how, by means of a subtle lie,
To keep my wing within your hand.

A twilight freshness comes
To you at every flutter
Whose stroke held in captivity
Moves back the horizon delicately.

Dizziness! behold how space
Is shivering like a great kiss that, crazed
About being born for no one, can neither
Gush forth nor be appeased.

Do you feel the fierce paradise like shrouded
Laughter flow
From the corner of your mouth
To the bottom of the unanimous fold!

The scepter this is of shores rose-hued
Stagnant over evenings with gold imbued,
This closed white flight and you now place it
Against the fire of a bracelet.

PETIT AIR

Quelconque une solitude
Sans le cygne ni le quai
Mire sa désuétude
Au regard que j'abdiquai

Ici de la gloriole
Haute à ne la pas toucher
Dont maint ciel se bariole
Avec les ors du coucher

Mais langoureusement longe
Comme de blanc linge ôté
Tel fugace oiseau si plonge
Exultatrice à côté

Dans l'onde toi devenue
Ta jubilation nue.

LITTLE TUNE

I

Some place or other isolated
Without the swan nor the quay
Looks at its own disuse in the gaze
That I abdicated

Here from the vainglory
Too high to touch
In which many a sky paints itself gaudily
With the golds of the setting sun

But languorously goes along
Like white linen taken off
Such a fleeting bird if dives
Exultantly nearby

In the wave become your incarnation
Your naked jubilation.

PLUSIEURS SONNETS

I

Quand l'ombre menaça de la fatale loi
Tel vieux Rêve, désir et mal de mes vertèbres,
Affligé de périr sous les plafonds funèbres
Il a ployé son aile indubitable en moi.

Luxe, ô salle d'ébène où, pour séduire un roi
Se tordent dans leur mort des guirlandes célèbres,
Vous n'êtes qu'un orgueil menti par les ténèbres
Aux yeux du solitaire ébloui de sa foi.

Oui, je sais qu'au lointain de cette nuit, la Terre
Jette d'un grand éclat l'insolite mystère,
Sous les siècles hideux qui l'obscurcissent moins.

L'espace à soi pareil qu'il s'accroisse ou se nie
Roule dans cet ennui des feux vils pour témoins
Que s'est d'un astre en fête allumé le génie.

II

Le vierge, le vivace et le bel aujourd'hui
Va-t-il nous déchirer avec un coup d'aile ivre
Ce lac dur oublié que hante sous le givre
Le transparent glacier des vols qui n'ont pas fui!

Un cygne d'autrefois se souvient que c'est lui
Magnifique mais qui sans espoir se délivre
Pour n'avoir pas chanté la région où vivre
Quand du stérile hiver a resplendi l'ennui.

Tout son col secouera cette blanche agonie
Par l'espace infligé à l'oiseau qui le nie,
Mais non l'horreur du sol où le plumage est pris.

Fantôme qu'à ce lieu son pur éclat assigne,
Il s'immobilise au songe froid de mépris
Que vêt parmi l'exil inutile le Cygne.

III

Victorieusement fui le suicide beau
Tison de gloire, sang par écume, or, tempête!

SEVERAL SONNETS

I

When the shadow menaced with its fatal law a certain old Dream,
Desire and disease of my vertebrae,
Pained at perishing beneath funereal ceilings
The Dream folded up its indubitable wing in me.

Luxury, ô hall of ebony, where to charm
A king some famous garlands twist in their deaths,
You are only a pride belied by the darkness
In the eyes of the solitary man dazzled with his faith.

I know that in this night's background, yes,
The Earth emits the unusual mystery of a great brightness,
Beneath the hideous centuries that obscure it less.

Space alike itself whether it increases or denies
Itself revolves in that ennui some vile fires as witnesses
That the genius of a festive star has lit.

II

Will the virgin, hardy and beautiful present time
With one stroke of an intoxicated wing tear free
For us this hard, forgotten lake haunted under the rime
By the transparent glacier of flights that did not flee!

A swan of old remembers that it is he
Magnificent but who without hope sets himself free
For not having sung the region in which to live when the ennui
Of sterile winter glittered resplendently.

All his neck will shake off this white death agony
By space inflicted on the bird who denies
It, but not the horror of the ground where the trapped plumage lies.

Phantom assigned to this place by his pure radiancy,
He immobilizes himself in the cold dream of scorn put on
Amid his useless exile by the Swan.

III

Victoriously the beautiful suicide fled
Firebrand of glory, blood through foam, gold, tempest!

O'rire si là-bas une pourpre s'apprête
A ne tendre royal que mon absent tombeau.

Quoi! de tout cet éclat pas même le lambeau
S'attarde, il est minuit, à l'ombre qui nous fête
Excepté qu'un trésor présomptueux de tête
Verse son caressé nonchaloir sans flambeau,

La tienne si toujours le délice! la tienne
Oui seule qui du ciel évanoui retienne
Un peu de puéril triomphe en t'en coiffant

Avec clarté quand sur les coussins tu la poses
Comme un casque guerrier d'impératrice enfant
Dont pour te figurer il tomberait des roses.

IV

Ses purs ongles très haut dédiant leur onyx,
L'Angoisse, ce minuit, soutient, lampadophore,
Maint rêve vespéral brûlé par le Phénix
Que ne recueille pas de cinéraire amphore

Sur les crédences, au salon vide: nul ptyx,
Aboli bibelot d'inanité sonore,
(Car le Maître est allé puiser des pleurs au Styx
Avec ce seul objet dont le Néant s'honore).

Mais proche la croisée au nord vacante, un or
Agonise selon peut-être le décor
Des licornes ruant du feu contre une nixe,

Elle, défunte nue en le miroir, encor
Que, dans l'oubli fermé par le cadre, se fixe
De scintillations sitôt le septuor.

O laugh if over there a purple is getting ready
But my royal absent tomb to spread!

What! of all that brightness not even a shred
Now lingers, it is midnight, in the shadow that entertains
Us except a presumptuous treasure of a head
Pours out its caressed nonchalance without flames,

Your head yes ever the delight! yours yes
Alone that from the vanished sky may withhold
A bit of puerile triumph by dressing

Your hair in it with light when on the cushions you repose
Your head like a martial helmet of a child empress
From which to image you there would tumble roses.

IV

Her pure nails consecrating on high their onyx,
Anguish, this midnight, torchbearer, supports
Many a vespertine dream burned by the Phoenix
That no cinerary amphora stores

On the sideboards, in the empty parlor: no ptyx,*
Abolished bibelot of sonorous inanity,
(For the Master has gone to draw tears from the Styx
With this sole object honored by Nihility.)

But near the vacant casement in the north,
A gold is dying perhaps according to the décor
Of unicorns flinging fire at a nixie,

She, deceased nude in the mirror, even though, inset
In the oblivion enclosed by the frame, there fixes
Itself with scintillations at once the septet.

---

* For some thoughts about the word "ptyx," see the introduction, p. 8.

LE TOMBEAU D'EDGAR POE

Tel qu'en Lui-même enfin l'éternité le change,
Le Poète suscite avec un glaive nu
Son siècle épouvanté de n'avoir pas connu
Que la mort triomphait dans cette voix étrange!

Eux, comme un vil sursaut d'hydre oyant jadis l'ange
Donner un sens plus pur aux mots de la tribu
Proclamèrent très haut le sortilège bu
Dans le flot sans honneur de quelque noir mélange.

Du sol et de la nue hostiles, ô grief!
Si notre idée avec ne sculpte un bas-relief
Dont la tombe de Poe éblouissante s'orne,

Calme bloc ici-bas chu d'un désastre obscur,
Que ce granit du moins montre à jamais sa borne
Aux noirs vols du Blasphème épars dans le futur.

EDGAR POE'S TOMB

Such as into Himself eternity changes him finally,
The Poet rouses with a naked sword his century terrified
At not having recognized
That in that strange voice death reigned triumphantly.

They, like a vile start of a hydra hearing of yore
The angel give a purer meaning to the words of the tribe
Proclaimed on high the sortilege imbibed
In the dishonorable wave of some black mixture.

Of the hostile earth and the cloud, ô grievance!
If our idea with it does not sculpt a bas-relief
With which Poe's dazzling tomb may be adorned,

Calm block fallen here below from an obscure
Disaster, let this granite at least show forever its boundary to
The black flights of Blasphemy dispersed into the future.

LE TOMBEAU DE CHARLES BAUDELAIRE

Le temple enseveli divulgue par la bouche
Sépulcrale d'égout bavant boue et rubis
Abominablement quelque idole Anubis
Tout le museau flambé comme un aboi farouche

Ou que le gaz récent torde la mèche louche
Essuyeuse on le sait des opprobres subis
Il allume hagard un immortel pubis
Dont le vol selon le réverbère découche

Quel feuillage séché dans les cités sans soir
Votif pourra bénir comme elle se rasseoir
Contre le marbre vainement de Baudelaire

Au voile qui la ceint absente avec frissons
Celle son Ombre même un poison tutélaire
Toujours à respirer si nous en périssons.

CHARLES BAUDELAIRE'S TOMB

The shrouded temple divulges through
The sepulchral sewer mouth slobbering mud and rubies
Abominably some Anubis* idol all its muzzle blazing
Like a savage baying

Or until the recent gas should twist the squinting wick that wipes
Away you know opprobriums undergone it lights
Up haggard an immortal pubis whose flight
According to the street lamp sleeps away from home all night

What withered foliage, votive, in the cities
Without evening will be able to bless, like his Shade to sit
Down again against the marble vainly of Baudelaire

Absent in the veil that girds it with shivers,
This his Shade a tutelary poison to be inhaled
Forever if we perish from it.

---

* Anubis, the Egyptian god of tombs and embalming, was depicted with a jackal's head. He led
the dead to judgment and weighed their souls.

TOMBEAU

Anniversaire—Janvier 1897

Le noir roc courroucé que la bise le roule
Ne s'arrêtera ni sous de pieuses mains
Tâtant sa ressemblance avec les maux humains
Comme pour en bénir quelque funeste moule.

Ici presque toujours si le ramier roucoule
Cet immatériel deuil opprime de maints
Nubiles plis l'astre mûri des lendemains
Dont un scintillement argentera la foule.

Qui cherche, parcourant le solitaire bond
Tantôt extérieur de notre vagabond—
Verlaine? Il est caché parmi l'herbe, Verlaine

A ne surprendre que naïvement d'accord
La lèvre sans y boire ou tarir son haleine
Un peu profond ruisseau calomnié la mort.

TOMB

Anniversary—January 1897*

The black rock angered that the north wind rolls
It will not stop either beneath pious hands exploring
Its resemblance to human misfortunes
As if to bless in it some fatal mould.

Here almost always if the ringdove coos
This immaterial mourning oppresses with many nubile
Folds the ripened star of tomorrows of which
A scintillation will silver the multitude.

Who seeks, surveying the solitary bound
Just a while ago exterior of our vagabond—
Verlaine? He is hidden amid the grass, Verlaine

Only to surprise the lip naïvely in agreement
Without drinking from it or exhausting its breath
A shallow, calumniated rivulet death.

* Verlaine died on January 8, 1896.

Toute l'âme résumée
Quand lente nous l'expirons
Dans plusieurs ronds de fumée
Abolis en autres ronds

Atteste quelque cigare
Brûlant savamment pour peu
Que la cendre se sépare
De son clair baiser de feu

Ainsi le choeur des romances
A la lèvre vole-t-il
Exclus-en si tu commences
Le réel parce que vil

Le sens trop précis rature
Ta vague littérature.

Of the soul all things
Summed up when we exhale it slow
In several rings of smoke
Abolished in other rings

Some cigar attests to this
Burning knowingly if only
The ash parts company
From the fire's bright kiss

To the lip soars in this style
The chorus of ballads exclude therein
If you begin
The real because vile

Too precise a meaning erases your
Vague literature.

AUTRES POÈMES ET SONNETS

I

Tout Orgueil fume-t-il du soir,
Torche dans un branle étouffée
Sans que l'immortelle bouffée
Ne puisse à l'abandon surseoir!

La chambre ancienne de l'hoir
De maint riche mais chu trophée
Ne serait pas même chaufée
S'il survenait par le couloir.

Affres du passé nécessaires
Agrippant comme avec des serres
Le sépulcre de désaveu,

Sous un marbre lourd qu'elle isole
Ne s'allume pas d'autre feu
Que la fulgurante console.

II

Surgi de la croupe et du bond
D'une verrerie éphémère
Sans fleurir la veillée amère
Le col ignoré s'interrompt.

Je crois bien que deux bouches n'ont
Bu, ni son amant ni ma mère,
Jamais à la même Chimère,
Moi, sylphe de ce froid plafond!

Le pur vase d'aucun breuvage
Que l'inexhaustible veuvage
Agonise mais ne consent,

Naïf baiser des plus funèbres!
A rien expirer annonçant
Une rose dans les ténèbres.

III

Une dentelle s'abolit
Dans le doute du Jeu suprême

340

OTHER POEMS AND SONNETS

I

Does every Pride of evening smoke,
A torch that one shaking motion choked
Without the immortal puff's being competent
To suspend the abandonment.

The ancient chamber of the heir of many
A rich but fallen trophy
Would not even be warmed if he
Appeared through the corridor unexpectedly.

Necessary pangs of the past
Gripping fast
As if with talons the sepulcher of repudiation,

Under a heavy marble that the console isolates
There blazes no other conflagration
Than the console which fulgurates.

II

Risen from the rump and the bounding up
Of an ephemeral piece of glassware without decking
With flowers the bitter vigil the unknown neck
Stops abruptly.

Two mouths have never drunk, I really
Believe, not her lover nor my
Mother, from the same Chimera, myself,
A sylph of this cold ceiling.

The pure vase of no potion
But inexhaustible widowhood only
Is dying but does not agree,

Naïve kiss most funerary!
To exhale anything that announces
A rose in the darkness.

III

A lace annuls itself totally
In the supreme Game's uncertainty

A n'entr'ouvrir comme un blasphème
Qu'absence éternelle de lit.

Cet unanime blanc conflit
D'une guirlande avec la même,
Enfui contre la vitre blême
Flotte plus qu'il n'ensevelit.

Mais, chez qui du rêve se dore
Tristement dort une mandore
Au creux néant musicien

Telle que vers quelque fenêtre
Selon nul ventre que le sien,
Filial on aurait pu naître.

To half-open like a blasphemy
A bed's eternal absence only.

This conflict unanimous and white
Of a garland with the same,
Fled against the pale windowpane
Floats more than it shrouds from sight.

But, in him who gilds himself with the dream
A mandolin* sorrowfully sleeps
With its nothingness hollow and musical

Such as toward some window according
To no womb but its own womb, filial
One could have been born.

* *Une mandore*: See the note to Mallarmé's "Saint," p. 317.

A la nue accablante tu
Basse de basalte et de laves
A même les échos esclaves
Par une trompe sans vertu

Quel sépulcral naufrage (tu
Le sais, écume, mais y baves)
Suprême une entre les épaves
Abolit le mât dévêtu

Ou cela que furibond faute
De quelque perdition haute
Tout l'abîme vain éployé

Dans le si blanc cheveu qui traîne
Avarement aura noyé
Le flanc enfant d'une sirène!

Concealed from the overwhelming cloud
Sandbank of basalt and lavas
Even from the slavish echoes
By a horn without power

What a sepulchral shipwreck
(You know about it, foam, yet slobber there)
One wreckage supreme among the wrecks
Abolishes its mast stripped bare

Or this that in a raging condition
For want of some kind of high perdition
All the vain abyss spread there

In the so white thread of trailing hair
Will have drowned avariciously
The childish flank of a siren's body!

Mes bouquins refermés sur le nom de Paphos,
Il m'amuse d'élire avec le seul génie
Une ruine, par mille écumes bénie
Sous l'hyacinthe, au loin, de ses jours triomphaux.

Coure le froid avec ses silences de faux,
Je n'y hululerai pas de vide nénie
Si ce très blanc ébat au ras du sol dénie
A tout site l'honneur du paysage faux.

Ma faim qui d'aucuns fruits ici ne se régale
Trouve en leur docte manque une saveur égale:
Qu'un éclate de chair humain et parfumant!

Le pied sur quelque guivre où notre amour tisonne,
Je pense plus longtemps peut-être éperdument
A l'autre, au sein brûlé d'une antique amazone.

With my books closed again on the name of Paphos,
It amuses me to elect with nothing but genius
A ruin, by a thousand foams blest, far away,
Beneath the hyacinth of its triumphal days.

Let the cold run about with its silences of a scythe,
I will not howl any empty funeral song
To it if this very white frolic along
The ground denies the false landscape's honor to any site.

My hunger that with no fruits here regales
Itself finds in their learnèd lack an equal savor:
Let one fruit with human and perfuming flesh burst out!

Where our love pokes the fire, with my foot upon
Some wivern, I think longer perhaps madly about
The other one, about the burned breast of an ancient Amazon.

INDEX TO THE *INTRODUCTION* AND *A NOTE ON TRANSLATION*

349

INDEX OF FRENCH TITLES

INDEX OF ENGLISH TITLES

VERLAINE

MALLARMÉ